From the Crack House to the White House

Turning Obstacles Into Opportunities

Denise Stokes

Life's Work Publishing

Life's Work Publishing Company, LLC
2045 Mt. Zion Rd
Suite 319
Morrow, GA 30260

Denise Stokes
Visit my website at www.denisestokes.com
Follow me on Twitter @denisestokes

© 2012 Stokes, Denise A.
From the Crack House to the White House:
Turning Obstables Into Opportunities
Life's Work Publishing, LLC

ISBN 978-0615595573

First Printing: February 2012

Printed in the United States of America.

For my predecessors in recovery and in the fight against HIV – your light still shines. To the Backroom for teaching me to stand, to Sandra McDonald for showing me how to march, to Tony Mercedes who convinced me I could fly... and to my father Charles Edward Olar who I never knew but always loved.

"If we are to stop this cruel disease
we'll have to have brave people like Denise
to reach out with candor and compassion
to those at risk. I really admire her very much."
~ **William Jefferson Clinton**

Contents

Part I

I felt a funeral in my brain,
and mourners, to and fro,
kept treading, treading, till it seemed
that sense was breaking through.
And when they all were seated,
a service like a drum
kept beating, beating, till I thought
my mind was going numb
And then I heard them lift a box,
and creak across my soul
with those same boots of lead, again.
Then space began to toll
As all the heavens were a bell,
and being, but an ear,
And I and Silence some strange Race
Wrecked, solitary, here.

~ Emily Dickenson

"It's five minutes before the hour or 2 o'clock and a sweltering 95 degrees in the southern bell of the south. Good afternoon Savannah. I'm Gloria. How are you? I'll be in control of your airwaves until 5 o'clock - pumping out some of the sweetest sounds around town. If you've got a request, give me a call and you know miss soul will oblige. So girls, guys, close your eyes. Sit back, relax and enjoy the ride. This is Donna Summer and you know she works hard for the money - right here on 93.1FM – eeee-93."

1

The Barber Shop

"Hair brings one's self-image into focus; it is vanity's proving ground. Hair is terribly personal, a tangle of mysterious prejudices."
~ **Shana Alexander**

Mama was always a pretty woman. With skin like amaretto coffee drowned in heavy cream and long cinnamon hair sprinkled with nutmeg swirls, she put the Max factor models of the sixties to shame and the go-go girls of the seventies out to pasture. Her eyes were a mysterious shade of brown that met glares with the kind of honey a man's feet could get stuck in. Old people said she had a figure like a "brick shit house" and it was true because young girls always checked themselves with renewed insecurity when she passed them with her rose appliqué jeans clinging to her curves.

Her smile parted congested walkways to let her through and she stepped on floors like she had built them. My mother owned her movements as if "unsure" was a word foreign to her vocabulary. She ruled her domain with an iron fist coated in caramel to sweeten the force of her blows and always knew what she wanted and exactly how to get it. People called me "Little Miss Soul," because they said I looked like her, but my reflection did not make the light in the mirror dance the way it did when she stood in front of it and brushed her hair; my words did not make the world bow to my will. I was not Gloria and no amount of housework or good grades would make it so. My mother was a Siren and I was nothing like her.

There was no shade of Posner that could make people cling to my words like the ones that flowed from her lips and no brand of grease would make my hair dance on the wind the way hers did. So I resigned myself to navigating the wide-toothed comb through my uneven lengths and grades just long enough to make the cowlicks lay down before dashing away from the contradiction that was my reflection.

I wasn't sure why Mama hadn't sent me to get the comb when I got up for school because our day always started with her cussing and fussing while she did battle trying to get my naps out. Thinking she was still mad because she found sores in my scalp the day before, I thought it best that I keep her calm by trying to fix it myself. My little sister, Tracy, had fine, wavy hair that didn't need to be done. Mama would always just wet a brush and put some grease on Tracy's hair and it would magically curl up or lay down or perform feat she wanted it to.

My hair, on the other hand, was a different story. It napped and kinked and frizzed at the mere mention of water. If you put it in a ponytail, it would soon overpower the rubber band and stand straight up as if to say, "I cannot be tamed." So, Gladys had to tackle my hair on the weekend so that my mother stood a fair chance in her morning battle. She had been doing my hair since before I could remember. And even when we began to move away and stay a while, we would always come back to town and, sure enough, Gladys would still be doing hair. She wielded the hottest straightening comb in all of Savannah, Georgia and mothers of nappy-headed children all over town knew it. She was like an evangelical minister of sorts and, like church her shop was equal parts social gathering and confessional.

I didn't like getting my hair done because it never looked the way I wanted it to after I got up out of the chair, but I did like going to the beauty parlor to listen to the gossiping ladies. It was a rare, unguarded peek into what women really thought when they weren't wearing their "mother hats." They came out of the woodworks on Saturdays to gather at Gladys' shop on

Augusta Avenue to tell some of the wildest stories I'd ever heard anywhere.

More so than casual conversation, it seemed like these women went out of their way to know everybody's business, then saved up all of the juicy news they found so they could spill it over the shampoo bowl. I could easily picture these would-be tabloid reporters sniffing all over town for the hottest dirt and gossip, then rushing straight to Gladys' shop to blurt out their latest exclusive.

The best part about it was that they didn't 'shoo' nosy little kids like me away – so I heard it all. I heard that Rev. Smith used the collection money to buy his wife a new Cadillac; that Roy Albertson was taking people's money and not representing them as a lawyer and that Sut and Tamp got to fighting in the juke joint over some lady named Pickle who didn't want either one of them. I laughed at most of the gossip, but some of it was mean. Like when they talked about poor Leroy like a dog just because he had a boyfriend instead of a girlfriend, so I didn't listen too much when they brought his name up.

Other subjects were so popular they were a running item in the shop; it became like a serial to stay tuned into each and every week. Although I didn't think it was roll-on-the-floor funny the way most of the women did, my ears would still start burning when they updated each other on the always-unfolding drama of Crawford and Marie. They were a sometimes homeless couple who seemed like they loved to get drunk and fight. It was sad, because most of the time, Mr. Crawford got the best of Ms. Marie and the police would come and lock him up for a few days. But there was that one time when Ms. Marie surprised Mr. Crawford by chasing him out of the house with a butcher knife.

This time I knew ladies weren't lying because I'd seen them yelling and screaming with my own eyes. Mr. Crawford kept ducking around the big oak tree in my grandma's front yard trying to get away – and he was butt-naked! People talked about that for two years until poor old Crawford and Marie just got their shopping cart and started hanging out in Carver Village instead of West Savannah.

I even heard about my own Mama one time when my head was hidden under the hair dryer and the lady didn't know I could hear her. "She think she so much because she a disc jockey on the radio, but Gloria just drop her kids off anywhere so she don't have to deal with them." Part of me wanted to jump up and tell her to stop talking about my Mama, but the other part that stayed put in that chair figured that maybe the lady was just a little bit right.

My Mama had five kids and all of us had different fathers and only two of us lived at home with her. Even though we lived at home, Tracy and I still spent most of our time being kept by other people. Tracy stayed at Mama Lula's house a lot because Ms. Lula Mae Clark was sanctified and Mama said that it was good for Tracy to be around her. I guess she thought I had too much devil in me for even the Holy Ghost to deal with, so I just got shuffled around from cousin to aunt to friend of the family – until finally nobody wanted to keep me and I was just left at home in peace peace with my books.

People said I was bad, but I didn't really know if I was or not. I knew I was different and it was hard for me to tell people what I was thinking. They asked me all the time, but the way they asked me made me think it was a trap. So when I was a little girl, I learned the two most useful responses of my whole childhood: "I don't know" and "Yes Ma'am."

"I don't know" was good for most things because, when I was a kid, people always wanted to know "how come you did this" or "what were you thinking when you stole that?" They never asked me IF I did it; it was just generally assumed that, if you were a kid you were up to some kind of no good and any adult was suddenly the judge and the jury. So I would just look right at them and say, "I don't know," because there wasn't much trouble to get in for not knowing. They would "hmmph" and shake their head and let me go back to play.

Other times, Mama and other people in charge of me would have these long conversations about whether they thought I was crazy or not and usually decide that I needed some kind of "cure." So they would come up with these solutions and ask me if I thought that would be good. I would just listen and wait for my chance to say, "Yes Ma'am." It seemed to make them happy enough to leave me alone.

So, after I got dressed and Mama took one look at my hairdo I buckled down for a cure as she spent the rest of the morning raising hell about the Negro state of my hair. When she finally asked me if I wanted it cut, well, "Yes Ma'am" seemed like the right answer. I didn't think a little clipping would hurt – and the ends did look kind of stringy. I followed Mama outside to the car, and set aside my disappointment for missing the gossip at Gladys' shop on Saturday and got a little excited about getting my hair done on a Monday. Maybe there would be ladies I had never met who would spill fresh news over the shampoo bowl!

Dawn was just breaking across the sky as we headed away from our home on Hunter Army Airfield into town. We drove up Montgomery Road right past Pulaski Elementary School until we got to Victory Drive. Then, to my surprise, we headed right. Gladys' shop was in West Savannah, to the left. Afraid of being yelled at for asking "why," I just sat there and watched the city as we drove past.

Mighty oak trees stood on both sides of the wide street. Their massive gray trunks may have been riddled with gnarls and knots, but still they stood at attention – allowing only their tops to lean toward the middle forming a canopy over the road. It was like driving right down the middle of a charming old oil painting. Thick gray moss hung from the lowest branches like great southern clouds that had come to rest for a while as squirrels scampered up and down their own private highway to heaven.

The houses that lined Victory Drive were worthy of the trees that stood sentinel before them like only fine southern gentlemen would do for a lady. Huge porches wrapped around each house like overskirts welcoming the weariest of visitors to sit and rest for a spell. I could almost smell the tart sweetness of the lemonade that surely worked its magic on the ladies and gents fortunate enough to rest their heels beneath the wicker rocking chairs and wooden swings. Driveways wide enough to send parades marching through generously separated each mansion from the next before meandering lazily toward the back of the property where the guesthouses stood. Each home bore some resemblance to the next, so that you could not mistake them from being old, stately and full of wealthy families.

Yes, they were old houses, but they were well-kept and much-loved like the ones in the early part of Gone with the Wind. As a matter of fact, most of Savannah was like that. Old bricks, old cobblestone roads at the riverfront and old money proudly defined this city from any other. But like most places, streets, houses and driveways knew both race and station and separated one from the next. Victory Drive was a trinket in the pocket of only the white and well to do. So, we cruised through the oil painting enjoying its beauty only long enough to run into Waters Avenue and head toward the place where black and brown people lived.

Here, the houses also had an air of antiquity, but they were not as well-kept or beloved. Small, dulled houses sat hiding behind fenced yards barren of grass and tiny wooden porches offered refuse to the brow beaten renters who lived there. Old women shuffled down cracked sidewalks in search of something better and old men sat on the porches drinking beer and hoping they would find it. Here and there young children clad in dirty t-shirts and diapers ran toward the rickety gates as if they knew they should be somewhere else. The quiet but elegant cars that shuffled down Victory Drive gave way to old Cadillacs and Impalas with loud stereo bass rising from their bellies like a growl. I settled deeper than ever into my seat, wondering how long a man's skin would decide which lot he lived in life.

Our middle-class army family vehicle headed up the middle of Waters Avenue until we veered left somewhere in the middle of the east side. We slowed to pass the parking lot of a small, whitewashed brick building connected to some dusty row houses.

"Shit," Mama proclaimed as her reconnaissance told her whoever she was looking for wasn't there yet. Without another word, we headed back the way we came through town and passed through the military security gates. I sat back wondering who on the army base could possibly clip and curl a little girl's hair. We drove down the main strip, past the PX and around the hangars before we finally came to rest at what looked like a row of barracks houses. I looked at Mama, unsure why we were getting my hair styled on base, but she just urged me on impatiently.

Once inside, she greeted a tall, deep black man wearing a black smock over military pants. I got nervous looking at his erect shoulders and clean buzz cut. Mama chatted with the man for a few minutes while I looked around. I strained to see if maybe he was the manager and there was a lady doused in Impulse body spray waiting in the wings to do my hair. The shop was small, but neatly arranged.

Whitewashed walls pronounced the deep grey of the floor and set the backdrop for the shiny black and chrome chairs lined up against the right wall like soldiers sitting at attention. Someone had taken the time to clip pictures from magazines and tape them to the edges of the plate glass mirror behind the service chairs, but they were all little boys sporting variations of the military cut. Where were the frilly curls and smiling young girl faces I was used to when Gladys worked me over?

In the center of the room, black plastic chairs sat in formation facing the chairs as if at some military assembly. There were no cute little kid's chairs tucked in the corner, no outdated magazines spread out on a coffee table, no hooded dryers at the back and not a single gossiping lady in sight. On the left side of the room two shampoo bowls sat at the beginning of a row of empty chairs and I wondered where the dryers were. The doorway in the back of the room had a sign that read "latrine," so there was no other place in the small shop where they could be hidden. Slightly suspicious now, I scanned the room for the familiar hot comb stand and plastic roller trays, but didn't see any. Just as I gave up on trying to figure out the strange décor, the man walked up to me and ran his large, thick-fingered hand through my hair with a frown.

"All of it, ma'am?" he asked cryptically.

My mother nodded and in a flash, with no time to comprehend let alone argue the situation, I was sitting in the first chair wrapped in an apron watching my hair fall to the floor like unwanted feathers off that night's chicken dinner.

Every time the scissors snipped, a pile of hair would fall and soon I was flinching at the mere sound of them. Then, the clippers whizzed around the nape of my neck and made my scalp itch.

Like a true craftsman at work he buzzed and zipped until he was satisfied, then in one smooth motion removed the black apron from around me with a flourish, like a matador signaling to the bull with his cape. The last bits of my hair fell to the floor and my mother paid him with a smile. It took less than 10 minutes and, just like that, all my hair was gone! I thought of how complaining about sitting under the hot dryer at Gladys' shop for so long had somehow cursed me. Was this mama's ultimate "cure" for all those nagging complaints? Too stunned to protest, I followed my mother back to the car and we retraced the winding main road of the military base in silence.

As we neared my school, Mama finally broke the silence and tried to explain that all of my hair had to be cut because I had "sand sores" in it. I distantly listened to her weak explanation while trying to convince myself that I looked okay. But the harder I tried, the worse I felt. My mind inevitably took me back to the piles of feathery black tresses that had been discarded carelessly onto the sterile barber shop floor. Nobody asked me if I wanted all my hair cut off!

For Mama, cutting it was just easier than watching me squirm when she combed it each morning. And it was easier than taking me way across town to Gladys' shop every Saturday. But it wasn't easier for me to go to school! I was already considered an outcast as it was; this would be social suicide. It was partly because most of the kids knew who my mother was and they either despised me with jealousy or they teased me because I was not the fair-skinned, talented beauty that she was.

The ones who didn't get caught up in the legend of my mother's "Miss Soul" radio persona shunned me because I didn't take any crap from the boys who picked on me. I had learned that skill from the best teacher around. Angel, the youngest Kelly boy in West Savannah, had beaten me up so many times that I learned how to fight back and not cry. It was his loving, brotherly way of toughening me up so I could fend for myself. And fend I did! Admittedly, I was also considered boyish because I was already 4 foot 9 and a half inches tall at ten. I was already taller than anyone else my age and people just stared at that. Getting my hair cut was the worst possible thing that could happen to me at the end of the school year. It almost guaranteed that I would have a long, boring, lonely, "you're not invited to the party" summer.

I sat in the car looking straight ahead and prayed that Mama would do something, anything, to make me feel better. When I finally got the nerve to look at her I knew that she had no more on her mind than getting me to school and making it to work on time. I thought about a story my grandmother, who defiantly and affectionately called Mammy, had once told me.

She said that Mama had hopelessly tangled her hair while trying to braid it herself. At the time, Mama was a teenager living in New York with my grandfather, Walter. He couldn't do a thing with the tangles and had no choice but to cut it short. Mammy said it broke her heart when she saw "Little Gloria's chopped up hair" and that my mother cried her eyes out. I tried to imagine my mother throwing the kind of crying fit that Mammy described, but couldn't. I looked at her once more and admired the long, shiny brown mane that fell into her eyes when she bent her head. I was no Gloria. I was just a tall, lanky, skinny, now bald girl.

We pulled into the schoolyard and I looked around to get some idea of what time it was. I hoped that it was so late that the school buses were there and Mama would turn right around and take me back home. But, there were no buses in the way as we pulled into the concrete semi-circle in front of the main building.

I spotted the science teacher lining his class up just outside the library. They quickly fell into order and trotted down the corridor past the main office, past the double doors of the lunchroom and up the first wing. I looked beyond the glass of the front lobby and examined the other three classroom wings for any sign of activity. Everyone else must have been in class or at the other end of the school on the playground. Mama interrupted my reconnaissance with her mantra:

"Hurry up, child – you slow as shit."

I had my own mantra; I was so sick of hearing "hurry up" that I often had to bite my lip when it was said so I wouldn't suck my teeth and get them knocked out. I pushed the car door fully open and stepped out as quickly as I could. And without another word she was gone. With no other choice, I smoothed the wrinkles out of the front of my blouse and headed for hell. No sooner than I'd taken a single step, I became painfully aware of my bare shoulders and the wind on my neck. Fifth grade would not be kind. I listened to the sound my shoes made as they clicked on the empty concrete wing. The echoes seemed to be saying, "Bald-Head, Bald-Head!"

I was glad that it was not lunchtime because then the wings would be crowded with students, each one restless and eager for someone new to pick on. My pulse quickened when I approached the last door on the left. I squared my shoulders and took a deep breath before grabbing the classroom door. I pulled it open just so and eased into the room, hoping to go unnoticed, but I had no such luck.

After a brief silence from my classmates, no doubt they were as stunned with my new look as I'd been, the laughter literally exploded. It was like cannons had gone off in the formerly pristine room, peppering the walls and myself with verbal shrapnel.

"She's Mister Clean!" I heard roar from my right.

"Denise is a boy!" I heard boom from my left.

Even my only friend in the world, Frankie, had her hand over her mouth in a weak attempt to hide her shock (and, no doubt, amusement). I had hoped that she would smile at me encouragingly or give me the "thumbs-up" sign like we promised we'd do for each other if we got picked on. She was my spirited red-haired pal who lived on the army base, too, and I thought she understood what it was like to always be the "odd girl." I guess she forgot, because as I neared her desk, she burst into hysterics with the rest of the class. I was disappointed and humiliated as I passed her and made my way against the stream of laughter to my seat.

Ms. Barlow settled everyone down, but even she looked at me in curious wonder. I sat there and wished myself invisible, but nothing eased the burn of cruel eyes on every side of my bald head. I was most worried about my boyfriend, André, because we had only been a couple for a few weeks. He sent me a note one day during lunch saying he thought I was pretty. At the bottom he asked, *"Do you like me too? Yes or No."* I checked the "yes" box and it was a done deal. He never knew it, but I only checked yes because he was the best fighter in the school and I was the second best. Being a couple meant that we would never have to fight each other. Or so I thought.

He was the only one not laughing that day so I watched him closely, trying to figure out what he was thinking. Frankie had once told me that André only liked me because my hair was a good length and he thought it would soon grow as long as my mother's, but I didn't believe her. Suddenly I wasn't sure what to believe anymore. I emptied the contents of my book bag onto the desk and found some blank paper and hoped for the best. A hollow feeling in my chest threatened to swallow me, so I lowered my head and did what I always did when I was in pain; I wrote.

I spent a lonely lunch hour sitting alone, but at least the laughter had stopped. After lunch, we practiced marching for the parade. At first I didn't want to participate because a few of the kids had started pointing and laughing at me again. But the alternative was to draw more attention to myself by sitting out and inviting everyone to point and laugh at me again. So, I lined up at the back of the center row and did my best to pay attention to Mrs. Barlow's instructions.

After a while, I thought a little less about my hair and started to focus on the big event. Savannah was known for its St. Patrick's Day Parade, although I'm not sure how many Irishmen actually lived there (if any). They decorated all of the city squares and made green beer all over town. They even dyed the Savannah River green! Every school in the city either marched in the parade or got bussed downtown to watch it. I let the last thoughts of hair go and began to feel light-hearted for the first time all day when I thought about our uniforms. They were blue and white with gold tassels swinging from them. Not bad for a bunch of 10-year-olds.

I smiled at the fact that my uniform was going to be long enough for my lanky legs, which was a big change from the doom I had felt earlier in the school day. I glanced down through my happy thoughts and noticed my shoelaces threatening to trip me, so I stopped marching and bent over to tie them. As I looped a pretty bow and pledged to see the glass as half full from now on, I looked up to see André standing directly in front of me. I was glad he was going to finally speak to me so I smiled, but he only sneered at me in return.

"You look like a boy," he spat through almost closed lips.

WHAP!

Before I could dodge him, he drew his foot back and gave me a swift kick in the mouth. The classroom reeled as lightning crashed across my face and traveled down my arms into my hands. My fingertips numbed and my pretty shoestring bow fell limply from my hands. My body felt like Play-Doh that someone had left in the sun too long as it oozed toward the classroom floor. I tried to offset the sinking feeling by scrambling to my feet and fighting back, but my body would not do exactly as my mind told it to. My arms and legs reacted in slow, disconnected movements and my attempts at standing gracefully were as futile as a newborn colt struggling on wobbly, knobby knees.

I tried to avoid the many eyes that had once again pinned me beneath their disapproving gazes, but found that I could not focus on any one thing. They became a sea of blurry eyes following my strange, bloody dance. The pain was unbearable but still, I instinctively made my way to the classroom door half-walking, half-crawling. I had no idea where I was going and it seemed very far away, but I was desperate for the safety it seemed to promise. As much as I'd wanted to, I had not cried earlier. Not at the piles of hair on the floor, not at the retreating taillights of my mother's car, not at the taunting laughter as I walked back to my desk, not even at Frankie's lack of support. But with the fiery impact of Andre's tennis shoe burning its way across my face, and the shame squeezing me too tightly, I finally gave in.

Tears stung my face as they poured from my eyes into my open mouth. I distantly heard myself gasping for air then sobbing in pain. Once outside the classroom, I leaned against the cool red brick of the school wing for a minute to steady myself then decided to make my way toward the office. I held my hand up to my face to try and stop the blood gushing from my mouth and splattering onto the gray concrete at my feet; it didn't work. Though my ears were pounding loudly, I began to hear voices behind me, but they did not make sense. My thoughts became fuzzy and I began to imagine that they might be one of the three trolls under the bridge and so I tried to walk faster, eager to put some distance between us.

Reality slipped completely away from me by the time I reached the front office. It seemed that a giant grabbed me and asked if Jack had sent me to climb his beanstalk. Then, suddenly, I was floating on a bed with wheels. We zoomed down a narrow passage, but I was unsure if it was a cave or the familiar brick of our rustic school wings. In a second of clarity I realized that I wasin the infirmary, but it quickly turned to a blur again.

There were more voices. Something about an ambulance and someone was sorry that "her pretty face" had to be stitched. I tried to wipe the tears from my face, but I couldn't feel my fingertips. Sirens flooded my ears and I thought I heard scissors snipping at me, too. I tried to speak, but my words were twisted through my swollen tongue and bleeding gums. I told the man in the blue uniform that someone "had cut my feelings" and "kicked my hair really bad." He couldn't tell me why all the evil stepsisters were going to the ball and I had to stay home and sew my face. The last thing I remember was an ominous black tunnel swirling about me, so I closed my eyes to keep from falling in.

2

Like A Virgin

From the treacherous passage through elementary school straight to the maze of high school, it seemed that I was always the "most popular" unpopular girl at every school I went to. Shortly after moving onto Hunter Army Air Base in Savannah, (my new military stepfather) Willie got orders to move to Germany so we shipped out right after the summer started. US Army Europe was headquartered in Bamberg, but there was no housing available for us yet and my mother did not want her new husband to live in the barracks while she waited for housing stateside. We settled instead into the small town of Altendorf, 20 kilometers south of Bamberg – and any other Americans.

It was actually a stroke of luck for me because soon after reading The Diary of Anne Frank in the 4th grade, I became interested in the fascinating foreign words I had found in her story. I began to take German lessons but had no idea that it would pay off the very next year! Actual moving to the country I studied in school gave me the opportunity see the places and experience customs I had only read about in books and imagined. I marveled at the expanse of the Black Forrest, giggled at the silly sound of glockenspiels and actually touched a piece of the very wall that divided an entire country. (It was more than 10 years after we left Europe that the Berlin Wall tumbled down and I was always sorry that I wasn't there to see it happen.)

Germany itself was beautiful with its patchwork fields and clay-topped houses, but I was even more excited to finally become more than a disappointment to my family; this was my chance to finally shine. I was the only one who spoke fluent Deutsch and it was my responsibility to communicate with the neighbors, answer the phone, and even translate the antics of Benny Hill being broadcast over the BBC in England.

It didn't last long, of course, but for a brief time at least it felt good to feel wanted. My mother and teachers were so proud that I was excelling at the language, but naturally it carried no weight with my more discerning peers. As a matter of fact, when we got back to the United States two years later, knowing this foreign language, in particular, seemed to help seal my fate as a bona fide nerd. Knowing German was not "cool" like speaking French or even "hip" like knowing Spanish. It did not sound sexy or exotic or street chic. It was just foreign, and to hear the guttural noises easily slip from the mouth of a little black girl made it stranger still. The teasing was predictably endless.

I did have some reprieve during my 8th grade school year in Lawton, Oklahoma. Almost all the other kids at my school were military dependents, too, so their fathers had been assigned to the weirdest of places – like Korea and Guam and the Philippines. Like me, they spoke bits and pieces of "strange" languages and talked animatedly about the customs they were exposed to while abroad.

In Oklahoma, at least, I didn't have to pretend not to know the answer when the teacher called on me. And I was elated that I did not have to stop by my locker at the end of every class so no one would know just how many books I needed to get through the day. I even made the pep squad and I was a shoe-in for the junior varsity cheerleading team the next year. At last, I was a nerd no longer.

For a brief spell I was accepted and well-liked – it was sheer bliss. No catcalls in the hall or hushed whispers as I sauntered by in class. But, as "sheer bliss" is apparently hard to maintain, my happiness did not last long. Before I could claim those coveted Lawton High Cougar pom-poms, my mother and Willie Wright divorced, and we headed back to the South where social cliques were the status quo and I, for one, was definitely not included. It was a quick rise and sudden fall but there I was, back at the bottom of the social heap once again. The school population became decidedly hip and cool, two things that I was not. So, I did what I could get over loosing a pretty good "dad" and focused of fitting in again.

During my 8th and 9th grade years I tried a million "get popular quick schemes." First I dressed more grown up, but that didn't work because my sense of fashion had not yet developed – neither had my hips. Then, I pretended not to be so smart by hiding my report card at the end of the grading period like everyone else did, but my homeroom teacher always ruined it by posting my name on the Achievements board.

I even went punk rock for a minute or two, complete with the ripped jeans and Kool-Aid dyed hair, only to figure out that the fad had not yet traveled from the mid-west across country to the south. (I couldn't even get props when I was ahead of the curve!) Finally, I decided I was just going to try and quietly hang around the cool kids until I was considered one of them. In some weird version of social osmosis, I thought that maybe if I didn't talk very much but was seen with the right people (or even just in their general vicinity) I would eventually earn my credentials. One of the quickest ways I knew to get in the middle of the "in-crowd" at Windsor Forrest High was to sit at the back of the school bus going home. I thought it was a simple plan but, logistically speaking, found it next to impossible. I gave it serious effort for some weeks, but no matter how fast I ran to the exit when the final bell rang there was always a long boarding line to the bus. Then, I would reluctantly sit on the third or fourth row and stare over my shoulder enviously at the less seating-challenged kids the whole way home.

Although I looked older because I was tall, the other girls seemed to be so much more mature than I was. They dressed differently, for one thing; more like women. And they wore make-up and stylish haircuts. I was vehemently against getting my hair cut, so I wore a natural looking jerry curl with bangs falling over my left eye. I liked it because it mocked classic Prince style, but I always wanted to know what it was like to be considered "pretty" and be worshipped – like Angelic Norwood.

Angelic! Even her name was heavenly. She was the queen mother of the pretty girls. She had a body that would've put Vanity to shame and how she got into those tight jeans every morning was a mystery to me. Her hair was long and straight and it was the richest shade of natural brown I had ever seen in my life.

Her skin was light and flawless and she always wore just the right amount of make-up. Her signature was the deep aqua blue liner she painted around the rims of her eyes and no other girl in school even dared to try and copy her. From those days to this one, I have never seen anyone wear blue eyeliner with as much class and impact as Angelic did. I often wondered why I never saw her face and body on the cover of a magazine in later years.

The Knights of Windsor Forrest were also some of the most memorable boys I have ever known. Ritchie Mole, Bobby Kenner and Chris Tabermena were all gods to me. As far as I was concerned, and I was the authority on heavenly bodies, they were

angels who had given up their wings to play high school football and basketball. I would have given my soul, or at least my grade-point-average, to date any one of them, but guys like that didn't even speak to me.

The only boys I ever attracted were the ones that nobody else wanted. Library-bound geeks who recited Keats and Shelly, only I wanted to hear Chicago and De-Barge. No matter how many clubs and teams I joined, or how many fly-on-the-wall, back-of-the-bus schemes I tried to become popular, I was never really considered one of the "in-crowd." It was painful always wanting to be a part of something and always ending up on the outskirts of everything. So, deciding upon a more realistic attitude, my best offense became having a good defense. I tried to console myself by saying, "I didn't want to hang around them anyway." Then I would find what peace I could in making myself invisible.

Mama worked late into the evenings and Tracy's school bus didn't bring her home until almost 4 o'clock. I got home at

2:45 or 3:00 and loved it because it gave me some alone time to lose myself in a daydream or to the beat of music, which, at 13, was my favorite pastime. Most afternoons I would hit the apartment door with a sense of excitement. Because it was both her profession and her passion, my mother had the best stereo equipment and music in the world.

She loved it so much that I ended up sharing a room with my little sister because the third bedroom was strictly for Mama's stuff. Piles of albums were stacked against the walls and there were so many components that the extension cord pile looked like a jungle just waiting to burst into flames at the flick of a switch. I was absolutely forbidden to even walk into the room, but every chance I got I cranked up the volume knob, adjusted the EQ and threw my own private concert. I read all of the equipment manuals and I could run the whole system then put it back exactly the way it was before anyone else got home. No wonder the bookworms and AV geeks were all over me!

I was engrossed in the normalcy of my first teen year when it happened. Prince had just come out with a new album, so I ran home, powered up the system, and sat mystified as the words of "When Doves Cry" graced my ears for the very first time. Ever since I had been 10 years old and got my hands on his first album, I had been fascinated with everything Prince had to say. Most people thought that the second album was odd because he was naked sitting on top of a white winged horse. But I gravitated to it not because of the mystical symbolism or even overt eroticism; I was drawn to the cover art because there was something about his eyes. They were soft and deep and mystifying, and the rims of them held distinct traces of pain that made you wonder why someone would hurt him, and if there was anything that you could do to make it better.

When I listened to his words I knew that, in Prince, I had found a friend I could relate to. He often made more sense to me than the world I was surrounded by and many days his music became the only relief in my life besides my own diaries. Intellectually, rationally, I could not explain what was making those doves cry, but something deep in my gut understood. I couldn't wait to get the album on tape so I could take my time and hear it properly. With some powerful new

19

lyrics floating around my head, I cleaned up behind myself and laid my homework out for Mama. Then, I headed to my room to change out of my school clothes.

As I often did, I examined myself closely in the mirror while getting undressed. I started with my bottom lip running my tongue along the inside of my mouth to feel the ridge of the scar left from my 5th grade stitches. Although it had been years since André had left his shoe print in my face, I still needed reassurance that it was not visible to the outside world. My recovery had been long and painful.

For three weeks after surgery my face was warped so badly that I had to suck watered down baby food through a straw. Although no one else ever seemed to notice, I still feared that if someone looked too closely they would still be able to see the lack of symmetry left by the whole ordeal. Only partly satisfied, I let my eyes wander down to my long, lanky legs and slender hips that did not quite separate from my torso. An imaginary straight line ran from my ankles to my waist. Then, suddenly, the line was broken with the recent addition of breasts. Over the summer of my 8th grade year, they just popped up with no warning at all. Without hips and a rounded behind, I thought they just made me look funny. So, I took to strapping them down to my body as tightly as I could. I still played a lot of basketball and after developing breasts, getting elbowed on a jump shot gave pain a whole new meaning!

Tracy finally made it home so in short order I had my daily fight with her. We didn't hate each other, exactly, but fighting had been a part of our relationship since our sister Sabrina left to go live with her father. In the old days, Sabrina had been the peacekeeper between us because she was the oldest. Tracy decided that, in Sabrina's absence, it would be unfair of me to assume the position of the elder so most of our fights – whether they were about whose turn it was to wash the dishes or take out the trash – were really for the right to have the last say.

Once in a while we got overly zealous and one of us would end up with a scratch or a bruise, but mostly we just argued and shoved each other around harmlessly. It never mattered that I was three years older; Tracy was on the heavy side so our fights were more than fair! She was not the traditional little sister, either. Tracy did what she wanted and didn't care very much what I thought about it. And she always, always got me into trouble. She would come up with a hair-brained scheme and, silly me, I would buy into it. As soon as we got caught, she would cry and point her finger at me.

It worked every time. So I stayed sore from the belt and she got ice cream for having been "misled because she didn't know any better." That accounted for a lot our fights, too, because although it was hard for me to express myself to my mother, I had no problem giving Tracy a piece of my mind. Mama came home before Tracy and I could get into a good fight that day and tore into some fussing of her own. Usually, she scolded me about my messy room, but that day it was about the dishes. I went off to the kitchen to do what I had forgotten and Mama disappeared to her room and closed the door.

As I often did after a good tongue lashing from my mother, I thought about my father. I used to dream that he would come from Philadelphia one day and rescue me. I knew almost nothing about him except that he was extremely handsome and generally soft-spoken. I learned those things from his mother – my sweet Grandma Olar.

My mother often told the story of how my daddy put her head through a wall, but for some reason I couldn't picture the tall, thin man I had met on my grandmother's porch as a hell-raiser let alone a wife beater. So armed only with little bits and pieces of people's opinion and my own imagination to guide me, I drew a picture of a kind and soft soul who wanted nothing more than to find his daughter and sweep me away from everything that hurt. Who knows - maybe he'd even swoop down on the same white-winged horse Prince rode?

I swished the suds around in the sink and was saddened because I would never know if I was right or not. The year before, my mother had broken the news to me that my father had died of a sudden heart attack. Not long before that, my Grandma Mammy and my Aunt "BB" had also died. They were the three kindest souls I knew – and with them gone, I knew that there was no one left to save me from this household of fierce, feisty women so expert at making me the villain. But I held on to daddy's soft eyes and gentle spirit anyway because

21

I loved him so much that sometimes even the "what if's" I imagined were enough to comfort me.

Mama came out of her room and made one final pass through the kitchen to criticize the way I had stacked the dishes in the rack and I scowled silently to myself in her wake. It was so constant that I began to wonder if I was unfairly comparing her to people like Aunt BeBe or Mammy, who unlike Mama were always delighted to see me. They used to say nice things and encourage me, especially when I messed up. They would even stand up for me when the grown-ups in West Savannah told ugly stories about me.

Maybe some people just expressed themselves differently. I didn't know. All I knew was that it looked like I would spend the rest of my childhood waiting for my mother to love me and most days it seemed to be out of the question. I went to school with girls who seemed to have wonderful relationships with their mothers, so I knew it was possible. My friend Evelyn laughed and joked with her mother and Anita even talked to her mother about boys; it was almost like they were friends. Monique's mother was very strict, but still when they shopped together they chatted about all kinds of things and actually looked forward to hanging out together.

Don't get me wrong; my mother had a nice side – I had seen it – it just wasn't reserved for her children. She gave all the niceness to my cousins or she used it all up at work on the air before she got home. I would sometimes turn on the radio and listen to her show if only to get a glimpse of her the way other people saw her. Her voice never cracked or became loud and angry over the airwaves. It was always what her many fans expected of her; smooth and sweet and intoxicating. She laughed often on the air and, to me, it sounded like easy jazz club melodies coming out of the radio.

The men who listened to her thought so too, because they were always proposing marriage to her right there on the radio. I wasn't sure if she was popular because she was a disc jockey or if she was a disc jockey because she was popular. All I knew was that people loved her and even worshipped her. She was one of the "Angelic Norwoods" of the world and I most definitely was not. And just like I did with Angie, I watched her closely trying to figure out how to be her. How to smile the way she did and how to charm people the way she always had. But there are some things you either had to be born with or taught by someone with time, inclination and patience and I had neither advantage.

I restacked the dishes, making sure to wipe down the kitchen counters and neatly lined the blue canisters up against the polished white tile back splash. Then I shook out the crescent shaped rugs, swept the floor and hurriedly took out the trash so I could go outside before my sunset curfew. As usual, I grabbed my Walkman and hooked it to the waist of my cut-off blue jean shorts. Next I combed my hair over the headphone band and smoothed the wrinkles out of my faded 1999 Prince T-shirt. Then, without a second thought, I charged out of the apartment to the gritty all-American beat of John Cougar Mellancamp's Pink Houses tape. I bounced to the beat along the pavement and looked at the Spanish style apartments we lived in. They were two-story beige stucco buildings with wide archways and white wooden patios. The grass was green and immaculate with tiny bursts of bedded flowers everywhere. It was considered very nice – especially for a single black mother in the Deep South in the early eighties.

Our building was in the middle of the complex right in front of the swimming pool, although we were seldom allowed to go swimming. The playground was located just beyond the building behind the pool, but most of the older kids avoided it and headed across Abercorn Street to the arcade of Skate Town. Tracy and I were only allowed to go to Skate Town on Saturdays, so I went the other way to the back of the complex and crossed White Bluff Road to see what was happening at the construction site just behind our complex.

Much like most of the southern outskirts of Savannah, all the land around our apartments used to be marshland. For a reason unknown to me, more and more people were deciding to make Savannah their home. So, construction sites full of men dumping fill dirt into the marshes became a common occurrence. It was all very exciting to the tomboy that had always lived just beneath my surface; that latent Y-chromosome that still thrilled to hear the rumble of a bulldozer or the churn of a cement mixer in the general vicinity.

A sense of adventure welled up in me at the thought of investigating the construction site and, with adrenaline pumping I dashed across the street like a gazelle and jumped the ditch. My long legs might have been a hassle on some days trying to get pants to fit, but on most days, I put them to good use with a variety of mostly unseen, and overwhelmingly unacknowledged, acrobatics. I knew that the buildings in the front of the newly forming complex were finished and already locked because I had investigated them during the previous week. So, I walked to the side of the buildings under the cover of trees until I reached the back. To my surprise, what had up until only recently been three concrete slabs with frames were now buildings with windows and all.

Looking around for potential witnesses, I carefully negotiated the muddy foreground until I reached the landing of a staircase. I checked my footing on the first step to make sure it was safe then climbed the surprisingly sturdy staircase to find a lovely oak door. I tried the antique bronze knob and the door opened with the faintest creak. Not the loud creak of an old, raggedy house, but the inviting sound of a brand new thing that had not yet been used. What girl could resist? I crept through the front door and looked around carefully. No one was there. It was a huge apartment and even nicer than ours.

The spacious living room sprawled out beyond the front door lavishly, finally giving way to a well-lit dining room. A cream-plastered archway framed the kitchen, which was considerably larger than ours and had a dishwasher! The beige carpet was so clean that I couldn't even see the pattern of a vacuum in it. Afraid of damaging it with the mud from my shoes, I just tipped onto the hardwood landing just inside the door and carefully slipped my sneakers off. Then, I headed up the hallway in my stocking feet to find two small bedrooms with a bathroom across the hall and a larger bedroom with its own bath.

The tall, expansive windows throughout the apartment flooded the rooms with the golden honey shower of late afternoon sunlight and made the carpet seem to glow. The daydreamer in me came wide awake and I pretended the larger space would be my bedroom because it could easily hold an antique four-poster bed like the one Mammy used to sleep in. I decided that none of the rooms in the apartment would have curtains because they all faced the woods and the dappled light was so beautiful there would never be a need to obscure it. Then I made an exception for my bedroom. It would have to have sheer white curtains that moved like a ballerina in the soft wind. The perfect room for my desk was the middle one. Every serious writer has to have a desk, and mine would be made of the Alligator Juniper wood I had seen in a magazine once – complete with the natural curves and gnarls it was born with. I imagined it right in front of the window that looked out over thickest area of the woods. This was no ordinary desk; this would be a kind of "tree-god" desk looking over the living trees in the woods as a king might watch over his loyal subjects.

From my writer's perch I could gaze out at the knotty gray oak tree trunks and catch the scent of the shade their canopies provided. As I stared into the woods, new words twisted around my imagination and demanded to be written on the keys of my brand new Smith-Corona. I sat on the floor with my legs folded and with every ounce of Poe, Dickinson, and Angelou I could muster up, I let the lines form in my head and take shape. I rolled down my tube sock to retrieve my ever present pencil then began to passionately spill the words onto some of the paper I always carried around in my back pocket for an instance just such as this. I don't know how long I had been sitting there lost in thought, but my neck suddenly burned as if eyes someone's eyes were fixed there. I shook off the feeling and concentrated harder on my words.

Just then, I was sure that I heard a rustling noise. I turned around on the floor and looked up to find a giant. He was so tall I thought he would bump his head on the door frame. I got a sinking feeling in the pit of my stomach because I knew I would be in trouble. I had been quiet, no one could have possibly heard me dancing around in my stocking feet and dragging my pencil every so lightly over the blank paper, so I gathered that he must have seen my shoes at the front door and come in to see who was trespassing. He was sure to take me home by the scruff of my neck and tell Mama where I had been. God alone knew the hell there would be to pay for such a slight.

Idly wondering about the criminal liabilities of trespassing charges for a minor, I slowly rose from the floor and re-folded my paper, tucking it deep into my back pocket. He asked me what I was doing in "his" apartment and my heart thudded loudly in my chest. Not only had I gotten busted, but it seemed I had been caught by no less than the construction boss himself. I stumbled over a few apologetic words and hoped he would be kind enough to just run me off and forget about the intrusion.

Curiously I watched him cross the pristine, sun-soaked floor in his mud-caked boots and I wondered why he was dirtying the beautiful floors. As he neared me the lines in his face contorted into an expression I had not seen before. He closed the remaining distance between us to a few inches and I instinctively backed away. He looked down at me and asked if my mother knew where I was. My fear was confirmed and I knew I would get a good whip-ping for being where I wasn't supposed to be.

Did I catch him doing something he wasn't supposed to? Was he drinking on the job? My eyes searched around the apartment for some clue - nothing. He leaned closer, invading the narrow distance between us until I could feel his breath on my face. Unable to decipher the situation, my heart pounded erratically. I looked behind him at the door and boldly took a sideways step to leave. He matched my movement and stood in front of without a sound. Panic worked its way from my gut to my chest then to my ears. Although he had not yet said an angry word to me, his large frame blocking the door seemed hostile and made me feel trapped. I studied his dark brown skin and thick black mustache.

He had on a battered hat that said "John Deere" and it reminded me of the mean, racist rednecks I had often encountered in the South. His shoulders were broad and muscular and his hands were as big as my entire face. Several of his fingernails and fingertips were stained an odd brown color and there was an angry redness at the center of his bottom lip, similar to the way old man Sut's mouth looked.

Nervously I tried again to sidestep him, but just like before, he matched my movement and remained squarely in front of me. He put his hands on his buckled hips and chuckled as if he were taunting me. My bladder began to ache and I wondered if I was going to pee myself. Although my breath had become irregular, I managed to inform him of my mother's rule to "be in before dark." This time, he laughed out loud and in one swift motion his huge arms swept me off the floor like I was a piece of litter. I panicked and swallowed the last precious air that was in my throat. My mouth gaped open, but no sound came. He was carrying me to the back of the apartment and I struggled to catch my breath. I managed to fill my flat lungs enough to scream, "Let me go!"

He grunted angrily and un-wrapped one hand from around my body. I thought that he was letting me down, but instead, he reached for a closet door.

"No, Mister! No!" I whined in a voice that was octaves higher than the one I knew. "I'm scared of the dark!"

Ignoring my high-pitched pleas, he stepped into the closet carrying me and closed the door behind us. It was pitch black except for a small shaft of light coming from the bottom of the door. Shocked and speechless, I was silent as he pushed me to the floor then knelt between my legs and covered my lips with his large, dry mouth. He leaned his massive weight against me and even if I had the courage to, I could no longer move or cry out. The smell of the red dirt in his clothing brushed past my nostrils and incited a wave of nausea behind my suffocating lips.

He pinned my shoulder with one ham-like fist and grabbed at my shorts with the other. I squirmed to try and free myself, but the more I moved his grip on my shoulder only got tighter. I felt the hot tears slide down the sides of my eyes and I choked back my sobs. Desperately, I scrambled to free myself but only managed to slip my mouth from beneath his. I gasped to regulate my breathing as he reached for my zipper. I kept trying to get up as his hand fumbled awkwardly around my waist until he slammed my back to the floor in frustration. I whimpered at the pain of harsh floor against soft skin and then his voice came to me in a low, crude hiss, "Take them off or I'll cut them off."

I had squeezed my eyes shut but the sound of his threat made them fly wide open. I easily adjusted to the dim light and caught a glimpse of something shiny. Panic had kept me from noticing too much at one time, but now my brain acknowledged the knife he held in his right hand. He pressed the cold blade against my lower thigh and terror shot up my spine to my arms. Terrified of being cut, I reached for my zipper to help him, but my hands trembled so badly that I couldn't unzip it either. Sobbing uncontrollably now, I pleaded between exasperated breaths like a rosary, "Please let me go, please let me go, please let me..."

He pressed the knife deeper into my flesh and I abandoned my defense. I tried once more and heard my shorts zip down. Dizziness engulfed me and the closet walls felt as if they were closing in on us. He jerked my unzipped shorts to my ankles and ripped my panties down unceremoniously. Then, he reached down and worked one of my legs free. Waves of fear gripped my entire body, helping to keep me pinned against the floor. He easily undid his zipper and the sound made the panic rise up in me again. I squirmed with all my strength trying to slip from beneath him then, finding no escape in that quarter, desperately turned my head to the side and bit the hand that was holding my shoulder. He grunted and pulled his knee up, striking me between the legs.

The pain was dull and pounding. I feared he would do it again even more than I feared the sound of his zipper so I tried to control my shivering, determined to keep still no matter what came next. He positioned himself over me and that's when I felt it. It was warm and hard pressing against me. He pressed so hard that I began to feel pain down there. He grunted impatiently and with one more burst of energy, shoved himself in me. I felt my insides open violently. The pain was sharp and burning. He immediately began to move with a frantic rhythm and the pressure inside me got worse. The bitter contents of my stomach rose to the back of my throat and I swallowed to keep from choking.

Despite my promise to keep quiet I cried out in a kind of agony I had not known before. Not when I tore my leg on the fence, not when I accidentally busted my head, not even when I spilled the boiling water on my bare chest. The kind of pain he was inflicting on me was foreign and deliberate and vicious and cruel. Indeed, he seemed to enjoy the sounds the pain drew from my lips and grunted more loudly and moved faster and harder if only to hear my agony come to life.

Time shifted, stopped, stood still or sped up; I lost all track. My thighs ached from his weight pressing them open and my breathing was raspy at best. I was just about to pass out under him when suddenly he grabbed my neck and arched his back, pressing even deeper into me. The motion made him cry out and become frigid. He jerked himself violently and a warm sensation flooded my groin. Then, he collapsed on top of me and rubbed his face against mine. The sweat falling down into my eye sockets and across my lips made the bile once again rise to the back of my throat and threaten to spill over. Afraid of choking on it, I drew a deep breath in through my nose and gave him a shove. He barely moved. He leaned up off of me and the shaft of light flooded his face. His eyes, wild and red, looked down into my face as he scoffed. He slipped to the side to allow me to breathe then growled breathlessly, "If you tell, I will find you and I will kill you." The tone in his voice left me no doubt that he was a man of his word.

Then he simply stood up and zipped his pants, as if he'd done no more than stand at a urinal and relieved himself after lunch. He let out a long, contented sigh and wiped his forehead with the back of his hand. As I lay trembling in the same spot, he added to his threat, "Don't you get up until I'm gone or I'll kill you now."

I numbly nodded my head as he opened the closet door. As if judging me, the sun streaming through the window was blood red. Angry clouds had drifted across it and it, too, seemed to make a scowling face at me. He brushed the wrinkles from his shirt and adjusted his hat. I watched his broad shoulders duck through the doorway and, like a giant ogre vanishing at the end of a Grimm fairy tale, he was gone.

Just like that, I was left alone to the empty closet. I sat up and my head swirled. I looked at my clothes hanging from me. I pulled at my torn panties and slipped my shorts back on. I was so sore that it hurt when the seat of my shorts brushed the tortured flesh between my legs. I felt like I was moving in a dream. I was there, but not all of me at once; some parts rushed to catch up while others seemed to scatter in the light of the truth. I brushed the wrinkles from my t-shirt and looked at the floor. There was my pencil, lying broken where I had just been. I picked it up tenderly and my eyes flooded. I cradled it in my hand and cried for it. Through my tears, I searched out the spot in the middle room where I had left my Walkman and clipped it back to my shorts, as if refastening it to my belt could somehow send me back in time to when the sound of John Mellencamp meant little pink houses and not sad, wretched, lonely apartments.

My feet numbly took me down the stairs back to the path that had brought me there. Retracing my steps I flew back over the ditch, and back down the road. My mind did somersaults with each car that passed me. Their motors seemed muffled and distant. The wind assaulted my face, drying my tears and his sweat together into a grim potion that would haunt me for years to come. As if trying to escape, my thoughts raced; my heart fluttered dangerously in my chest.

As I walked, I began to understand that terror was not a girl screaming in the grand finale of a movie. Terror was the smell of red clay on a stranger's clothes; terror was the monster that could invade daylight and steal your very soul with the dim rush of midday traffic zooming past just beyond a tiny, closed closet. Desperately trying to feel safe, I called for my daddy, praying that somehow he would hear my thoughts and come to me. The blare of a horn broke my daze and I narrowly dodged a passing car.

As if for the first time, I looked at my surroundings and realized that I had walked a long way from home. I turned and flew toward the apartment as fast as my long, once graceful legs would carry me. It was pitch black dark and fear was attacking me from every corner. Was he there, just out of sight, following me in the dark? Would he make good on his threat, even though I hadn't told anybody? Would never tell anybody? Wouldn't dare dream of it?

My heart pounded as I ran back down the pavement nearing my apartment. The lights in the window accused me. I reached for the doorknob with shaky hands. As soon as I turned the knob, Mama's voice boomed from the back of the apartment.

"Where the hell have you been? I thought I told you to have your black ass in before dark! Why is it that you just think you can do what the hell you want to do?" She flew up the hallway with belt in hand.

"B-But mama..." I stammered, trying to tell her about the man. A loud whap interrupted my sentence as the belt landed squarely on my bare thigh. I sucked in the mad scream that was rising in my throat and took my whipping in silence. Each blow reminded me of hands, large powerful hands, pinning me to the closet floor. After the beating I floated up the hallway and gathered my nightclothes and towel without a word. I ran the water for my bath and shut the door to take my clothes off, again. I peeled off my panties and gasped when I saw the blood.

My eyes flooded once more as I opened the sink faucet and stuck my panties under the cool stream of water to wash away the stains so Mama wouldn't see them in the morning laundry pile. As my virginity disappeared down the drain, I felt a heaviness settle over me that I knew would live inside me for a long time.

I eased my sore body into the tub and just lay there for a while. Everything hurt, especially between my legs. I put as much soap on the washcloth as I could and tried to scrub away the insult and the terror and the indignity and the shame. Determined to make it right again, I ignored the pain. Tracy knocked on the door and sneered, "Mama said hurry up girl, you slow as hen shit."

Instantly I heard Mama scold Tracy for cussing as I let the stopper out of the tub. I got out on rubbery feet and slipped my nightgown over my head. I stared into the mirror at my big brown eyes and noticed how different they looked. I glanced down at the Smurf on my gown and thought of how ridiculous little blue men were. I slowly crossed the hall to the bedroom and grabbed my Walkman. It had a speck of red dirt on it. I wiped it off with the back of my hand and crawled into bed, rolling myself into a tight ball that would take all night to uncoil. I pulled out John Cougar and reached for the Prince tape on my nightstand.

I fell into a tormented sleep as he sang the words of Purple Rain:

I never meant to cause you any sorrow.
I never meant to cause you any pain.
I only wanted one time to see you laughing.
I only wanted to see you laughing in the Purple Rain...

3

The Morning After

The blaring sound of the alarm clock tugged me from the safe arms of sleep. As the early morning sun crept in through a crack in the lacy white curtains, my whole body ached. Tracy had already gone. She must have decided to go up to Nikki's house so they could catch the bus to school together. I was glad because I was not in the mood for her smart remarks this morning.

I opened my closet door and looked at the rack bulging with clothes. Chic, Braxton, Lee – the trendiest jeans in the world lived in my closet. But a diamond tiara couldn't make me feel good after what had happened to me. My crotch burned and my shoulders and thighs were decorated with the purple and green evidence that a stranger had been there. I had no choice but to wear long sleeves and long pants. I reached for the pair of jeans closest to me, then grabbed a T-shirt and topped it off with a blue sweatshirt. Without looking in the mirror, I brushed my teeth and quickly ran a comb though my hair.

Most mornings the mirror was an intriguing curiosity. Magical changes in my growing body seemed to take place every week and I watched them with fascination like the morphing colors of a kaleidoscope. But today I was afraid to look into my own eyes for fear of what I would find. The ride to school was dull and uneventful on the outside, but my head was tortured with thought. Knowing that the seat I took was a highly political decision, I usually gave it a lot of thought; can't sit too close to the nerds, can't seem too desperate to sit next to the cool kids. I didn't care where I sat that day. I just took the first seat I passed. I didn't know if seats were open in the back because I didn't even look up. I just plopped down and randomly opened my history book, landing on a chapter about the ancient Mesopotamian people.

I stared at pictures of people with bright pink skin and raven black hair. I was sure that ancient Mesopotamia was a place in Iraq and wondered why the people who wrote my schoolbook didn't color the people darker. Unable to deal with the ugly backlash of racism, I closed my book and looked out of the window. We were just passing the new apartments on White Bluff Road. It was as if fate had pulled me out of the history book and back into the here and now at just the right – the wrong – time.

The morning was fresh and the day was new and, in the simmering sunlight of early morning the apartment exteriors looked so harmless and, oddly, inviting. How many times had I looked up as we were passing them before, all without a second though? Now they seemed as spooky and cheerless as a haunted house high atop a craggy cliff.

My skin grew hot and flushed; I was sure the whole bus knew what had happened and were secretly whispering behind my back. I took a few random peeks around but no one was looking; not at me, not at the apartments, not at the secret shame spilling through the thin veil of my skin.

I clutched my stomach desperately as fresh memories threatened to spill from it. Relieved that I made it to school without incident, I bypassed the breakfast line and quickly made my way to homeroom. The day seemed to stretch on as one class gave way to the next. Watching the clock only made it worse, but I was powerless to look away as each minute ticked inexorably, painfully by. By the afternoon, the pain between my legs seemed to have spread. It was unlike the bellyache I had after eating too much or the cramps I got in my side from running after drinking a lot of water – only this ache was hot and low in my stomach and it felt as if it were even seeping into my lower back.

As soon as the lunch bell rang, I left the library where I had hidden out and headed for the bathroom. Suddenly the dull, throbbing ache had turned into a fiery knot and I doubled over in the first stall. After feeling a warmth spread to my upper thighs I gently pulled my pants down to investigate. Blood! There was blood everywhere. It was different from the bright red spot of blood that I had seen the day before. This blood was thick and dark and heavy. It was the woman's blood I knew would come one day. My mother's sex talk popped into my head.

"Don't let no little boys touch you before you're married," she had warned me a thousand times before this day. *"God don't like ugly and only ugly girls do that. Everybody will know that you're a hussy and you will never be able to live it down for the rest of your life. No one will forgive you and you won't have any friends left. Once you start having your period, you can have a baby and Denise, I'm telling you, you better not bring your black ass in my house with no baby. I will put'cho grown ass in a home for unwed mothers and throw away the key."*

I replayed her words over and over again, especially the part about God "not liking ugly." I wondered if God was punishing me for having sex with that man. Before I knew it I was sobbing as I tried to clean up the mess with toilet paper, then stripped down to my t-shirt and tied my blue sweatshirt around my waist. I left the stall and ran cool water over my hands. Two girls stood in the mirror painting their lips red. Unable to handle another red thing on an already queasy stomach, I finally let go of the contents of my stomach and heaved in the sink.

One of the girls said, "Oooh, shit, gross!"

And the other said, "Damn, bitch!"

But I had no energy to confront them so I ignored the insults and made my way down the hall to the nurse's station. I had only been to her office once before. Two freshman twins were playing around in gym class and one of them tried a wrestling move he had seen on his brother. Turns out, the damned thing worked and before the whole class, Larry slipped limply from Barry's sleeper hold and fell to the floor cold. We all rushed to the nurse's office where they had taken him to see if he was dead.

I remembered the toothbrush charts on the walls and the odd silence that seemed to engulf my ears as soon as I stepped in from the hallway. Lots of kids went there to lie down and relieve their headaches, so it was famous for being quiet. The quiet bothered me because another girl was seated in the row of chairs against the wall apparently waiting for her mother to come pick her up. Did I have to do this in front of an audience? Nurse Thomas appeared from the back of her office with a wide smile and a concerned look on her face.

Her face was round and her auburn hair formed a perfect circle around it, making her head remind me of a basketball. She asked what she could help me with and I glanced at the other girl and choked. She was such a nice lady, what would she think of me when she found out what I had done? I couldn't say out loud that there was blood between my legs. I couldn't let anyone know what the man had done or the whole world would know that I was not a virgin anymore.

I looked at her dumbly until she instructed me to follow her. We went to the back of her office where the bed was and she motioned for me to sit down. I looked at the white sheets and froze. The nurse looked suspiciously at the blue sweater tied around my waist and nodded as if she understood.

She stood in front of her shelf full of pamphlets and my heart pounded as she scanned the titles. To my relief, she bypassed the one called "Sex and Birth Control" and selected something from the "Adolescent Health" section instead. She opened the file cabinet where her linens and medical supplies were stored and handed me a small brown bag and instructed me to go into her bathroom and open it. I took the bag and disappeared into the small bathroom with pink plastic flowers on the sink.

I folded out the pamphlet she gave me and the words stared up at me '*SO YOU GOT YOUR PERIOD?*' No shit, I thought and read on, relieved that she didn't suspect that I was having sex. I read about cramps and about the 28-day cycle. Curiously, I did not see any of the warnings my mother or aunts had given me. Nowhere did the pamphlet say, "Don't take a shower when you're on your cycle or you will bleed to death" It did however assure me that I would still be able to be active when on my period, but regardless of the author's cheery language I just couldn't see making jump shots with a huge Kotex stuck between my legs. I opened the bag to find two maxi pads that had been folded in threes, a hospital rag and a tiny bar of soap. I cleaned up again and placed the pad in the seat of my stained underwear. Unsure of why it wouldn't stay in place, I looked at the pamphlet more closely until I found the part where you are supposed to peel the back off so that it could stick in place. On the second attempt it fit just so and I smiled with a sense of grim satisfaction.

Ms. Thomas greeted me tactfully in the waiting area and I assured her that all was well. I was grateful that she did not make a fuss about it in front of the other student. She offered to call my mother, but I knew that Mama would be upset if she had to leave work early. I looked at the clock and to my surprise it was already 2 pm; time to go home anyway. I told her that I would be fine and faked a smile to keep her from calling Mama anyway after I left. Satisfied that I was okay, Ms. Thomas told me to come back and see her anytime I needed to. Regardless of the quiet kindness she had shown me that day, I silently hoped I would never have to come to her office again.

I slipped back out into the hallway just as the last bell rang and merged with the crowd that was headed for the bus ramp, hoping no one had seen where I had just come from. Carefully walking so that the pad in my stained pants wouldn't shift and bulge out from the sweatshirt I had tied back tightly around my waist. I slowed my steps just so it would not shift and followed suit until we got to the bus. When I climbed the steps and looked for an empty seat, I did not see one. My eyes scanned the length of the bus and came to rest on a seat two rows from the back. The elite section.

My heart sank. Of all days!

I immediately turned around and got off the bus. As the long yellow procession chugged away from the school, I walked across the baseball field and took the wooded path home instead. I found what comfort I could in the confusion of the day. Mesopotamians might be pink, but Edgar Allan Poe's

Raven was still stark black. My mind filled with visions of his poetically painted scenery as I drug my feet over the leafy path.

Maybe the bus would have been a better idea after all. Suddenly I smelled the red clay that was stuck to the man's boots and hat again. My body trembled with the memory and I could feel the flow between my legs, so I rested on a tree stump to comfort my misery. I slipped my pencil from behind my ear and stared at a blank page in my spiral notepad. Blank pieces of paper had long been the only peace I could find in my young life and, over the next two years, I would reveal things on paper that would never cross my lips and reach another person's ears.

As the blank page filled me with inspiration I thought of the little girl who had left her house and then thought of the end she had come to – and the ungainly woman who had returned. I knew that I would miss her. Another wave of pain burned its way across my abdomen and I drew my pencil across the paper to ease the pain as I let my thoughts fill the page...

My life is the sky and my feelings are birds
Vast emptiness with a sudden flutter of words
A rose to grow with the sun
and whither in rain
My life is filled with the graceful
ecstasy of pain
Like irony in motion, the owl defies fate;
The black widow spider devours her mate
To rise with the moon and sleep with the sun,
Afraid enough to stand with the courage to run
My feelings destroy me as lies gain trust
Like dust to ashes, ashes to dust
Deep like a puddle, shallow like a well
Death is escape and life is hell
As bright as black and as dark as day,
The vulture swoops down to carry me away
To tear apart my flesh and taunt my soul
I freeze like the fire and burn like the cold
Now flying in the ocean
and swimming in the sky,

The buzzard arrive to watch me die.
A quick eternity,
A prolonged end
He repents for righteousness
and celebrates sin
I was born to die... and be reborn again.

4

Prince Charming

I examined the cover of the book I was reading closely. Never had I read such a love story. I was glad I had given myself a short break from serious literature to see what the rave over romance novels was all about. I had to look down at my feet to make sure they were still tucked neatly under the break room table. My head rushed with the tender emotion that had delicately unfolded on the pages of the Harlequin romance burning a hole in my hands.

I felt like I was returning home from a long journey as the last chapter assured me that my heroine would live in her ancient castle for an eternity with her love happily beside her. I smiled and slipped the book back into my purse and prepared to clock back in from my lunch break. I rose from the chair and stretched my limbs. I knew that it would be a long night because two guys had called in to say they were sick. I knew just the kind of "sickness" they had, too.

That night, the two most popular high school football teams in Cobb County were playing each other. Whenever Osborne played Marietta High, two things were bound to happen: one, we got a rush crowd at McDonalds and, two, most of the guys that worked on the grill called in sick. I thought of the pep rallies we used to have at Windsor Forrest before a game and felt a pang of regret sweep over me. I missed my old school, but leaving Savannah was inevitable.

Mama was not happy and hoped that moving to the Atlanta area would be helpful to her career. It didn't hurt that she had fallen in love again, either. Sgt. William Jay House was the new love in her life, only he was recently retired from the military. This, at least, meant that we would not move halfway across the world. Both Tracy and I were crazy about him and affectionately called him "Sergeant House" so, all in all, the move wasn't too bad, but still, my heart would always belong at Windsor Forest High School.

I sighed and went to the sink to wash my hands. I thought of the noisy crowd hurling insults at the each other across the stadium and decided that maybe I wasn't going to miss much after all. I fixed my paper hat bearing the golden arches and sped to the front of the store to resume my duties at the drive-through window. I found greater satisfaction knowing I would get a paycheck at the end of the week than in joining the rest of the gang in the bleachers.

I had only been working for three months, but already I enjoyed the idea of doing something grown up and responsible. I was 15 and I woke up and went to bed thinking about driving. In just six shorts months I was going to be 16 and two of the highlights of turning 16 were getting a learner's permit and going to the junior prom. I was anxious – and needed cold, hard cash – for both.

My mother had promised me that as long as I kept my grades up I could use my money any way I wanted to. Of course, most of it had to go into a savings account as I earned it, but my 4.0 grade average was going to guarantee I'd be one of the kids driving to school and parking in the senior parking lot the following year. With high spirits, excitement tingled in my toes as I rounded the grill area and approached the fry bin. I met my manager at the shake machine and she asked if I had been trained on the grill. I looked at her face and knew that we were going to have a rough night with all the "no-shows" who had left us stranded and short-handed.

"Yes," I told her. "I worked with Troy for two weeks last month." Without further ado, she rearranged her limited staff by plopping me on the grill. I giggled inwardly as I stood in front of the sizzling cooking surface. All of the other girls thought they were too cute to work the grill, but money was money. And besides, no matter where in McDonald's you worked, you looked and smelled like grease, so it didn't matter to me.

"Cha-ching!" I chimed along with the front cash drawer as I counted dollars in my head while laying out frozen burgers in a row. This opportunity to work the grill on busy nights like Fridays would mean at least four more hours a week to help make up for "sickness" shortages in the near future. I grabbed a hand full of frozen patties and spread them out on the grill with a smile.

"Two-Four-Six-Eight... How many Big Macs does it take... to buy a car, that is?" We worked feverishly for hours. In fact, the Friday night game rush lasted so long that by the time I caught my wind it was almost closing time. I squirted a healthy helping of special sauce on the last batch of Big Macs and scanned the lobby for straggling customers. There was not a soul in sight.

I gratefully headed to the bathroom to relieve my over-burdened bladder. Afterward I wiped the back of my hand across my forehead and headed toward the front counter before I realized I had left my paper hat on the bathroom sink. Stringy strands of smoke filled hair fell limply into my eyes as I rounded the front end to the lobby. *WHAM*! I collided with something solid and suddenly felt an icy wave spread across the front of my uniform, soaking through to my chest. I looked up from beneath a tangle of hair to see an angry customer staring back at me.

I apologized instantly and sincerely tried to help him. I reached for the crushed cup in his hand just as he was reaching toward the counter to set it down. *KAPLAT*!! The remaining contents of his cup went flying into our faces. A roar of laughter leapt from the drive-thru bay where all of my coworkers had quickly gathered to get a good view of the unfolding catastrophe. I whined helplessly while orange soda streamed down my face.

"Damn man... you a'ight?" Someone behind the man snickered. He was a tall, thin man with flawless dark skin and a thin-lipped smile. Apparently unable to contain his laughter any longer, he burst into a loud belly laugh and pointed at me. I looked down at the orange puddle on the floor and, although I wanted to run, I was unable to move from the embarrassment.

"Hey... it's OK. I'm fine," said the soda-drenched man. I looked up into his face for the first time since I had attacked him with a crumpled soda cup. His eyes were slightly squinted and his cheeks rose high on his face. A small stream of soda that was trickling down his cheek mesmerized me. I felt the blood spread across my cheeks and his eyes seemed to soften. With great effort, I uprooted my feet from the floor where they had attached themselves and finally scurried away to find a mop.

I brushed past my co-workers as quickly as I could to avoid any more insults. As I retrieved a bucket of warm water and a clean towel, Trina finally came out of the manager's office to see what the commotion was about. Seeing my obvious discomfort, she did her best to rectify the situation. I glanced up from the mop bucket to find the man staring at me intently. It should have made me uncomfortable, but instead I had to quickly lower my head so that he couldn't see me smile.

As the last bit of orange moisture from the floor disappeared into the mop, Trina had soothed him with a fresh order and an apple pie and ice cream as a bonus. I breathed a sigh of relief as he smiled and gave her his new order. As quickly as the relief came, so did my next wave of panic. He ordered a specialty Big Mac. He had no idea that he was giving me another opportunity to make his night miserable! I begged my manger to let me close down the lobby instead of making his Big Mac, but she just grinned and put her hand on my shoulder. She asked me why I was so nervous, but I honestly could not say. I looked up at the gentleman as if to get his opinion.

He smiled crookedly and said, "Yes, Denise... I'm sure you can handle it." His reassuring smile made me feel strangely comfortable. I smiled back and went to work on his burger while he went to the men's room to work on his shirt. The heat from the open grill made it hard to see through the cubbyhole to the front counter, but I was sure I felt someone staring at me. I blinked and looked closer. There he was with that terribly cute, crooked smile on his face. He would not take his eyes off of me.

At first, I thought he was still angry about his clothes, but his eyes twinkled rather than accused. I immediately blushed and looked away. I didn't know why the hell I was blushing, so I tried to ignore myself for being so silly - maybe it was heat exhaustion from the grill. Instead I concentrated on what I was doing and expertly sent his Big Mac racing through the shoot. I searched the lobby to find him still there and, yes, he was still staring.

My co-worker, Rachel turned toward the grill to fix him another soda and looked at me with a puzzled expression. I gave her a questioning look back. I scraped the grease from the grill and he glanced at me one more time before he took his tray and disappeared around the corner of the lobby. Cheryl popped into the kitchen from drive-thru waving her vamped red nails.

"Damn girl," she said with a slight hint of envy in her voice, "you have got to be the luckiest heifer I know." I tried to act as if it didn't matter that he was staring at me, but all the girls on shift knew – even before I did – that I had been bitten; and not by a mosquito, either. Since everybody had a good laugh off of me so the late night clean up went fast. One by one, the crew trickled down to Trina and me. I gathered my purse and headed for the door so the alarm could be set.

Even with all the last-minute excitement and the do-over Big Mac, we had managed to finish about half-an-hour before my mother was scheduled to pick me up so I plopped down on the curb of the drive-thru bay and took in a long breath of the greaseless air. Trina finished up with the alarm and headed for her car. Seeing me still on the curb, she asked if I wanted a ride home. I looked at the almost-fall sky and shook my head "no." She was hesitant to leave me there so late at night, but I assured her I was okay and she smiled and drove on.

The night was clear and cool and I needed a moment to come down from the adrenaline rush before Mama came anyway. I knew that when I got home I wouldn't be allowed to turn the TV on because Tracy would already be asleep. I swear, when Tracy turned seventeen and I turned twenty, we would still have to share a room. And as much as I tried to grow up, having a little sister seemed to keep me little, too, since we still had to share the same space. I had left her in the pre-teen days and moved ahead to such responsibilities as having pads and tampons and bras to hide. That gave Tracy plenty of cause to spend her spare time torturing me for turning "girly" on her.

She played in my toiletries and tossed my bras around the room like confetti. She even had taken to reading my diary; that is, when she could find it. I guess for as long as we were sisters, we would always find a reason to fight over something. Even slightly irritated, I had to smile, though. Tracy was Tracy. And of all the little sisters in the world, I was still glad she was mine.

I tilted my head to the sky and let the breeze lift my bangs from my forehead. It felt so nice that I closed my eyes and just relaxed. The lines of the romance novel I had finished earlier that day began to dance on the night air and I let them sweep me away to a world of romance, riches and fantasy. Even as the orange soda continued to dry on my polyester uniform, I imagined myself the heroine standing at the top of a craggy cliff weeping in despair. My hair blew out behind me and tears slid down my face and throat until my breasts were moist with the pain of my lost love.

I teetered at the edge of the cliff, ready to thrust myself into the oblivion below. I could not live without him. Suddenly, I heard his voice rise on the wind behind me and I spun around startled – my feet coming dangerously close the edge. He instinctively lunges for me and steadies my wavering body. My breath comes harshly from me. "But My'Lord," I imagined myself saying, voice low and horrified, "you were killed in battle. Father brought me your battered helmet as proof. Surely I am not mad." His eyes softened to me.

"My sweet darling," his ghostly image replied, "'tis true 'twas my helmet, but not my blood that stained it. I had taken a blow that threw me from my horse and another soldier donned my plumed crown. When he was killed, our enemies thought they had won the battle and sent word to your father pompously. Meanwhile, my love, I could not let them march their muddied boots on the virgin soil of my beloved Sedonia. I gathered what little men I had left and we assaulted their ranks from behind. 'Twas a fierce battle and the men fought bravely but, alas, I am but the only one of your father's soldiers left."

He held me tighter in his grip and continued his story. "I had no thought but to deliver the news of our victory to the king - and to taste the sweet nectar of your lips again. Perished? No, my love... death hasn't a grip mighty enough to wrestle me from your arms." Hearing of his journey and his sweet words of reassurance, I fell deeper into his arms. I floated on gossamer strings as he called my name sweetly.

"Denise... Denise." Hearing my name, I smiled broadly.

"Yesss" I panted breathlessly. I opened my eyes to find a shadowy figure blocking out the twinkling sky. Startled from my daydream, I leapt to my feet in surprise.

"Hey... it's OK. It's just me," the formless shape said hurriedly. My eyes adjusted from fantasy to reality and I took a closer look. It was the man from the lobby!

"Hello again," he purred. "I didn't mean to scare you, are you okay?" He looked at bit worried. I smiled at his concern.

"Yes, of course," I answered quickly. "The question is, are you okay? After all, you almost drowned tonight." We both broke into an easy laughter. I was glad that he wasn't angry with me. I looked at the large orange stain in the middle of his white shirt and stopped laughing.

"Oh, don't worry," he assured me, following my gaze. "I'll tell everybody it's tie-dyed." I looked into his twinkling eyes and we both started laughing again. "So," he asked, spying the dark and empty parking lot, "are you okay out here?"

"Oh yes, I'm fine. I'm waiting for my ride." Then it dawned on me. "What are you doing here?" I asked a bit nervously.

"I don't live very far from here and thought I'd come back to speak to you."

"Oh really" I asked suspiciously. There was no way to block the sudden images of the deserted apartment and the red-clay covered boots from my mind; they were like a lens filter casting an ominous shadow at the corners of my mind.

"Yeah, I figured since we already shared a soda I could at least tell you may name." Despite my concerns, the shadows quickly faded and I relaxed again. His voice had a sure and easy flow to it. I looked closely at him, unsure of what to say. He was barely equal to my height, but somehow I felt he'd be taller if he stood up straight. His broad shoulders slumped lazily into his chest. His jeans were fitted enough for me to tell that he had quite a muscular build, despite his average sized frame. I smiled as I looked down at his feet and noticed that he was terribly pigeon-toed. I quickly brought my gaze back to his face. He almost looked like he was mixed with Korean. There was something beautiful about those high cheekbones and slightly squinted eyes.

"It's Richard," he said.

"Huh?" I asked, dumfounded.

"My name; it's Richard."

"Oh, yes," I fumbled. "Mine is Denise."

"Yeah, I heard." he said, clearly amused at my obvious discomfort.

"So, you waiting for your mother, right?"

"Yeah," I mumbled embarrassed.

"Hey, that's cool. My mother picked me up from work until I was 19!" He giggled.

"Oh yeah? So, how old are you now?"

"I'm 22."

"Wow, you don't look 22."

"So, what does 22 look like?"

"I don't know. Just… not… like you."

"So, I come all the way back up here to speak to the beautiful girl who said hello by baptizing me in orange pop and I get insulted."

"Nooo. I didn't mean to insult you." I tried to think quickly how to fix it and realized that he had just called me beautiful.

"I – I…" I stammered and tried not to blush.

"Did the moon just turn pink or are you blushing?"

I held my head a little higher and looked up at the sky again.

"It does look a bit flushed," I said defiantly. We both laughed uncontrollably. As we let the last few giggles out, the night became silent and even the breeze ceased it's whispering. Our eyes locked in the moonlight and I was fixated. The softness of his gaze drew me into them deeper, but there, just behind the deep brown, was a fire that made my stomach flutter. Unable to look away from him, I silently hoped he would say something, anything. The silence continued. I finally found a small voice and said, "You, um, you had better go. I'd hate for my mother to pull up right now. She'd have a fit."

I was surprised by my honesty but, oddly, I was no longer embarrassed.

"Yeah, you're probably right," he said, still captivating me.

He slowly let his eyes fall from mine and I felt their absence instantly. "Well, can I pop back in and see you here?" he asked casually. My heart raced at the prospect of seeing him again. I parted my lips to tell him I wasn't allowed to "date" yet. Just then a car slowed on the highway and put turn signals on. I craned my neck to try and make out the car.

"Oh! That's gotta be my...." I looked back toward him and he was gone. Poof! Just like that. I couldn't have turned away from him for more than five seconds and he was gone! I looked up and down the parking lot but there was no sign of

him. My heart sank as Mama's car pulled up to me. She reached over and opened the passenger door for me.

"Come on girl; get in!" she urged impatiently.

"Yes ma'am."

I slid my body into the seat, but my eyes were still scanning the lot for him.

"What's wrong with you, child? You look like you seeing ghosts."

"Oh no," I lied. "I thought I saw a shooting star."

"Well, Mammy used to say if you see one you could make a wish. Did you make a wish?" I thought of my heroine wrapped in her hero's arms on the windy cliff of my daydreams.

"Yes ma'am, I made a wish." I turned my head to face away from Mama and smiled to myself all the way home.

5

My First Time

Meeting Richard was the beginning of a great and memorable adventure. Most people remember their first love unfolding with the new leaves of spring, or sizzling with the heat of summer. But mine drifted in on a chilly autumn wind and nearly blew me away.

At first, it was a slow, graceful dance that made me giddy, but soon it took on an uncontrollable energy that pushed me from threshold to pit before I even understood where I was standing. While Richard might have blown the hinges off the door to my heart, we both had to keep a tight leash on our schedules to make sure our illicit affair wasn't discovered. I worked from 4 p.m. until closing time, and Richard worked 3rd shift at a nearby carpet mill. He would sneak into McDonald's every evening on his way to work, deftly trying to avoid both my mother and my manger.

At first, it made me nervous to see him sitting out there with his legs crunched into one of the brown plastic booths just watching me. I was afraid that I would do something clumsy and embarrass myself in front of him, or worse, that my mother would make a surprise visit to the store and find out that I was seeing "a boy." But I never doused anyone else with soda, Mama never popped up unexpectedly and our secret stayed safe.

Sitting there, Richard would just watch me and smile. After a while, I began to anticipate his arrival. I would stand behind the front counter and ring up orders only half paying attention.

Like a marionette controlled by some unseen force, my neck would crane toward the door just before 10 p.m. every night and my eyes would stretch wide open so I wouldn't miss an inch of him strolling in. I was sometimes bold and would take long breaks and crunch myself into the booth with him where we would talk about anything that crossed our minds.

Some nights, my mother would be late picking me up and Richard would entertain me with stories of his high school days back in his hometown of Indianapolis. I was fascinated by the idea of growing up the way he did, normal and stable, not nomads like with Mama and our family. He lived in the same neighborhood and had the same friends all through school. I heard so many colorful descriptions of school dances and double dates that I almost felt like I was there. He let me in on some of the schemes he dreamed up with his best friend James and I could almost taste their good times together. When he talked lovingly about his little brother, Mike, I could tell that they were very close and felt badly for not being closer to Tracy.

I even listened to him talk about his first love, Dawn. He told me very private things and it made me feel like he really trusted me. So, following his lead, I began to disclose some of my own most closely guarded secrets. Before I met Richard, I had never opened up because I was too afraid of being scolded or criticized. But I just felt like it was okay to talk to him or, more specifically, like it was okay to think out loud. He never laughed at me or judged me, no matter what I said or how trivial – or poignant – the revelation. He just did what I needed him most to do; he listened.

And I began to feel like a bird finally ready to spread my wings and take flight. I explored feelings and talked about dreams with him as easily as I did in my lines of poetry. I knew that he was special; maybe even beyond special. I was unsure of exactly what name to put on what I was feeling, but I did know that it felt good to be with him and just then I really, really needed to feel good in my life.

Feeling good soon gave way to waiting to look good. Before I knew what hit me, my tomboyish days completely ceased and made way for a femininity I didn't know existed in me. I replaced my crew-necked army green T-shirts with thin white cotton ones with lace running around the shoulder straps.

High-cut satin panties took the place of my remaining pink and blue flowered cotton drawers and suddenly my nails felt bare without at least a wash of pale pink or mauve. I added beauty magazines to my list of mandatory reading and before I knew it, I was officially fashion conscious. When he was not headed to work, Richard was a sharp dresser and was surprisingly helpful as I developed my own "adult" tastes.

With his encouragement, it seemed that I developed a knack for the couture and an eye for the classic. I meticulously evaluated my current wardrobe and came to the conclusion that it was completely unacceptable. In a premeditated campaign worthy of Patton himself, I pretended that my flowery dresses were "too tight" and helped my mother replace them with slim pencil skirts and tailored blouses. After finally "wearing out" the elastic waistbands on all of my baggy pants, I convinced my mother to replace them with fitted waistlines and boot cut legs. I even convinced her to let me have a double-belt or two to twist around my jeans.

By spring, I went into sixteen a tall, lanky, clumsy kid with a not-quite-up-to-date hairstyle and emerged a well-dressed, statuesque young lady with soft, dark, hair that framed my face and shoulders. To my awe and wonder, people began to look at me the same way I used to look at Angelic Norwood. I felt like the girl on the cover of Vogue, only without the ton of make-up. College guys mistook me for a sorority girl and I sometimes even found grown men staring at me.

At least once a week, someone asked me if I was a fashion model. At first, I thought it was just a new pick-up line guys were using but, to my amazement, women would stop me and ask the same thing. It was all very exciting and, in my eyes, I owed it all to Richard. I thought that if he had not come along, I would not have blossomed. I didn't understand that time was unfolding and that all girls eventually finished developing and the odd clothing choices of adolescence inevitably gave way to a more sophisticated, personal style. Some silly, romance-novel-reading part of me just needed proof that fairytales were real; that every girl could get rescued by her very own Prince Charming if only she wished on it long enough.

All the fantasies I ever entertained culminated in my head and Richard was my knight-in-shining-armor. I thought that he was valiantly slaying all my dragons of low self-esteem and awkwardness. Somehow, I gave him credit for "saving" me and, true to storybook form he was due the just reward of my everlasting love. So, without formality, I decided that I truly loved Richard and that he was the man I was going to spend the rest of my life with.

Of course, in real life, Richard was twenty-two and could come and go as he pleased. I had just turned sixteen and was barely at the threshold of dating. There would be no mind-blowing evenings on the town or cozy winter nights in front of the fireplace for us. Quite frankly, the only way I could even make time to see him without having to reveal my whereabouts was to skip school. As much as I loved school, I never would have dreamed that ditching class was in my future. But I had also never been head-over-heels in love with anything besides books before, so I abruptly began my academic demise.

Once my mind was made up, I became unbelievably brash about it. In fact, I skipped the first day by walking right past the bus and meeting Richard on the very next corner. He picked me up in his old brown Nova and off we went to his apartment. We talked for hours about music and fashion and family. Before we knew it, it was time for me to go home. He dropped me off right on the same corner just before my bus arrived and I walked home with books in hand as if I had been at school all day.

No truant officer followed me home, no principal called while I was gone, my mother and little sister never found out. In fact, it was much easier to do than I imagined. So, two weeks later, I did it again. I'm not sure how many times I skipped school just to talk to Richard, but an unstoppable device had been set into motion and its springs were drum tight. There was no place else for it to go except catapulting forward. It was early one Monday morning and I had decided ever since the Friday before that I was going to ditch school to see him.

Without a hitch, we met at the corner past the bus stop and rode out to Powers Ferry Landing, where he lived. We stepped into the apartment just as the orange early morning sun was spreading itself across the carpet and winding up the spiral staircase. It was quiet except for the sound of our breathing. I plopped down on the beige leather sectional in the living room and he walked into the kitchen to grab a soda. And just like that, a brand new feeling came over me. A vicious swarm of butterflies attacked my stomach and did not give in until they had spread all over my entire body. I watched his tightly-fitted Levi's clinging to his thighs and buttocks as he glided across the floor and my breathing escalated to almost panting levels. In the previous weeks I had thought about him, I had written him love notes and I had even etched his name on the girl's bathroom wall, but I had never gotten butterflies in my groin watching him walk to the kitchen before.

He turned on the stereo on his way back into the living room and Foreigner was crooning "I Wanna Know What Love Is" and suddenly I was careening from entranced to complete enchantment. Instead of bobbing my head to the smooth beat like I normally would, my hips connected to the sensual undertones and swayed almost involuntarily. Nerves mixed with anticipation and caused me to let out a silly giggle that seemed to linger in the middle of the room for a moment before it fell to the floor in an awkward crash and burn. Richard smiled a sly, crooked smile and, as if I had cued him in some secret language of love, moved closer to me. He took my hand and I let him gently pull me into his arms.

The music surrounded us in a cocoon and we floated back and forth across the carpet in an awkward dance. That song melted into the next one and then the next one and still, we danced. The last remnants of adolescence disappeared with the orange glow of the late morning sun and I looked up into Richard's eyes, ready to be kissed for the first time. He paused and held my gaze as if he were savoring the moment and recording it for future recall. He placed his hands tenderly around my face, framing it like a picture then let out a long, deep sigh as if the very sight of it pleased him to no end.

My heart was beating so wildly that it almost made me dizzy. Then, just as he leaned closer to me and bent his head down to meet my lips, the radio announcer's voice boomed through the room and broke the magic spell. As if a drug had worn off, the carpet stopped floating and my hips stopped swaying. I wanted so much to be kissed, but a terrifying wave began washing over me until I was sober. My head stopped swirling as I realized what was unfolding: Sex. I was on the verge of having sex and there was no stopping the panic that followed. A thought began to rise up in me like a scream after having been long been buried under books and poems and silence.

Flashes of cold stainless steel shot out of my mind like shrapnel. Old wounds were ripped open and ugly memories began to ooze from them. Although the circumstances were entirely different, the man in muddy boots from the construction site fell out of my memory and into the living room and all I could focus on was the carpet. It reminded me of the brand new carpet in the apartment where I was raped. I remembered every detail of that day in a flash and the brutal memory left me weak in its wake. My hands trembled and tears filled my eyes. I felt ashamed of my reaction, but any hope of remaining calm was already gone. I was so overwhelmed that I plopped down on the couch and cried in Richard's living room.

I finally cried about how that man had made my insides feel all those years. I cried because it was only then that I fully understood what he took from me. Long before I had even had a chance to meet the person who would give me my first kiss, the man had complicated me. He took the beauty out of it and left me trembling and afraid of what it might be like to be brutalized again. I was angry with him and tried to grasp why he would hurt me that way, but I could not. I finally understood that I would forever remember losing my virginity without candles or music or even a shred of romance. I would instead always recall a dark closet with a switchblade pressed between my thighs and the weight of a man far too heavy pressed against my chest.

Frustrated and ashamed, I looked at Richard for help with my emotions. True to form, he was gentle and gracious. He wasn't angry or impatient with me. He didn't try to make me do anything. He just sat next to me and held me and waited. So, I decided to tell him what was wrong. I had never told a soul, but Richard was my best friend, so slowly and in detail I shared my memories with him. He was compassionate. He spent hours calming and soothing me until my tears were gone and my hands had stopped trembling. Then we talked about what sex was, as he remembered it. He talked in detail about what he and his ex-girlfriend used to do and I learned things I had never known before. His voice was full of emotion and intrigue.

Like an exorcism, the fear began to lift from me. His tenderness left me calm and relaxed and ready to let him show me what it should be like. It seemed that by sharing my memories with him, it gave them less power. The images and smells could not go bumping around in my head unchecked anymore because not only had I recognized them, buried them and unearthed them, but I had finally taken them out and shown them the light of day; like vampires their power was only strongest in the dark. It felt like the worst of my fears were behind me and the hope of Richard was standing in front of me. I felt ready to move into the unknown. I was glad to know that the thing men and women did behind closed doors did not always hurt you, shame you, disgrace you and scar you for life. The hollow fear in my stomach moved aside and gave butterflies room to flutter again.

Richard rose from the couch and stood there with his hand reached out to me. It looked strong. It looked safe. The softness in his eyes assured me. So I stood slowly, reaching for the hope he offered. We crossed the living room floor and wound our way up the spiral stairs to his bedroom and made a new memory together – one that I would long treasure and hold to me like a healing garment over my bruised self.

And what we did at the top of those stairs was too precious to write about in the secret pages of my diary or even to find its way into the languishing lines of my poetry. I felt a beauty that I had often thought I was not privileged enough to become familiar with. It was mine, and his alone.

And finally, it did not matter what had happened before.

6

The Great Escape

I wish I could write that all the time I spent with Richard was as beautiful as those first few months – but seasons change. The magic glow of the rising morning sun soon gave way to the full heat of the afternoon and my life changed as well. Being with Richard activated a chain of events that altered my life so profoundly that I still sometimes wonder if I am the same little girl he met at McDonalds. Without warning, my anthem went from a soft, sweet, low love song to a biting rebel yell. The worst part was in the beginning when we got caught. The consequences were great and my mother made sure that I knew she had every right to hang me if she chose to do so.

Oblivious, Richard and I were lost in the fantasy of love even if the rest of the world was disgusted with the idea of a 16-year-old girl and a 22-year-old man being together intimately. They did not see the sweet talks we had in the afternoons or hear the comforting words he spoke to me when something was wrong at home. They cared little about our zodiac signs being aligned and even less about our mutual love of the artist still known as Prince. He was a man and I was a girl and, as far as the rest of the world was concerned, we were in a whole lot of trouble.

My mother was angry and this time she had the laws of the State of Georgia to back her up. So when the shit hit the fan it spread all over the world. It was like a bad car wreck. One thing just piled into the next thing and it couldn't be stopped until the worst had been done. It was too late to hit the brakes or slow down, so my life just spun out of control. I was forbidden, absolutely forbidden to even so much as whisper Richard's name.

Suddenly, with the weight of the law behind her, my mother went from mean to vicious and what was worse is that she was right. Even so, it was like I had been given wine after years and years of being thirsty. It was much more than I could handle but too sweet to let go of just yet. The more my mother pried my bony fingers from Richard's grasp, the tighter I would cling to him. Our family life was an already smoldering fire; Richard just came along and fanned it into an inferno. Eventually, it would have burst into flames anyway because I was naturally coming of age and needing understanding. I needed Mama to tell me why she had always been so angry with me and why she didn't love me. She'd always made me feel like it was my fault that she wasn't happy with her life and no matter what I tried I was helpless to change how I made her feel.

She often told Tracy and I that having children was the reason she had to marry so many men who didn't treat her well and who sometimes beat her. According to her we made her miserable and we brought her shame and it was too much for me to handle. It may have been too much for any child to handle. I felt unloved and unwanted and I was holding onto Richard so dearly because he seemed to give me the illusive acceptance I needed. He never cursed me, or yelled at me or told me I wasn't shit. He never ridiculed me and never went on and on about how horrible I was.

I bravely kept trying to explain my feelings to Mama, but she thought self-expression was unruly and disrespectful. I never raised my voice or cursed in the process of trying to be heard. I never cut my eyes or stuck my hand on my hips to try and make a point. But I'd never had the courage to try and talk to her before and it just didn't go over well when I finally did. I would stand there almost stumbling over my words trying to get the feelings out and, in between my adolescent ramblings she kept blaming Richard for everything. I was getting steamrolled over so I retreated.

It seemed that any ray of hope we might have had for becoming close was overshadowed by Richard's presence, so I just gave up. The atmosphere became unbearable. I alienated what few friends I had and began to slack up on my schoolwork. It just became too difficult to concentrate. A horrible depression settled over me and wouldn't go away. No matter what happened around me, I couldn't quite connect to anything anymore. Not being able to see Richard wasn't the only problem; although that had a lot to do with instigating the feeling, it was more like a deep hatred of my entire life.

I was distraught over things that had happened to me and mortified by the things that were unfolding around me. There was so much I needed to understand and I couldn't. Everything that hurt me came to mind at once and it almost drove me crazy. I wanted my daddy and my grandmother. I wanted to know why my sister Sabrina had been ripped away from me and sent to live with her father. I wanted to know why my mother had never told me I had an older brother and sister and I wondered if I'd ever get to know them. It was all too much to think about and far too much to feel. I would sometimes sit in a corner in my room and rock back and forth for hours trying to sort my feelings out.

Sometimes I would be so emotional that I couldn't breathe. So, I did the only thing that came to mind: I ran. I woke up one night and looked over at my little sister sleeping in the bed next to me and wondered where the hell I was. I grabbed one of my stepfather's green army duffel-bags and packed as much stuff into it as I could carry. Then, without a second thought, I slipped out of the back patio door and just kept walking. Far from being afraid, every step I took away from the house was exhilarating. I felt the further away I got the safer I would be, so I picked up my pace. I ran down the two-lane street as fast as I could. I had no idea where I was going to but it felt so good to just run after so many weeks of sitting there, inert, rocking back and forth in the corner of my bedroom. It was the first proactive thing I had ever done and, in my own way, I felt like I wasn't just running away from home; I was defending myself.

I was taking a stand without having another confrontation. I was escaping the deep loneliness and confusion that was making me feel like slitting my wrists open. At first, my escape was sweet. I spent a week or two hiding out at Richard's place, pretending that nothing was wrong. To the best of my ability, I ignored the turmoil of my life and just played house for a minute. I laid low and kept quiet. But I wasn't a very savvy criminal and it wasn't long before the charade was over.

With my mother almost catching me, and the Cobb County police on constant watch for me, I had become an easy target at Richard's apartment. So, I called my God-brother, Al, who lived in Mississippi and, soon enough, it was the Kelly boys to the rescue. He drove all the way to Atlanta and picked me up at the Greyhound bus station to let me hide out there. He tried getting to the bottom of what was going on and sending me back home, but even at the thought of it, I would slip into horrible fits of crying and screaming. He said that he felt better at least knowing I was somewhere safe and not out on the streets. So, he did what he thought was best under the circumstances; he took me home to Mississippi and watched after me in hopes that I would soon change my mind and return to my mother.

And I tried. I wrote letters to my mother, but never got the courage to mail them. I picked up the phone and dialed all but the last digit, then panicked at the thought of talking to her. I even began to dread calling Richard because talking to him meant dealing with the situation my life was in. I kept trying to force myself to make the right decision and go home, but before I could come to a resolution on my own, Al's sister, Linda made a decision for me. With Linda's help, my mother had gotten wind of my whereabouts and was vehemently threatening to put Al in jail for interstate kidnapping of a minor child.

In fear for her brother's freedom and with little choice of her own, Linda called the local authorities. Within minutes, my great escape came to a screeching halt and the State of Mississippi cuffed me like a hardened criminal and shipped me straight back to Georgia. Before I could blink, I was locked in a concrete room with steel reinforcing beams at the Cobb County

Youth Detention Center. I was there with girls who had robbed stores and assaulted people with pistols. But in the confines of those walls, there were no explanations of our crimes or their severity and we were no longer little girls.

In the eyes of the state, in our own eyes as well, we were all inmates. I spent the first night of my incarceration yelling through the bars of my room, begging someone to bring me a maxi- pad. My period came on without warning and because it was my first night and I had come in late, there were no sheets or pillows on my metal-framed bed and the sparse mattress. There was nothing for me to use to collect the blood, so I crouched in the corner of the room trying to confine the mess.

Despite my weak attempt at civility, I could not stop the blood that ran down my thighs and collected in the crevices of my knees before finally resting in pools on the floor. I trembled with shame and dreaded the guards finding me like that. They ignored my screaming all night and the next morning when they opened the door, I was trembling with my lower extremities covered in my own half-dried blood.

They found it disgusting and marched me off to the shower with all the other girls laughing at me. I had never been so humiliated in my life and felt less like an inmate, which was bad enough, and more like a rabid animal. How different my life had become from the lovely nights I would spend outside of McDonald's chatting with Richard and waiting for my mother to pick me up. The confinement and subsequent free time to sit and dwell now only made those magnolia-scented nights on the sidewalk seem more romantic and fantastic than ever.

My mother came to visit me and after a few weeks it was left up to her whether she would take me back or allow the state to have custody of me. In a cruel twist of fate, I was placed in a room with her and told that I had to communicate in order for her to see if she wanted me back. I laughed because it was all I had ever tried to do, and look what it took for me to finally have the opportunity!

As soon as we were alone, she lit into me. "What the hell were you thinking? Do you know how many goddamned nights I rode the streets of Cobb county looking for your black ass?

You must have been out of your mother-fucking mind if you thought I was just going to let you lay up with that butt-faced mother-fucking Richard. I did everything I knew to make you happy. I work my ass off to give you nice things and put your trifling ass in nice apartments and this is how you repay me? By running off with that bastard, then going to Mississippi to hang out while I rode the streets looking for you in a ditch? That's the thanks I get?"

She paused and let the tears she had worked up fall as if to validate her point. To me, they were like little exclamation points running down her cheeks. Her pale face was accented by the bright red pain in her eyes and around her sniffling nose. I was scared for me, but I was also hurt for her. I wouldn't want a child like me either. Although not immune to her words, the sting of them was not quite as sharp as I watched her cry.

As if she could feel my compassion, she looked at me as if searching for a reason. She calmed herself and asked almost genuinely, "Tell me what's wrong, Denise."

I was stunned. My pulse was erratic. Could it be that after all the years of silence she could be willing to hear me? Could she be earnestly concerned? I swallowed hard and tried to capture one of the thousand painful memories already rushing through my head just begging to be heard. I thought of how loving Richard was after I told him about being raped and wondered if I dare expect that from my mother.

Forcing myself to speak before the moment passed, I said in a dry, cracked voice, "A man raped me when we were still living in Savannah. That's how I lost my virginity; not to Richard." My words hung there for an odd moment then proceeded to stun my mother, not into empathy, but back into her bitter rage.

"Well what the hell do you expect me to do about it now?" she asked bitterly, all traces of previous concern or empathy vanished from her face. She went on for a while longer, but I was already deafened by her words so the rest of the sermon was lost. I stiffened my quivering lips and cursed myself for spending all of 2 seconds hopeful that this would be a good thing. Knowing that the situation was impossible, I took a cue from my mother and surrendered to the dance we had danced all of my life.

One-Two-Three "...bitch." *One-Two-Three* "...grown heifer." *One-Two-Three* "and I bust my ass to provide you with nice things." *One-Two-Three* "ungrateful mother fucking..." Like an exorcism the familiar rhythm of pain sent my mind trailing off where my mother's dancing fury could not find it.

Over the next weeks, I smiled and pretended to be happy and well-adjusted. My early life lessons had just been reinforced. Don't talk, don't ask questions and don't show anyone how you feel. I retreated back inside myself and just said what everyone expected me to say: I'm sorry, I was bad, Mama. I won't do it anymore, Mama." And the Cobb County authorities let me go back to my happy home.

7

Banished

As hard as I tried, and as may fake smiles as I could muster, it was impossible for me to pretend that I was okay for very long. Every part of my being ached with indignity and shame from what I had just gone through, but the final insult was my mom's indifference. It was clear to me that in my mother's eyes I would never be anything but a disappointment and, what's more, an inconvenience. She felt as if I was a screw-up that could not quite be disposed of.

Richard was a problem, to be sure, but he wasn't the root of the problem. He was just another excuse to yell louder and not have to hide it from the neighbors. I was dazed and numb on most days and my body was exhausted from crying all night. Eventually, sleep began to elude me and the smell of food began to make my stomach flip and knot.

Yes, I was in love, but more seriously, I was in hate.

I was in deep hatred of my stupidity for loving my mother so much. I despised myself for always wishing that I could be like her and dodged my reflection in the mirror because my eyes and nose had taken the shape of her eyes and nose. Most of my early days were spent trying to escape the outside world, but something in me shifted and I began the long and painful process of trying to escape myself.

Deep thoughts found their way to the surface of my head and the walls and barriers of protection I had built threatened to fall with the crumbling foundation of my sanity. I did not know it at the moment, but I was at the beginning of the darkest years of my life. I was in the corridor of insanity, fumbling around looking for the light switch and on the brink of disaster, teetering just on the edge.

I had always thought that I messed my life up running toward Richard's love, but I knew the truth was that I damaged myself fleeing from my mother's hatred. I could not hide the intense desolation I felt and did not even try. My pain was so great that even my mother's cold heart was affected by it. She tried to console me by offering Richard up like a consolation prize.

After she was sure that she had proven to me that she was in charge, my mother allowed Richard to come visit me at home. It was a strange time in my life, considering our intense but short-lived history together, because even the sight of him did not calm me. It was like seeing him in the far distance but not quite understanding how to reach him.

The visits were surreal. Richard sat across from me at the dinner table on Sunday evenings and ate the food my mother had cooked. It was as if our illicit past had been erased, sterilized and approved for mass consumption. Nonplussed, I would watch his mouth mimic strange words like, "Thank you, Mrs. Wright, dinner was great." Then, after a dinner heavy on politeness and skimpy on actual conversation, we would be ushered toward the front door and allowed to take little walks through the neighborhood. It was courtship in reverse.

It was as if we were an exotic pair of wild animals tamed by the permission of my mother and propped up in a glass front window for onlookers to gawk at. Everyone in the neighborhood and at school knew that I was the nasty little belligerent girl who dated a grown man and ran away from home like a whore, only to be locked up, an inmate bloodied and cowering in the corner of her cell.

My days and nights began to melt together in a seething soup of wariness and battle fatigue. Textbooks no longer charmed me with their secrets and listening to the truth in Prince's music began to hurt so much that I couldn't breathe. I became desperate for relief and hoped that Richard could save me. I decided that the reason his visits did not console me was because I needed to see him alone, away from my mother, away from our street and the prying eyes – and ears – of neighbors more loyal to Mama than romance. Then, I believed that the magic would take hold again and the hurt would go away.

So after only a short time back at home, I did what most hardened criminals do and repeated my crime. I got up one day and without even bothering to take my books with me I left the house and walked right past the school bus stop. I went to the nearest phone booth and called Richard.

He was shocked that I would take such a chance so soon after my liberation, but I told him that I just needed to be in a safe place away from the house for a few hours to get my head together. And so, the final minutes on the clock began to tick. Before long, his car rounded the corner and he pulled up to the phone booth to collect me. He held my hand between shifting gears and we putted along Cobb Parkway, finally arriving at new apartment he and James rented on Franklin Road. We crossed the parking lot and disappeared into our tiny sanctuary to conference.

As I sat in the middle of the floor, fixated on Richard's words, I was unaware that the school had quickly called home to see why I was absent that day. Meanwhile I poured my heart out to him, searching for a way to keep the peace at home while, across town, Mama was cranking up her car and crossing the miles to Richard's apartment to find me.

Richard held my chin in his hand and encouraged me to keep my head up all the while Mama was closing the distance of the parking lot outside and holding the handle of the building door in her hand. And as the doorbell rang, it never even dawned on me that Gloria would be standing there filling the frame with her fury when Richard opened the door. As it all unfolded, I froze to the spot and waited for a violent scene to begin to play, but it did not.

My mother calmly reached down beside her and produced a large plastic bag she had brought from our cozy little townhouse in Smyrna. Her expression did not change as she hefted it forward across the threshold and into the middle of the living room floor, just inches from where I was standing.

The bag popped open and my little yellow sleeveless sweater peeked out at me – the one I wore to my modeling interview. Beyond it I saw my most comfortable panties cowering behind my favorite blue jeans and gym shorts. My eyes slowly rose from the gaping mouth of the open bag and fell into my mother's face. It was a familiar look of disgust, but on that day it was laced with a bitterness I had not seen so openly before.

Her words came in a low and dangerous hiss: "Here goes all your shit."

Then, she turned and looked Richard squarely in his face before announcing in a louder voice, "She's your problem now, buddy." With that, she disappeared through the doorway and I was officially kicked out of the house.

Home Away From Home

At first, the pain was still too fresh for me to smile about anything. Every time the door to Richard's new apartment opened I panicked, thinking it was my mother or the police. Eventually, my tense days and nights mellowed into quiet weeks and I finally knew that I was really on my own.

Although I wasn't sure if I had been freed or forgotten, I finally knew that my mother would not be back to collect me. It was not a victory so much as a reprieve. I was glad to put some of the pain behind me, but still afraid of what the next days might bring. Without the violence of my mother's words to greet me, I began my mornings in solitude. When the alarm rang for me to get ready for school, Richard was still at work and his roommate, James, had either just left the apartment or was quietly on his way out. Some mornings, it was like moving in a dream. I thought if I moved too fast, I would wake up and my mother would be right there to scream at me or, worse, take me back home with her.

At first, going to school was terrifying. The complications of my running away had caused my teachers at Wills to watch my every move. I was starting to be uncomfortable and then I got news that Wills High School was going to be converted to a middle school to accommodate the influx of residents and all of the high school students would be rezoned at the end of the year. I was glad for the opportunity to be transferred from Wills after my 11th grade year because Marietta High offered me a fresh start.

Not many people at Marietta High knew of me and, for that, I was grateful. Although Cobb County was quite close to the busy city of Atlanta, it still held much of its small town appeal and word tended to travel fast – good or bad. Marietta seemed to be more lenient in that regard. I was not sure if it was because it was a different school or because I was a senior. I just knew that I was grateful not to have to answer a million questions before lunch period every day.

Instead, I was allowed to just quietly move from class to class, bypassing both principle and counselors. Before long, I was right back in the swing of things and my grade-point-average soared as if I had never missed a class. To make matters easier, one day when I was still at school, my mother called Richard at work to say that I was now an "emancipated minor" and that he didn't have to worry about the law anymore.

With that bit of news, I did my best to erase the last memories of where I had come from I lived my life as if I had always been right there with Richard. It was no longer a sleepover for me, but in fact a do over. I never played in my days of childhood, but I began to recall what I had seen on television shows and in movies and literally "played house." Cleaning things up came easily to me since not cleaning up properly had always been one of the main reasons my mother fussed. I learned, through Richard, that the way I cleaned up was just fine. All I had to do was do what I thought was sufficient, and then wait for my mother's voice to echo in my head. I would do whatever I thought she would raise hell about and, voila, the house was clean!

Laundry was more of a challenge because, at home, I was not allowed to run the washing machine. I was only allowed to fold the clothes after they were dry. So, I ran it through my head backward. I remembered which clothes came out of the dryer together and knew that they had also probably been washed together. Aside from a few items that never appeared in the laundry at home, it worked like a charm and Richard always forgave me for the occasional pair of pink boxer shorts or blue tube sock.

Cooking was not so easily mimicked since I wasn't allowed anywhere near the kitchen when Mama was cooking. I tried to think back on the days I spent at Mama Lula's house with Tracy, but those memories were of little help. The two of them were always thick as thieves. They would stand wide hip next to wide hip in front of that old chipped white porcelain stove and stir pots of pork-laden collard greens and turn out pans of hot water corn bread like an assembly line.

Since I never acquired a taste for such delicacies I was labeled "white girl" and banned from their kitchen, too. So, I checked out a recipe book from the school library and took it to Richard's kitchen with a vengeance. (I doubt the librarians at school ever intended their patrons to "play house" and cook for real, but that's exactly what I was doing.)

At first, James protested. He told Richard that hot dogs and hamburger helper were just fine. Then, I lucked up on a garlic mashed potato recipe that gave me just the leverage I needed. Before long, 3 out of 5 dishes were edible and just like that I was the official head of cooking and groceries! And so my life went on as I began to make neat little loops of school, homework, cooking, cleaning and waiting for Richard to get home. And just when I thought I had a handle on my new life, it changed again without warning.

James' girlfriend Venus moved into the picture like a black cloud threatening rain at every turn. She had a long history with James – dating all the way back to his days in Indianapolis. But she was an off-again, on-again girlfriend, so I never saw her a lot. Once I moved in, that changed quickly. Standing a full six feet tall, her pale beige skin was so delicate that you could sometimes see the tiny green veins just beneath it.

She had small breasts, but had shoulders broad enough to make you forgive God for the oversight. Her waist was almost non-existent and gave way to a pair of hips both wide and slender all at once. Her long, wavy hair was a black so stark that it gave off an electric blue shine when she tilted her head back and it caught the light of the sun. But with all the beauty with which she was endowed, none of it had seeped through her exquisite skin and settled in her heart.

Mythology's Venus might have been the Roman goddess of love, beauty and fertility, but our Venus might as well have been the goddess of strife. It did not take long for me to realize that Venus was suspicious and dry at best. But more often, she was accusatory and venomous with a particular verbal poison that never missed its mark. And from the day I moved into her boyfriend's apartment, I was her chosen mark. I remember running into her a few times when I would skip school to spend time with Richard. And when I had first run away from home, she spent the night with James almost every night but, even then, I seldom saw her because she was not a day person.

She only came out of his room late in the evenings when I was on my way to bed. By morning, she was usually passed out in James' bed after a night of partying. A few times, I tried to talk with her, but I just assumed that she was not responsive because she was hung over. So, I gave up trying and just stayed out of her way as much as possible. She seemed harmless then – but now that I was a permanent fixture, I was getting a totally different vibe.

I came home from school one day and headed to the kitchen to thaw something for dinner and there she was in a thin white robe and pink curlers. It only took one nasty look from her for me to figure out that she wanted me to get out of her way, so I conceded. I headed down the hallway to Richard's bedroom and noticed that across the hall she had taken James' space hostage. Unlike the times she came and went in the past, she had what looked like all of her possessions piled up on his bed and along the wall for as far as I could see. There were boxes and bags and suitcases of Venus' things in every corner of his room. She made herself a part of the landscape and I found myself walking on eggshells in a house where the odds were quickly stacking against me.

Venus' first order of business as the more established and more powerful woman of the house was to call in her girls. I wondered why I had never met them before, but quickly learned that where Venus went, her clan followed. Baby Girl, Shaun and Pam made up the rest of the guerilla crew and, for a time, it seemed that their sole mission in life was to bring me misery.

Pam was not as beautiful as Venus, but still prettier than most. Her shape was a little curvier and her frame was a little shorter, but she was Mike's girlfriend and since Mike was Richard's cherished younger brother, she carried "Goddess" status without question. No one pretended that Shaun was not hard to look at, but she was Pam's little sister and so the title was also hers by relation. I probably could have lived with the idea of Pam and Shaun running around boosting Venus up, but when I realized who Venus' little sister was I panicked. At first, when she came to visit I was oblivious.

Baby Girl was quiet and even seemed polite when I would run into her in the hallway without the other girls. She would give me a little half-smile then disappear into the ruckus they made behind the closed door of James' room. When Richard began to spend less and less time in the living room until finally retreating into our bedroom, I didn't think anything of it. Like me, he would opt for peace before war and I thought he was just avoiding the uncomfortable bottleneck of the often crowded apartment hallway. Then one Saturday morning we all ended up in the living room trying to watch TV at the same time. As they often did, the girls had gone to the mall the Friday before and boosted some clothes and cassette tapes and whatever else they could get their hands on.

Shaun lucked up on an untagged box of some of the newest VHS tapes at the video store and wrapped her sticky fingers around them without so much as a hesitation. Mike and Pam curled up together on the love seat while James and Venus stretched themselves out on the couch, sharing a beer.

Shaun sat in the chair next to the couch and Baby Girl tucked herself between Shaun's legs so she could have her hair braided while we watched

The Breakfast Club spin its tale in the VCR. Unpretentious and comfortable with each other, Richard and I stretched out on the floor in the middle of the living room and munched on cheese balls. Just after the movie got started, I made a dash for fresh drinks and swapped the empties around the room. When I got to Baby Girl, James broke into a wide grin and kicked Richard's leg.

He snickered and Richard turned around just as James was proclaiming, "Damn Rich, how you got your new woman serving your old woman? I wanna be a player just like you, man."

Richard jumped up from the floor and grabbed the falling beer cans from my arms and all hell broke loose. I stood aside in shock. I could feel the blood rushing to my head in shame as I realized that everyone knew that Baby Girl was Dawn's nickname – and Dawn was the famous first love of Richard's life. How could I be so stupid?! I never connected the nickname to the very same girl that Richard had spent hours and hours telling me about. I never suspected that the very same girl he told me he was so crazy about was Venus' little sister. I just assumed that she was long buried in the past back in Indianapolis. But there she was. Right under the same roof with me and in the middle of the hostile group that had invaded my newfound home.

Suddenly I understood Venus' hatred for me and why the other girls seemed so hell bent on running me off. They were all bitter and I was the reason. Venus jumped up and raised some hell and James had to stop Richard from smacking her. Pam and Mike did their best to calm the room down but I could see Pam looking at me nastily out of the corner of her eyes, too. Shaun jumped in to help Venus and James fend off Richard. Dawn and I stood looking at each other in silence. I had never noticed the pain in her eyes before that day. I just thought she was quieter than the rest of them and content with allowing them to raise hell while she watched.

I never knew that she was quiet because they were raising hell on her behalf. And I had never before that moment noticed how truly beautiful she was. Venus's hard black and beige lines paled in comparison to Dawn. She was shorter than Venus, but she did for short and voluptuous what her older sister could never do for long and lean. Her hair was a brownish blonde with frizzy curls that misbehaved invitingly. It flowed across her forehead and spilled down her back like waves of amber grain. Her skin was a browner shade of beige and decorated with tiny splashes of brown freckles across her nose and cheeks.

The more I drank in her features, the drunker I felt until finally I hung my head in defeat. We had waged our battle in silence and she had won. Between Venus and Dawn, it seemed that the market on beauty was cornered and they did not have to go out of their way to let me know I that had no stock in it. I was an intrusion into their perfect world. Two beautiful sisters had landed two handsome best friends and secured their bounty with the insurance of becoming best friends with Mike's girlfriend. The picture was complete and there was no room in it for me.

My heart sunk and fluttered all at once because I knew I did not belong. It did not matter if Richard loved me or not. They were all part of a family and I was an outsider. The commotion of that day came and went, but nothing – and no one – was peaceful after it. My insecurities fed into Richard's uncertainties and the arguments shortly began. At first they were just unsolved disagreements over silly things, but for every silly thing on the surface, there was a deeper feeling connected to it.

I tried to allow bygones to be bygones, but what was in the past was not buried. It was walking around the apartment in increasingly shorter shorts and in bikini tops that somehow always came untied at just the right moment. I became quieter and quieter until none of the voices in the apartment belonged to me. I cooked on my appointed days and cleaned out the bathroom despite the daily raids the other girls made on my things. I smiled at Richard whenever he would look at me and tried to make myself welcoming but, more often than not, it went entirely unnoticed.

After understanding the close ties between the family I had happened into, I learned how the hierarchy worked and why I was so disliked. So, I stopped trying to make peace and just did my best to avoid an all-out war. But trouble was in such abundance that it was hard to avoid it completely. At first, it was simple enough. My tampons and other toiletries would mysteriously disappear from the hall bathroom, so I started keeping them in the bedroom closet and locked the doors together with the lock I brought home from gym class.

Then the cold war spilled from the bathroom to the kitchen. Somehow, meat I left in the sink to thaw in the mornings before school would somehow escape the confines of its chrome prison and fly across the linoleum back to the safety of the freezer. Of course, this phenomenon would only occur on the nights I was designated to cook. This was a little harder to rectify than locked-away tampons and other toiletries, but I got in the habit of walking by the grocery store after school and picking up something fresh just in case.

After the opposing side saw that their tactics were not working, they graduated to more sinister crimes like finding and destroying the newest looking school book in my satchel and making sure that my homework somehow ended up in the kitchen garbage on spaghetti night. I tried not to run to Richard with every little thing, but where my schoolwork was involved, I panicked. Affronts to my toiletries were one thing, even with dinner I could turn the other cheek; but school was my future, and I'd be damned if these trifling girls were going to mess with that.

James and Richard soon began to have tension between them because both women living under their roof expected to be defended and justified. It was an impossible situation. Over time, Pam was less of a problem because she got pregnant with Mike's first child and came around less often as her stomach grew. Dawn lightened up, too, because I found out that she really didn't hate me and wasn't as angry with me as I thought. She was just caught up in the crowd and felt obligated to follow her older sister's lead. But Venus and Shaun never let me breathe easy. I was their own personal plaything and, with nowhere else to run, I was at their mercy.

More and more of my time was spent squabbling with them all day and then crying all evening once Richard got home. Our formerly happy home was never quite so happy again and my fascination with taking care of a man's laundry and dinner was reduced to frequent catfights and name-calling just like it had been with Mama and my little sister back home. Still, somewhere in the midst of the ongoing war, Richard and I managed to have some precious times.

Life was not ideal and peace did not last long, but when it came, it was worth walking through fire. We spent long nights staring into each other's eyes and coddling each other's dreams. We took long walks in the brisk winter air and held each other close and sacred. I learned more from Richard during those few months than my mother or any stand-in father had ever dared to teach me.

He swept my hair away from my face and told me how pretty it was. He bought me pants that suited my figure and convinced me that my long, lean frame was as sexy as any. He bought stock in my dreams of writing and he apologized for all the people who had ever hurt me. He made me feel safe and confident and hopeful and, for those things, he will always hold the esteemed honor of being my first love. There have been many times in my life since Richard that I have wished to be loved as completely as I thought I was loved then.

But the truest thing I have ever known in my short life is that change will come - and so it did. The warring household spilled over even into our quiet love and changed something between us. The squabbling between Richard and I got even worse, and subsequently I spent more and more of my time escaping the apartment for the pool house or the safety of the woods behind it. Although I was writing more than ever, I shared less and less of my poetry with him. Somehow, the safety he used to offer to me had been disturbed and, in its absence, I was left unprotected in a house of chaos. On the days when I wanted to stay home and venture out into the madness beyond the hallway, Venus and Shaun had begun openly smoking weed in the living room and the foul smell of the reefer kept me confined to the bedroom.

While I was in self-imposed seclusion, the rest of the house began circling the wagons. James and Richard settled back into their pre-Denise routine of drinking beers and talking about old times in "Nap-town." Slowly, a beer at a time, Richard began to agree with James' suggestion that I get a job to "help with the bills" and, to add to the emotional difficulty, suddenly school was also at stake.

Richard had conveniently forgotten my well thought out plan to save money my first three years of high school so I could focus completely on my studies senior year. But school was of little important to anyone else in the house, so I was suddenly the odd roommate out. Venus and Dawn had dropped out of school long before senior year, Shaun had always hated school and Pam was busy with her newborn daughter.

So, feeling cornered, isolated and out-numbered, I gave in to what Richard had promised me I would never have to do and got a job in the middle of my hectic senior year. In the moment of decision there was a deeply ominous feeling that passed in the silence between us. We both knew I was letting go of a vision I had held since I was seven years old. I looked into Richard's eyes for some last measure of safety, but found none.

So I released the wings of my hope and prayed it would not soar beyond my reach. My words reassured James and Richard that I would have a job by the end of the next week, and the very sound of them drowned out the sweet lines of the valedictorian speech I had been preparing in my daydreams. I stood at the threshold of my life draped in cap and gown – waiting to see if they would still call my name.

9

Sand Castles

Love.

I don't think I ever really figured out what defined our love. Was it the long moments we spent staring into each other's eyes? Was it the passionate expression of our bodies entangled? I don't know any word or gesture that could paint a true picture of what love really is, so we did not notice at first when the words and gestures became sparse.

I suppose we both thought it was just the routine of "real life" taking hold. We did not see the secrets we each began to hide away from each other and the trust float away on the evening air. So instead of opening my eyes along with my heart to see our beauty fade into an uneasy ugliness, I busied myself with the mundane; I worked and went to school.

I justified my plight with the fact that a lot of seniors did the same thing. But I knew I was not the average high school senior. My father was not waiting in the wings with the money he had lovingly stored away for my college education. My mother was not waiting at the end of each hard day to keep me encouraged with her love. I was shuffling between work and school and home in a dizzying effort for balance. But I did not feel balanced and I became less and less sure that Richard could – or even would – catch me if I fell. (And falling felt more and more likely with each passing day.)

My entire paycheck went toward household bills I didn't know we had and my only "reward" was Venus and James greeting me every evening with a sneer. I saw Richard less and less since my hours at work overlapped his hours at home.

Although we were not the same loving couple, he was still my only fan and his absence around the house left me vulnerable and insecure, and then it got worse.

One day, Richard just didn't come home. I did not notice right away because we had become a roving band of nomadic passers-by, the classic two ships passing in the night. Sometimes I came in from a long day at work and school and just passed out on the bed with my clothes on. Richard would come in from his shift and gently take my shoes off and tuck me into bed, still half-dressed. On that day when the alarm rang for me to get ready for school, I was still wearing my shoes and Richard was not snoring gently beside me. Only a little suspicious, I shrugged it off and showered and headed for the bus. As the day wore on, I wondered because I did not recall seeing Richard's dirty clothes lying on the floor by the hamper where they would always end up in the red-eye hours when he would inevitably drag himself in. Surely if he went for a morning jog after work he would have taken his work clothes off first! Suspicion gave way to concern. I skipped work and came straight home and see if my mind had been playing tricks on me. I tried to dismiss the concern and hoped to open the room door to find Richard sprawled out after an exhausting shift. I opened the front door and ignored the "dynamic-duo's" daily jeer and headed straight for our room. He was not there.

There were no dirty clothes on the floor and, come to think of it, I did not see the Nova in the parking lot on my way into the apartment. I stood in the open doorway of our room trying to get a fix on what was wrong, but I would not have to ponder for long. James slinked up the hallway and propped his hand on the doorway above mine.

"Looking for your old man?" he asked ridiculously.

"Did you see him this morning?" I asked in a tight voice.

"Pssss. Where you been? Rich got locked up last night. You didn't know?"

I wondered for a second if he was drunk, then realized he was just being his old facetious self. I answered anyway, "No James, I didn't know." Then the panic came. Locked up? In jail? "W-what, when was... what happened?" I stammered.

He sucked his teeth long and deliberately before passing off news like dirty coins to a beggar. "I told him 'bout driving the hooptie without insurance," he said slowly. "And you know he don't have license one?"

I leaned my head against the doorway in slight relief until James ruined it for me.

"He called me on my job and I'm telling you like I told him, he gon' have to do that lil' time cause that's my boy, but I 'ain't got no money to bail him out."

Knowing I didn't have twenty-dollars scraped together, I didn't even bother to ask how much the bail was. So I stopped breathing and waited for James to tell me how much time he would have to do. Venus beat him to the draw.

"Ninety-days" she yelled up the hallway triumphantly, almost laughing at my displeasure.

"Well, I hope you know that you need to pay his part of the rent while he gone. This ain't no free ride just cause the coppers gotch'a man."

I looked up at James and fought to hold my words. It was not the time to have beef with the man of the house. I sucked up my grief the rest of the evening, refusing to cry in front of them. But as night fell and the living room cleared, I sat in the middle of the couch and let my tears fill the empty room. What would I do for three whole months in this house alone? How would I get along without Richard here to protect and guide me? I was overwhelmed with fear and just sat trembling into the wee hours of the morning.

The first weeks of Richard's incarceration were the hardest. I tipped around the house trying to be unseen and unheard by the tyrants that were left in the power vacuum of Richard's absence. Sometimes, they were so into each other that they left me to my fear, but more often than not, James and Venus had a field day. Like a tortoise naked without its shell, it was like harmless target practice to them but torture for me. The more they drank, the meaner they got, so to gauge the rest of my evening I learned to count the number of beer cans in the garbage when I got home from school or work.

If there were too many, I dropped my books off and headed down the street for some solitude. It was too cold to hang around the pool house, so I had discovered a cozy little Mexican restaurant up the street where the waitress didn't care how long you sat on a $3 order and never checked ID. I pined over tacos day after day until I became a regular. I knew I was a regular when I began to notice the same faces at the barstool on certain days; the other regulars.

A couple of big husky guys came in with a pale skinny girl three nights a week and I began sitting at the bar next to them and chatting about nothing. It seemed like a better choice than trying to break down chemical compounds behind closed doors, alone. I liked the company of the strange people I had met and began looking forward to hanging out with them. Roger, Steve and Angie were their names.

Steve and Angie was a couple; Roger was Steve's cousin. They had moved to Atlanta from Harrisburg, Pennsylvania in search of higher paying jobs and lower rent. They said good jobs were hard to find in the north because the union had everything tied up and they weren't union men. They were just happy-go-lucky blue-collar guys not looking to be tied to the job. They wanted decent work, decent pay, and didn't want to sell their souls for the privilege. I enjoyed their brick-laden accent and easy spirit. Angie was a blast because no matter who said what, she would laugh – and she had an infectious laughter. It was kind of gritty and loud, but genuine. I couldn't help but to laugh with her, whether you got the punch-line or not. Before long, I found myself sitting at the barstool with my new friends, half sipping beer and laughing at nothing more often than not.

I'm not really sure why, since I needed to be working more these days, not less, but I took fewer and fewer shifts at work and studied less often, too. Walking into the Mexican restaurant in the evenings was like getting sucked into a black hole. I knew I should be doing something else, but it just felt so good to leave the worry outside on the curb for a while. Time passed quickly as I spent more time becoming familiar with the gang at the bar – and before I knew it, Richard was home. He reappeared just as abruptly as he had disappeared.

I had long stopped asking James for updates, because it was like pulling teeth. He knew he was the only one Richard could call because he could take collect calls at work. There had never been a phone in the apartment and there was no way for Richard to get enough change to call me when I was at work. I couldn't go see him because I was underage and James knew he was my only link. But he got more enjoyment out of being nonchalant about my suffering, to say nothing of Richard's, than he did from delivering messages to me. James knew that Richard was coming home and had not told me. James had also been "kind" enough to let Richard know where I had been spending my evenings the past months. So I was elated to see him, but our reunion was dampened by the innuendos that had been planted by his "friend" while Richard had been locked up. After weeks and months of waiting for him to come home, after whole paychecks had been consumed by the rent, after all the lonely nights in our quiet room while our roommates' beer cans filled the trash can (I would no doubt have to empty), I looked forward to him holding me again, but it was only a lukewarm reception.

I saw something in his eyes I had not seen before: distrust. It was in his eyes and in his tone and I did not know how to explain my long hours at the bar except to say, truthfully, "I was lonely." I told him about Roger and Steve and Angie, but all he heard was Roger. I told him again and again that nothing was going on but still he pleaded with me to tell him "the truth." I could not tell it more truly than I already had. We stood in the middle of the bedroom arguing before we could even unpack the orange Cobb County property bag still sitting at his feet. After an hour or more of going back and forth, he seemed to move from anger to guilt. I did not understand and thought he was being irrational. Finally, he tried to bargain with me.

"Tell me the truth about this guy," he urged, "and I'll tell you something, too."

I stood stock still, startled by this preview of an admission. I was afraid to move. My words betrayed my fear and slipped from my lips anyway. I had nothing to confess but, obviously, he did.

"What kind of confession do you need to make to me, Richard?" I cursed myself as soon as the words escaped me. I did not want to know. I wanted him just to believe me and let it go. And why not? The old Richard would.

Hell, the old Richard would have believed me at a moment's notice, would have never had anything to believe me about because the old Richard would have never gotten locked up and left me to this den of thieves in the first place! But it was too late. I had already asked. A quick flash of Dawn's beauty danced across my imagination and I tried to brace myself, but I could not have been prepared for the answer that was to come.

"You remember Korea, Denise?" he said without any further prodding.

"Korea?" I repeated, confused. Did Dawn visit him in Korea? She couldn't have been old enough then...

"Have you ever wondered why I got kicked out of the army?" he prodded, almost too eager to confess.

I thought about it briefly before responding,

"No. I guess I haven't, but what does this have to do with..."

Before I could finish he cut me off, blurting,

"I got a dishonorable discharge."

His shoulders seemed to shrink forward into his chest as he spoke. There was something distant about his eyes now, as if in that moment he had gone back to a place that haunted him.

He was stumbling forward now, the confession was coming whether I liked it – whether he liked it – or not.

"In Korea," he mumbled, "there was a group of us that liked to hang out together – all GIs."

I listened, afraid, but not knowing of what.

"We drank and partied with the prostitutes like most of the guys. But our motto was 'No Boundaries.' We were pretty tight and always just a little wilder and more adventurous than the other guys, you know, more willing to experiment."

He paused at that last word and looked into me; not at me, but into me. For the first time, that loving gaze I had always been so fond of felt... somehow... invasive.

He finally let out a long sigh and hung his head. "What I'm trying to tell you Denise is that when I was in Korea I slept with men. I had sex with men."

I don't know if he paused then or if his words were simply drowned out by the pounding in my head. Unable to control my reaction, I took a step back away from him as if he had physically struck me. Shock is a word too mild to describe the rushing of my heart and cold core in the pit of my stomach at his unexpected words.

The hairs on the back of my neck stood up and froze and my eyes glazed over a little. Then, right before my eyes, he seemed to transform. His shoulders looked suddenly droopy and his cheekbones seemed suspiciously delicate. Something in me connected and disconnected all at once. The long days at the mall made sense now. I could never put together my clothes the way he could. I never understood the warm undertones of just the right color blush the way he did. He had an opportunity to discover his femininity long before I did, and he was much more astute at it than I.

His words became audible again, "… and there have only been a couple of guys since then." I wondered if that tiny caveat – since then – was supposed to make me feel better; it didn't, not by a long shot. I stared at him with my mouth agape and tried to steady myself against the shifting scene in front of me. In one eye I saw a grown man with hard features and a macho stride. In the other I saw a delicate boy with a soft air about him, unable to square his shoulders. It was too much and too sudden. It was too big of a secret. I had been expecting the all-too-expected admission that he had been unfaithful with Dawn before being locked up. That I could have expected; that I would have preferred. I went somewhere inside myself and watched the rest of the scene play out through the fog.

I had heard the saying, "A house divided against it-self will fall." And so, the sand castle that Richard and I had so meticulously constructed and decorated throughout our love.

At first, it had only given a little under the pressure of everyday life and the challenges of school and jobs. But in that moment of blunt reality, the full winds of war tore at its walls until, in bitter defeat they fell away altogether, rejoining the anonymous dreams left by all the strangers who had walked the same shores before us. We would not make it and love was not enough to change that fate.

He said more, an apologetic tone replacing the hushed breathiness of his earlier admissions, but I could no longer hear him. It was as if all of a sudden his language had changed and I could not decipher the strange sounds that came from the strange man in front of me. Feeling lost and stunned, I stepped around him and his still-full property bag and half-packed a bag of my own.

Unmoved by his pleas "to stay," "to understand," even "to forgive," I headed toward the front door. The world beyond it seemed dark and forbidding, but the force of the collapse catapulted me forward still. With only a sideways glance at the home where I had found, then lost, my independence, I stepped into the rushing tide and waited for the world to take me where it would.

10

Out of the Frying Pan

My mind dazed in and out as I walked, but I did not cry. It was not a time for tears. My shock and sorrow were so great that the tears were afraid to come. I passed the clubhouse and thought of Bryan, the cute guy I always found Richard chatting with by the pool. I wondered if they were just friends – or more.

Then I remembered the wounded look in Dawn's eyes. Was this the thing that tore them apart? Had he left her for the army and come back a changed man – or had he always been that way? Did she live with the knowledge that she had shared the man of her dreams with other men?

More importantly, could I live with that knowledge?

I thought back to Vernon and Leroy and some of the other gay guys I knew growing up. I did not see Richard in them. They were who they were. They were soft or flamboyant or serious or whatever individual personality they were swathed in, but they were just people being who they were. Just like any other person you met, you could like or dislike them because of the way they mixed with who you were and that's all.

But Richard; I had never known a thing as terrifying as Richard. He was hidden in shadows, lurking dangerously just beneath the truth. It scared me to think I had opened my soul to a thing that could not open himself up to his own humanity. I shuddered at the dishonesty of it all. Was it just a cover? Were Dawn and I failed attempts to satisfy a judgmental society? Was everything a lie, or was there some truth to the lovely, thoughtful words we'd shared? Did he love me - ever? How could he love me and hide who he was from me, from himself?

There was no place in my understanding to find the answers I needed. I just knew that I could not be there under the weight of that lie and survive. I walked around the last curve of the apartment complex and hugged my feet close to the edge of the main street so lost in thought that I had not realized the day was coming to a close. Like the sun sinking low in the sky, the cindered ashes of my first love affair escaped on my long sighs and fluttered into the orange glow of the horizon.

Tired and stunned, I made my way down the length of Franklin Rd until Cobb Parkway stretched out before be urging me to choose. Unsure of where to go, I headed for the 24-Hour bowling alley and slipped in - duffle bag unnoticed. Crunched next to my bag in the women's stall staring at the love initials carved into the red metal door I knew that the home I had come to know was irretrievable broken and that somehow I had to stabilize myself enough to get to school and work.

I watched through the crack in the stall door as an early evening customer toppled into the bathroom and brushed her teeth to mask the beer scent from her mouth before changing her T-shirt and stuffing her things into a Pinky Tuscadero bowling bag. Like a hint from heaven her comfortable interchange in the bathroom eased my mind. The bowling alley had everything I needed! The sink and stall could keep me clean and the seating areas dotted throughout the dark crevices of the family fun center provided the perfect cover for a loafer looking to catch a few hours of sleep. Enthused by what little I could find to focus on I peeled last few crumpled dollars from my pocket and flattened them against the coin changing machine to separate my clothes into bowling lockers. I settled low into the hard plastic row of chairs furthest from the counter and fell into a tormented sleep.

The sound of bowling balls rumbling down the smooth lanes in search of the unsuspecting pins roused me from an uncomfortable doze. The uniform clad bowling alley attendant greeted my sleep drunk eyes with her arms folded and a scowl on her face. "Hon, you know you can't stay here. Dang near all week I don watched you loiter and ain't said a word." She reached past me and hurriedly tossed my nights' trash in the receptacle next to my book satchel. Almost regretfully she continued, "Now I don't know if you done run away or what's going on – but if I see you in here tomorrow I'm gon' have to call the police." Embarrassed but grateful I nodded my head as respectfully as I could and proceeded to the locker to repack the duffle bag that I had stuffed in the smaller locker to lighten my daily load. With an empty silence I brushed aside the fear of where I would go and took a minute to thank God for the warm, safe week I spent in the plastic chairs. Too daunted to think of how I would wash up for school the next day I threw my life over my shoulder and took back to the main road.

I walked and thought and instinctively ended up at the Mexican restaurant. The usually inviting smell of fresh fajitas sizzling against the heat of serving skillets suddenly turned my stomach. I sat in a booth near the door and tried not to let the greasy smell engulf me. I was lost in a hole that I had not seen coming and I was still falling.

I was so lost that I didn't even notice my friends come in the door and head to the bar. It wasn't until I heard a familiar high-pitched laugh that I lifted my head up to look around. As if she felt me stir, Angie caught my eye as soon as I glanced up. She stopped mid-laughter and slipped from her barstool. I had never asked how old she was, but as she approached me with a worried face, I realized she was much older than I had originally assumed. Something about that knowledge made me feel safer and I clung to her.

She did not seem taken-back or uncomfortable in my grasp. She just let me cling to her; just let me do that thing I needed to do the most. At first, the guys must have thought we were just goofing off, but as Roger caught a glimpse of my face, he too came to surround me with his friendship; Steve was close behind. It was if we had known each other much longer than the three months we had socialized at the bar. As we sat there crowded into that booth, we felt bonded more deeply. The silence was not harsh and the closeness was not intrusive.

We sat there just like that for a while until I found the strength to try and come out of the black hole to meet their concern. But a different kind of vacuum had hold of me this time. It was not the easy, relaxing energy that invites you in to sit a spell. It was brutal and demanding and I knew that I would have to fight hell and everything I wanted to be free of the force that took hold of me. Still half dazed, I began trying to put words together that made sense.

"Richard..."

"I..."

"He..."

I took a deep, exasperated breath and tried again, but Angie stopped me. "Hon', just let it go for now," she urged compassionately. I looked into the kindness of her face and felt the safety of Steve and Roger close by as well. I finally mustered a weak smile for my new friends and announced with only a tinge of doubt, "Richard and I are over."

They all looked down at my haphazardly packed bag and Roger asserted good-humoredly, "Yeah, you must be!" With that, we all broke into a round of laughter and I was glad they knew how to handle the pain because, frankly, I did not.

Steve and Angie spoke softly to each other for a moment then motioned for Roger to grab my bag. Slightly relieved, but still reeling, I moved without the slightest resistance when Angie grabbed my arm. I was so airless that the faintest pressure of her fingertips guided me up from my seat and toward the door.

Bag in tow, I floated up the road on foot, surrounded by my new clan. They were there to rescue me at a time when I could think of no one who could. Those months of laughing and drinking at the bar earned some well-needed friendships and I was grateful. When I walked away from Richard, I had also walked away from the only place I knew I could call home. I did not know where to go or what to do next. But I was now a part of this band and the thought comforted me as they whisked me away with them.

When I thought of what they were rescuing me from I knew I was willing to do whatever they asked to earn my keep. In a moment of confession, I had been elevated into the world of adulthood all too soon. As I took my first step into that world, I knew it meant walking away from all that I had known in my youth. So, the vision of a cap and gown fell completely away to make room for my first piece of armor.

11

High School Drop Out

I knew it had to be done, but it still wasn't easy to do. How do you ask a bird to give up her song or a cheetah to sit idly by on her haunches as the rest of the pack takes chase? How do you tell a child that reindeer cannot fly and how could I, who had never known any other dream, put that dream away?

I touched the handle of the high school door and stiffened when the cold of it reached deep into me. Had it been weeks since I was there? Had it already been months? I almost couldn't find my way because the rows all looked alike now. There was nothing distinct about the place anymore. It was just another cold, gray school hallway now with none of the old landmarks I'd thought I'd always recognize to show me the way.

I fumbled around corners until finally I saw the familiar blue devil staring at me from the door of locker # 254. He was not supposed to be there. All the stickers and graffiti left by the rowdy class before us had been neatly cleared; all, that is, except for him. He was just a one in a million blue devil sticker, but somehow he had survived the Windex and scouring powder assaults that had erased all the rest. The right side of his narrow face was slightly faded and a bit of his goatee had been rubbed away, but there he was just the same.

When my eyes met his, I shuddered because it seemed as if his crooked smile was mocking me. It was saying, "I told you so." After all the mornings I had been running late but still took the time to adore him before the second bell – he mocked me.

And what was worse was that I could not explain to him – to anyone, least of all myself – the reason for my decision. There was no combination of words that I could string together that could explain why I was abandoning the only future I ever imagined for myself.

How, after all those long nights of studying and longer days of dreaming about college and success, I could just walk away from the only thing I ever wanted to be. My stomach soured as the names of the academic and literary heroes I adored taunted me from the corner of my mind. The weeks and months of dust they had gathered did not slow the ache they caused as they fell from my memory one by one. Dickenson, Poe, Whitman, Thoreau, Dubois – even Homer himself – could see that I was plummeting into a place where dreams dared not go – and they were taking a final bow before they eluded me forever.

Of course, I tried to convince them that it was only for a little while; that as soon as I got back on my feet again I would be back for them as well. I would pick up where I had left off and not miss a beat. And even while I was away I would still read and study until I could wholeheartedly pursue my dreams of writing again.

I tried to convince myself, but there was a deep hollow in the sound of my locker door as it creaked open for me. Then, quickly, before I lost my nerve, I reached into the abyss and grabbed every scrap of paper my fingers could connect with. Such emptiness washed over me that I dared not read the neatly scrawled words that gracefully filled them with thought. But still, geometry notes and literary secrets peeped at me one last time as if pleading to be spared. But I was firm and spared no life.

Not Greek mythology, not the Laws of Probability, not even the Renaissance would survive my ultimate mission to search, to destroy… to retreat. I watched each piece of paper that now no better than scrap land squarely into the trash can I had borrowed from the guidance counselor's office.

Like the Devil sticker's, her expression had been full of questions as I told her my plans to leave school, but no matter her choice of words, she only said one thing to me with the look in her eyes, *"You are throwing your life away."* And the truth in her glaring eyes stunned me into silence – just as the gaze of the Blue Devil choked me into shame. Fear reached for me and held fast to my chest as I cleared away the last traces of my claim to academic notoriety and made certain that, at Marietta High School, my name would be forgotten by the end of the semester.

The knowledge of scholars past echoed throughout the halls, but Marietta was not ready for the kind of understanding I had already come to. The neatly manicured lawns and pretty public squares were not prepared for the misshapen truth of my own personal life. The mere mention of the word "homeless" was not even appropriate – unless, of course, I was doing a compassionate and insightful story for the Blue Herald. We were, after-all, a humanitarian community and at least mentioned the things we dared not touch.

No one here could understand or approve of my circumstances. I knew that Roger and Steve and Angie were not villains; they were kind souls who were intent on rescuing me. Their plans to help me learn to survive were honorable. They could not be held liable for not pushing me to stay in school. They knew work; they understood hard and manual labor. They knew progress by the sweat of their brow. They did not dream in chapter and verse the way I did. They knew the north and they were coming to know the south. Their lines did not extend beyond the borders of America and their thoughts did not reach into the blackness of space the way mine did. I would have to train my mind not to wander to such places; for now. I would learn to dream in pay wages and withholding taxes and time clocks and overtime hours until I could find room in my life for the dreams of my soul again.

With resolve, I took one last look at my future buried deep in the cracks and crevices of that locker and mustered up the strength to close them inside, once and for all. And as the door clamored shut one last time, I knew that I alone would remember its tragic sound.

I made my last passage through the hallway of hope and the doors of Marietta High School flew open and emptied me onto the sidewalk leading to uncertainty. A gentle breeze wandered through the campus trees and my mind closed to the laughter rising from the grassy hill behind the library. In the distance, gray clouds hovered in the blueness of the sky. I quickened my step and steeled my mind and I knew that not rain, nor sleet nor snow would keep me from the nowhere I was headed...

12

Into the Fire

It began again.

I adjusted to the rhythm of the house I called home with a pensive kind of hope still tarnished from the lessons of my past. In order to feel worthy, I quickly found things to do to make myself useful. I practiced the recipes I had learned and escorted the trash to the dumpster. I found that Angie was not prone to cleaning so I assaulted the layers of things that had grown on the shower walls and in crevices of the kitchen counter tops.

I worked long hours thanklessly because I did not want to always be the first one home in an apartment that didn't belong to me. I volunteered for every closing and every employee cancellation the restaurant had. I made sure that my check was always at least as good as Angie's and, sometimes, even as good as Roger's. He didn't work as often as Steve did, but the money

was good for a machinist. But as my feet began to settle into the grass on their side of the street, something felt dangerously amiss.

There was a noticeable dissention in the home and tension was building between Steve and Angie. Fewer nights were spent unwinding at the Mexican restaurant and more time was dedicated to drinking at home. Angie's laughter was no longer pleasantly infectious. Instead it was closed and bitter and seldom heard before at least a half-pint of her favorite brand of cheap gin.

In the wake of this souring mood, fear began to grab at me from where I slept on the tiny living room couch. I didn't know how long the thin fibers of commitment would hold the clan together and what would happen to me when they finally, inevitably (or so it seemed) broke. So, to the best of my ability, I tried to break the ice that had formed just beneath the surface.

I said nice things to Angie the way Steve used to do and I went out of my way to make Roger feel important, which is what seemed to make him smile. But all the extra effort made little difference. The quiet drinking with the scattered laughter turned into loud clamoring discussions and then, ultimately, to war.

Within weeks, Steve and Angie fell apart and Roger fell into the bottom of the gin bottles he bought on the way home from work every day. As soon as I had finished unpacking my things, it seemed, Angie was loading hers into the back of a taxi and headed back to Pennsylvania. I was only able to piece together bits of the final feud that precipitated her untimely departure, but it seemed that her unexpected pregnancy was unforgivable to the man who had impregnated her. So she decided to go home where her mother could help her raise the baby that Steve didn't want. I felt for her and loathed Steve for his callousness, but kept my opinion to myself since voicing it would probably mean that I would have to load my things into the back of a taxi as well.

What had begun as an uncertain environment quickly proved to be unstable and hostile. Steve became quiet and withdrawn. He went to work, came home and went to his room, where the television kept him company. As the days and weeks without Angie stockpiled, he stopped speaking to me altogether and mumbled only two- or three-word phrases to his cousin, Roger.

Roger, on the other hand, became increasingly more talkative; verbose, even. It seemed that without Angie around he longed for someone to chat with. At first, our conversations were light-hearted and anonymous; the day-to-day chit-chat of polite roommates. But more and more, he opened up his thoughts to me and before I could turn the pages myself, the next chapter began to unfold.

Roger was to be the opposite of what I had come to distrust in Richard. He stood more than 6'4" with broad, squared shoulders and large, rough hands. His jokes were harsh, his laughter was deep and his strides were sure and macho. He was not gentle and graceful like Richard. He preferred straight vodka or gin over the pretty green bottles of Heineken that Richard fancied. And as the liquid intoxicated his head, his voice became louder and harsher – unlike Richard's wistful, quiet drunken reveries.

Although we spoke more and more, Roger was not apt to talk about his feelings. He was matter-of-fact and blunt and we chatted about Harrisburg and football and, of course, warehouse machinery. It wasn't what I had become accustomed to with Richard, but the more I focused on the crudeness of Roger, the more I came to like it or, at least, respect its straightforwardness and lack of deceit.

In just a few months, I had traded the soft, feathered kisses of Richard's love for the harsh friendship Roger freely offered me. It was not like falling in love with Roger. It was more like falling out of love with Richard. I needed a man who was rudimentary, not complicated. I decided that I needed Roger's friendship more than I needed Richard's love.

Early in our friendship, Roger had taken to calling me "Princess" – and the more we sat around sipping gin and chatting about machines, the less he used "Denise." I was just "princess this" and "princess that" and it suited me just fine. We were not romantic; the subject had never even come up so I just took it as "little sister love." Our odd friendship seemed to satisfy his loneliness and it helped me "get by" while the memories of Richard loosened their grip on my mind.

I worked, helped to keep the apartment clean and looked forward to Roger coming home in the evenings with a bottle of gin and a safe, two-dimensional chat. I didn't so much like the taste of gin, but usually nursed a small glass for myself while Roger "got his head right." It wasn't long before I noticed how my glass would sit for hours waiting for me and Roger's glass would be in constant need of filling.

Over time, it took more and more gin to "get his head right" and I began to notice how much harsher Roger's words got as he drank. Uneasy with his increasingly angry demeanor, I began venturing outside the apartment for friendship. A nice family from Chicago lived in the building across the street and I began hanging out there in the evenings, talking to Max, the new friend I had made after work – avoiding Roger's increased agitation.

To my amazement, I came in one evening to find Richard, of all people, sitting on the couch listening to Roger's slurred words! Unsure of how they found each other and why Richard was there in the first place, I avoided the collision and spent more and more time with Max and his family across the street. I knew I had to get out of the volatile situation I had put myself in, but had no idea of where to go or what to do.

One evening I realized that not knowing what to do could have grave consequences. I came downstairs after taking Steve a plate of dinner to find Roger standing at the bottom of the landing with his 5th or 6th empty glass of gin. His posture may have been uncertain but there was no mistaking the intensity of his gaze; his watery eyes were blazing a dangerous red.

"Princess – what the hell is going on?" he slurred.

I shrugged and tried to figure out what had happened.

"Princess – Stevie? You picked Stevie?" he accused.

"What are you talking about Roger? I always take him dinner when I cook. He's sleeping anyway – I left it on the dresser," I tried to comfort.

"So, you fucking Stevie now?"

I gasped and stared at the scowl on his face. Instinctively, I was silent for a moment.

"I'm not getting no pussy, Richard not getting no pussy - and Stevie is getting all the pussy," he declared angrily.

"Roger – I am not having sex with Steve or anyone else!" I defended.

"Ooo-ooh!" he sang. "I know you not having sex wit' me or my boy Rich – but I watch you coming in and out of my cousin's room eee'vry night."

Frustrated with the effect of the gin, I took the last steps to the bottom of the stairs and tried to brush past him.

"Ah-ah-ah" he shook his finger at me, slurring. "Not 'till I get a ex-pun-ation."

"Roger, you've had too much to drink--"
WHACK!!

My words were interrupted by the white hot fire his hand brought to my face. Stunned, I stumbled backward against the bottom railing and reached out to it for support.

"You calling me a fucking drunk AND fucking my cousin? That's a lot of fucking, Princess"

Afraid to do anything, I gripped the banister and waited. My heart pounded loudly and my eyes raced from the staircase to the front door. I wanted to run, but I was afraid to move.

"Come on – I'm gonna 'dress this shit right now," Roger spat.

He reached around my head and grabbed a handful of hair at the nape of my neck and pulled me up the stairs like a rag doll. I tried to pry his fingers loose, but it was no use. I used my legs, scrambling to grab on each step to help ease the burden on my scalp until we reached the top of the landing.

With his grip still firm, he dragged me the short distance to Steve's room and pushed the door open with his free hand. I looked up toward the bed and yelled for Steve to help me but he did not stir in the commotion. An empty Beefeater's Gin bottle lay on the floor and he snored loudly even as I yelled out for him.

"Ain't that a bitch?" Roger declared. "You done knocked him out, huh? You dirty little Princess," he scolded me.

"Roger – you're wrong!" I yelled up at him, praying desperately that someone in the apartment next door would hear me crying out.

He loosened his grip on my hair and I fell limply to the floor at his feet, trying to regain myself. Then I looked up at him and knew that it was far from over; in fact, it had just begun. Before I could scramble to my feet, he had my upper arms locked in his grasp and was dragging me to the bathroom. He shoved me in the small room and as I fell over the toilet he stepped in behind me and closed the door.

Terrified, I grabbed the plunger and flung it toward him. He swatted it away unscathed and stepped toward me. Backed between his large frame and the small space between the bathtub and the toilet, I froze. I looked at his face and knew there was no reasoning with him.

"Take that shit off," he demanded.

I grasped the wrinkled blouse I was wearing, knowing it would not protect me. The noise of his breathing rushed into my ears like a cold northern wind. I thought about a switch blade pressed between my thighs and quickly removed my blouse. His eyes motioned for me to take my pants off so I fumbled with them until they fell free.

"Get in the fucking shower," he demanded.

I stepped back quickly, almost falling into the tub, and pressed my panty-clad body against the cold shower wall, silently waiting for what was to come next. In one motion, he reached for the cold water with one hand, turning it on full blast while reaching for his zipper with the other. I watched in frozen horror as he released himself from the confines of his jeans and begin to stroke him-self to arousal.

Panicked, I lunged toward him in a desperate attempt to open the door and run out of the madness that was taking place in my adopted home. One large hand connected with the center of my chest and sent me crashing back into the tub under the torrent of freezing cold water. Then blow after blow struck me until the water mixed with blood in a steady stream.

His fist struck my shoulder and head and face with increasing intensity until I could not feel them connect anymore. The water rushed into my eyes and partly blinded me as I tried to look up at him from my crouched position in the tub. His blows slowed and I could see his other hand still frantically stroking himself. He grunted and stroked until he could no longer seem to focus on the hand he was using to pummel my body with. The blows ceased and as the blood streamed from my mouth he ejaculated into the tub, sending a demonic mixture of pain and pleasure down the drain.

My head fell back against the tub as a dark figure opened the door behind him. Voices erupted then, but I could not make them out nor did their words interest me. My head stopped pounding and became suddenly weightless. I looked up into the shower head and was blinded by the water still streaming from above. I felt my body lift into the air and then there was nothing.

13

A Jim Baker Miracle

The sound of Jim Baker's voice reached out to me and delivered me from a hard sleep. I slowly opened my eyes to the sight of Reverend Baker pouring the gospel out to his flock and Tammy Faye shedding tears of witness behind him.

I slowly turned my head toward the window and felt lightning crash across my face and neck. I reached for my face and felt the large knots that had developed while I was at rest. Slowly, I eased myself into an upright position and looked around. I was in Steve's room. It smelled like old tennis shoes and gin. I tried to focus back in on Reverend Baker hoping that one of the miracles he performed through the TV would reach my aching head and body.

Steve eased the door open and looked in on me. "Can I come in?" he asked gingerly. It struck me that if his concern were available last night, I might not be tucked in his bed bruised and battered this morning. I said nothing and watched him cross the short distance and sit on the edge of the bed.

"Are you okay?" he asked tentatively.

"No, I'm not," I spat through swollen lips.

He glanced down at the tent-like T-shirt he must have put on me last night and quickly looked away from the purple bruises on my arms and thighs.

"Denise, you know Roger..." he began.

I interrupted, "I know Roger what, Steve?"

"He just drank too much," he continued weakly.

I said nothing for a moment and tried to make out the shape of Roger's closed fist in the purple bruises dotting my thigh. Steve rubbed his chin and stared at a spot on the wall.

I broke the silence. "I need to leave here; I need some pants."

I pulled my knees toward my chest in an attempt to swing my legs around Steve's frame and get out of bed. The pain shot through my stomach and back and made me whimper involuntarily. Steve scooted off the bed and hung his head. I continued, "Why did he beat me like that, Steve? Why?" I paused to let a sob settle in my throat. Then, choking the sob down deep I declared, "I'm going to call the police."

"Denise," Steve said, looking and sounding alarmed, "my cousin didn't mean it."

"I don't care; I'm going to call the police."

Steve's face hardened against my threat. "And tell them what, Denise?"

"I'm going to tell them how Roger beat me and..." I let my voice trail off, trying to form

words to describe Roger ejaculating in the tub.

Steve rubbed his forehead and took a deep breath, as if he didn't want to say what came next.

"Denise, if you call the police they are going to take you and Roger to jail."

"Bull crap, Steve! They can't take me to jail – I didn't do anything to Roger!" I cried indignantly.

"They are going to take you to jail because you are under-aged," he explained, almost as if he were reading a line from a script.

"I am an emancipated adult; they can't take me to jail for being under age," I said smugly.

"Is that even a real thing?" he pried. "I mean, have you seen the papers saying that you were emancipated?"

I paused as my breath got thin under the scrutiny of the question.

"N-No," I stammered, suddenly uncertain. "But my mother told Richar-"

Steve cut me off, "That was bullshit, Denise. There is no such thing and you are going to go to jail if you call the police.

They will find your mother and you are going to sit in jail until she comes to get you."

I hung my head, shaking. I remembered the cold steel doors at the juvenile detention center and the awful meanness of my mother when she finally came to liberate me. Defeat settled over me and I let the tears welling up in my eyes fall onto the bed. I wondered where Roger was as I watched Steve start away from the bed.

The thought of facing him after the beating and what he did in front of me made the tears run more freely. Afraid, I said nothing more. Steve shook his head again and crossed the room to collect a glass and bottle from his dresser. I watched him pour a long shot of gin and come back to the bed and bring it to my lips.

"Drink a little of this," he offered. "It will make you feel better."

I looked at the glass, knowing it was the reason I needed to feel better in the first place. I brought the liquid to my bottom lip anyway and it burned from the outside all the way down my throat. The tears slipped down my face and fell into the glass, making me a cocktail of regret.

"Just - don't leave now - stay until you feel better. Then, if you still want to go, I'll help you," Steve consoled.

I shot him a look that must have told him what I was thinking.

"Roger won't touch you again – I promise."

With that, he set the glass on the nightstand and quietly left the room. I sat in the absence of friendship and listened to Jim Baker give out his phone number and imploring faithful souls to support the ministry through financial donations. Without much money and without a Jim Baker miracle, I lay in Steve's bed for the days it took for my body to heal and the bruises to begin to fade. I heard Roger going to his room and going to the bathroom, but he avoided Steve's room. As soon as the swelling began to go down, I grabbed my Cover Girl compact, doctored the fading bruises on my face and made my move.

I waited until I heard Roger and Steve leave for work and headed downstairs and rummaged through the closet for my duffle bag. I gathered as many clothes and toiletries as I could lift and headed out of the apartment before fear of where I would go could make me turn around and stay.

Walking past Max's apartment, duffle in tow, I wondered if he knew what a relief it had been for me to escape my troubles into his daily family life. I wondered if he knew about the madness I had been living in right across the parking lot. With a mix of gratitude and sadness, I almost stopped to knock on his door then thought better of it. Maybe it was just better left alone. I would leave, but I would not say goodbye.

I thought vaguely of Tracy as I walked to the top of the apartments and onto Franklin Road. I missed her and hoped she was okay. Things might be messy at home for her, but I was glad she was not in the streets with me. It was true that life inside my mother's house seemed to unfold with a slow, unaddressed pain, but I was quickly finding that life on my own could unleash with a fury that was fast and brutal.

14

Fugitive

I didn't care where the road took me at that point. I just needed to be on it. I needed to be in a place where there was no Richard and no Roger and no empty school locker or left-behind devil sticker to contend with. The last time I had visited the Greyhound bus station it was to wait for Al to hide me out from my problems. Now, I waited as a legally ticketed passenger for the bus to South Georgia.

When I arrived, I found that Savannah was a gray blur of old memories and a white hot flash of new challenges. There were no want ads for 12th grade drop-outs and most of the jobs that came easily in Atlanta were manned by single mothers trying to keep their children off of welfare and by newly released parolees trying to stay out of the big house.

To add to my distress, the whispers of the ladies at Gladys's shop had spilled out all over town. Did I really run away from home to be with a grown man? Was it true that I had an abortion? Were the police looking for me in three states? I avoided the questions, but had to live with the accusations in people's eyes just the same. The grapevine was a tangled mess, but I did verify that it was true my mother had moved to Miami and took another radio job.

I was happy for her but, at the same time; selfishly I knew it meant that Sgt. House was a thing of the past. My sister Sabrina broke the news that Tracy was pregnant and on her own at 13. No one knew where she was. My heart sank. I had hoped that Tracy was having better luck at home than I did and imagined how much fun she was having in Miami. I never thought that she had only survived on a few months longer than I had at home and prayed that she had not yet run into a fist as furious as Roger's was.

I fried chicken at the local fast food establishment until the rumors came right onto the job and made my manager uncomfortable enough to ask me to a take a leave of absence. Then it was back to the classified ads.

Struggling to stay afloat, I drifted between distant relatives and friends – unwilling to come to terms with the fact that I was, quite literally, homeless. Small, insignificant paychecks got me by at one place just long enough for me to grab hold of another temporary residence until the rumors, or the competition, sent me packing yet again. But nothing lasted and nowhere welcomed me with open arms. I could not believe that 16 was about to give way to 17 and my life was in the state it was in. Mirrors became unfriendly adversaries and the rumors and whispers were a constant companion.

Finally, the news of my supreme failure reached out past the City of Savannah's street signs and beyond the Chatham County line to find my cousin Sharon in Virginia. In a heated moment of love and compassion she came to my rescue and whisked me away to her college-educated life in the suburbs. It was as if my father's heart had left the confines of the grave and motivated his sister's daughter.

She had always loved me. In fact, all of my father's family had always been kind to me. I remembered that much from my childhood. But I did not know her and did not know how to be around her. Everything about Sharon seemed so wonderful. She held me and nurtured me and cleaned what wounds she could find, but the deepest of them lived in the confines of my sharp and wounded soul and bled profusely no matter how tightly she hugged me or what salve she used to try and soothe them.

She lavished me with the loveliest cashmere dresses and the finest wool slacks, but thanks to the barriers I'd been building for months on the street, at that point I was incapable of gratitude. The more I spent time with her, the worse I felt about myself. I began to wonder just what kind of atrocity I was to have had the kind of life that was so different from hers. Maybe the things my mother said were true. I decided there was something inherently wrong with me and I was not good enough to hang out with nice girls like Sharon.

I thought maybe it was too late for love in my live; that maybe something wilder and more compelling had already taken hold of me to the point where there was no stopping my downward spiral. So she talked to me and welcomed me and promised me a life full of all the things I should have, but I was not strong enough to hold on to the hope Sharon offered. And no sooner than she relaxed her watchful eye and went off to her office building in DC, I absconded into the night.

The pain and guilt I felt for walking out of the home she opened up to me buried itself under the rest of the pain and guilt that lived in me – and I ran. I hitchhiked my way from the quiet safety of the suburbs into the city and sold her pearl earrings and whatever else my selfish hands had found in the few minutes after she'd left for work. Like an animal afraid of captivity, I fished in the bottom of my hand-me-down black purse for the last of the quarters I had stolen from her piggy bank and bought sandwiches for the long ride ahead. I tucked my legs into the back of the empty Greyhound seat in front of me and headed down the road again; a fugitive from my own mind, certain I had burned the last of my bridges behind me...

15

God's Tears

I sat in the large waiting area listening for my name while soldiers in uniform bustled about me performing their daily duties. I had been so impressed with the neatly-uniformed recruiter I remembered addressing the senior class of Marietta High school that, when Sgt. House told me I could only stay with him temporarily, I knew exactly what to do.

Richard and I had not lasted. Roger was a maniac. I had broken Sharon's heart. But I would not mess up the chance that Sgt. House was giving me. For no reason other than love, he had opened his doors to me after my flight from Virginia. No matter what he felt behind the break-up with my mother, he said that the place I had once called home would be open to me as long as I was trying to do something with my life.

So, without flinching, I promised him that I was not a "lost cause" after all and that the military was definitely a good move for an "adventurous" girl like me. I began to avoid the Wills high school buddies I had hooked up with when I first got back from Virginia since smoking weed didn't seem to suit me anyway. I knew I had to act more responsibly. *I would make Sgt. House proud*, I said, believing in every word. But now that it was time to put up or shut up, my nerves of steel turned to mush. My stomach began to churn and I wondered if going into the Army was really the right thing for me, after all.

What if I didn't make a good soldier? What if I couldn't do what they wanted me to? What if my commanding officer was a jerk? What if I needed to run away in the night and there were no pearl earrings to sell or piggy banks to break into? What if...

"Denise Stokes," my named blared over the intercom and broke my reverie. I rose shakily to my feet and tried to remember which door it was that I was supposed to enter. My first order and I couldn't even get it right. The enemy wouldn't be getting any classified information from me - that was for sure; I couldn't remember any of it! A skinny red-headed boy wearing K-Mart army fatigues read the confusion on my face and authoritatively pointed to the white door on the left. I mouthed "thank you" to the future officer and nervously put one foot in front of the other.

I opened the door and a pale man in a neatly starched and decorated uniform motioned for me to take a seat. I crossed the room feeling like I was under a microscope. I sat down, remembering to keep my chin up and my back straight. My recruiter, Sergeant Graves, had already told me to go ahead and start working out and jogging in the mornings because I would be doing "a lot of that" soon. It was not new information to me, since two of my mother's life companions were either military or retired military, but I thanked him for the "good advice" anyway. He shared as many tips and clues with me as he could, but even he had no explanation for today's unexpected appointment. He was just as confused as I was that they wanted me to come back down to the Military Entrance Processing Station after I had already taken my physical.

With an AFQT of 98 apparently I was one of his highest scoring recruits and could choose almost any military occupational specialty I wanted. Without a second thought, I had decided that I would be an Intelligence Analyst just long enough to qualify for Counter Intelligence. Worried that my MOS might be at stake, I kept pressing Sgt. Graves for more information but they just hadn't told him because of something called a "need-to-know" rule, which was the military's polite way of saying, "none of your damned business."

I nervously waited for the uniformed man with slightly graying hair to let me know why I had been recalled. A woman dressed in a military version of a nurse's uniform came through the inner door and handed him a folder without looking in my direction. I got a glimpse of my name written in bold black letters on the tab. Although enthusiastic for the opportunity the Army offered me to have a more meaningful life, I shuddered at the thought that I wasn't even government issued yet and my life had already been reduced to a simple, thin manila folder.

The man at the desk carefully cleared his throat and peered at me over the rim of his silver-framed glasses. The southern twang in his voice mixed with his stern military demeanor struck official fear in me as he asked,

"Miss Stokes, do you know why you have been called here today, ma'am?"

Unable to find my voice at that particular moment, I shook my head "*No.*" My lack of uniformed behavior must have irritated him because he hesitated long enough to shuffle his papers again while wiping the frown from his face. I could have kicked myself for not answering, "No Sir," but consoled myself with the fact that I was not army property yet.

He then proceeded to inform me that I had applied to enter the Armed Forces of the United States and before he could complete what sounded like a rehearsed speech I was pinching the inside of my folded hands to keep from laughing. I lightened up a bit and thought that maybe, with the natural assimilation skills I had learned movong all the time and trying to please my mother; I would fit into the army after all.

After I got past the formality of it, I realized that even the military was just as mixed up and crazy as the rest of the world. I calmed the inner giggles and re-focused my attention just as he was saying "...and a part of your application for the armed services was the completion of SF93 and the subsequent routine physical examination which took place right here at this processing station..."

I had no idea where he was going with his 'official talk' but tried to look well-informed as I follow him. His voice sounded so official, I couldn't help but to give him my official face in return and let it go at that until his hairy knuckled hand shuffled a document free from my manila file and passed it across the gray desk for me to read. He continued as my eyes made contact with the medical file, "...and it is unfortunate that your blood results for the HTLVIII test..."

His voice droned on but I lost all sense of composure and numbed to the tiny courier font letters typed just under my name.

"Miss Stokes, as you can see, your test results have come back unsatisfactory and, as a result of that, you will have to be classified as a permanent medical disqualification."

With no hope of regaining my stern facial expression I stopped trying to mask the numb confusion it had been replaced with. He paused to ask if I knew what my test results meant.

"No sir," I replied with a frantic sense of impending doom.

He cleared his throat again, this time almost regretfully. He took his glasses off and looked intently at my face as if to see if I was lying. Then his God-like voice assaulted my ears with the words that I would hear, over and over again during countless sleepless nights, for the rest of my life:

"Miss Stokes, you have AIDS and we cannot accept you into the any of the armed forces. Please do not reapply. Furthermore it is advisable that you do everything you want to now because you're most probably going to die before you even reach the age of 21."

His voice droned on but I was unable to accept the brutality of them all at once so I focused on stonewalling my face until he finished.

He shuffled papers again, only now it seemed he was moving in slow motion and deliberately avoiding my wide eyes. A thin veil of fog seemed to come down out of the ceiling and settle on everything in the white room, making the details disappear. His voice finally penetrated the mist and stung me again, "Do you understand what I've said to you?"

I could barely hear him because a succession of explosions had been set off in my head. One after another, they invaded the far recesses of my mind and set my entire brain on fire. Every part of my head was trying to run, but seemed to stumble over the thoughts that had run just ahead – causing a traffic jam. Suddenly, I was focusing on him behind his gray steel desk through someone else's eyes. The room began to spin and my body surrendered to the numbness that had washed over it and floated up out of the seat and spun with the room.

"Miss Stokes...? Miss Stokes?" I heard him call to me in his sanctioned drawl. I mumbled something breathlessly while he tried once more to make his words make sense to me. I nodded my head to whatever he was saying and tried to feel my hands to make sure I was really there. I rose from the gray steel chair and had to look down to see if my feet had a firm grip on the floor because I could not feel them.

Waves of blackness washed over my eyes and threatened to erase everything, so I focused on the lines separating the large white tiles in the floor. They led past his desk and guided me across the expanse to the door. Just as I put my hand on the door knob to leave, he called out to me as if he had just told me that I had a cold and should take two aspirin,

"Have a nice day, ma'am." I heard him shuffle my file one last time and as I left and imagined he was appropriately placing it in the "reject" file, never to think of it again.

In all of my life and in all of the pages of Webster I had read, there was no word I could find that explained how I felt at that very moment. Not "perplexed," because I was *way* beyond that. Not "shocked," because that was just an appetizer to what I was really experiencing. I was partly numb, partly on fire; half-scared, half-angry. Some places in me took off running and some places just plopped right down in the middle of the floor, weakened by the weight of the news and my inability to comprehend it.

It was if I had been suddenly smitten from the face of the earth and dropped into a black hole to stare into the face of hell. As hard as I tried, none of the justifications in my head offered any relief. Not my 3.8 grade average, not the gorgeous brown eyes my mother had given me, not the flowery words I often drew out on paper – nothing could save me. Sgt. Graves said they wouldn't care that I had dropped out of high school and gotten a G.E.D. because of my high ASVAB scores. I was not as disciplined as I promised myself I would be, but I studied just the same. Sometimes at Steve and Roger's place, sometimes on my break at work, sometimes with no place to lie down for the night, no matter what was going on I found the time to study.

My body was seventeen and graceful muscles rippled across my shoulders and stomach and legs just beneath the soft smooth surface of the caramel brown skin that held me together. My arms were ample and my fingers were precise. My mind was open enough to accept complex codes and to translate languages and my eyes were keen enough to see into tomorrow; it was beyond my comprehension that death could be so close. I was disqualified – from life it seemed.

In my mind, I saw an orange sun burning its way across the gray sky until it was a powdery blue. I heard brown thrashers and blue jays come to life with song and saw flowers turn their pastel faces toward heaven in thanks. There were no dark clouds and there were no pale and cloaked riders atop black horses breaking the horizon and coming for me in a clamoring of hooves and swinging scythes. How could the army not see how alive and capable I was? How could they just throw me away? And if they did, what was going to happen to me?

I stared blankly ahead and made my way toward the front door. Immediately the hush of the little white room was diluted by the bustling noise of the outer waiting area. I slowly pushed through the steady stream of bodies that seemed to also follow the invisible lines on the floor. I caught a glimpse of the golden afternoon sunlight streaming through the glass entry door and reached for the shiny, steel-barred handle. I was surprised when my palm actually made contact with it rather than passing through. I felt like a ghost; and shouldn't my body do ghostly things, too, like move through walls and pass through glass doors unmolested?

I shuffled my feet over the doorstep fully expecting to wake up from the awful dream that had engulfed me. I hesitated hoping the man in the steel-framed glasses would come running after me to tell me that somehow my file had gotten mixed up with another one and that he was wrong; that he was sorry. My gut churned in anticipation of hearing him say, "Welcome to the Army, Miss Stokes! Welcome to the rest of your life."

"Miss Stokes! Miss Stokes!" I heard a voice calling me. I turned in half-relief, only to focus my eyes on a burly black man standing in front of me instead with his armed folded across his chest. Sgt. Graves looked at me with questioning eyes.

He wanted to know where I was going.

So did I.

He wanted to know what had happened.

So did I.

He fired his questions at me with military precision, but they just rolled off and slumped over onto the cold, unattractive gray cement of the parking lot: "Miss Stokes is there something wrong?"

"No-sir... I mean Yes-sir." I struggled to make sense of my thoughts. "Sir, I won't be going into the Army," I stated matter-of-factly. He looked at me with a question mark on his lips, but I raised my hand to stop him from asking.

"Sir, it's on a need-to-know basis."

He looked offended, but did not press. He reached in his pocket for his car keys and we began silently walking across the parking lot.

We reached the car and I looked at the blue and white government tag on the back of the blue Citation. A pang hit my heart with such force that I gasped. He turned toward me and looked into my eyes. His questioning look had turned to one of concern. I couldn't face him, though. I couldn't face anyone.

I ignored his concern and sat in the car and lightly slammed the door as if to say, *"Let's go."* He sat behind the wheel and cranked the engine to life. It sounded like the roar of an angry lion, one that had been dethroned as king of the jungle and left to die alone in the bush. I closed my eyes and saw the wounded beast with his golden mane shaking with rage. I pitied him, but I couldn't help him. When I opened my eyes again we had already left the parking lot and hit the highway. I watched the cars in the other lane racing toward us. I silently prayed that one would swerve and hit our blue government Citation. They didn't. They just buzzed by, unseeing... and uncaring. I heard the gray haired man's words over and over. The imprint of the letters typed across my file seared in my brain before finally blurring into an incomprehensible pool of ink.

The icy fingers returned to tear at my heart and I turned my head to the sky with a bewildered look embedded in my eyes.

Dark clouds had covered the sun as if to block my view of God. Before I could blink again, the sky tore open and rained down on the gray world.

God was crying. He was crying because I couldn't. I was afraid that if I started, I would never be able to stop. So I tilted my chin to the crying clouds and rode in silence, my fate once again a blank slate upon which I was expected to draw a very uncertain future.

16

Worm in a Bottle

We pulled up to the driveway after what seemed like an eternity. Somewhere along the ride from Fulton County back to Cobb County, the rain clouds had emptied themselves of their burden and started to retreat back to wherever they lived when the sun came back out. I looked over at my would-be recruiter and could not ignore the worried look on his face. He asked again if I was okay, this time pensively. It was not simply the loss of a recruit that I heard in his voice, but a genuine concern.

Touched, I tried to thank him through my pain. "I'm gonna be ok." I paused to stop the sob from escaping me then continued, "Thank you for everything you've done Sgt. Graves. I'm really sorry that it didn't work out."

He pressed his lips into a slight smile and extended his hand to me.

"You call me if anything changes. You would make a fine soldier Miss Stokes."

His words finally brought tears to my eyes. I struggled to find the door latch before they spilled over into our conversation. I left his car and did not look back. He was such a kind man and I was really sorry to have disappointed him.

I heard him pull slowly away as I walked up the driveway. He turned at the top of Wells Drive and then disappeared onto the main road and I knew that I would never see him again. I also knew that I would never look at the olive and green patchwork of a military uniform the same way again.

My heart pounded frantically in my chest as I realized that I would never hear music the same way again or see a calendar the same way anymore. And I would never, never look at my own body the same way again.

What would I tell my stepfather? He would be back from his road trip in just a few days and want to know when I would be headed for boot camp. Tears streamed openly down my cheeks and the squirrels running across the rain soaked yard did not seem to care.

I opened the door of the charming little townhouse that used to be my home and the words of the neatly uniformed man once again assaulted my ears: "You have a permanent medical disqualification." I avoided the stairs afraid that my pounding heart would burst right out of my chest and plopped down onto the orange and brown sofa instead. I looked into the gaping emptiness of the fireplace and my mother's words swept down the chimney and across the bare hearth and lit a fire under my feet.

"You aint shit and you aint never gonna be shit. Look at you laying your lazy ass around like you the queen of motha' fuckin' Sheba or some shit. Get'cho stanking black ass up and clean up this nasty ass room before I..."

I tried to ignore the harsh words and untangle my thoughts. What would I do with my life now? Sgt. House was firm in his demand that I do something with me life – but he believed in me. How could I face him? And the army doctor – his words were ... Suddenly, the stale air seemed to take on a surreal quality and the sound of the clock reached me in slow motion. There was something my mind wanted to reveal to me, but I could not hear it clearly.

I rose from the couch and crossed the living room floor where my little sister and I had played Monopoly for hours upon hours. I dodged the cruel monologue of the fireplace and ran to the bay windows to look out onto the yard that I had helped to rake Saturday after Saturday. My head swirled with thought and with fear and I stumbled into the pretty brass and glass shelves against the creamy white walls. I remembered reluctantly dusting the delicate what-nots and knick-knacks that lived there year after year and reached out to steady the white unicorn whose wing was already chipped from an earlier run-in.

"You're not allowed in the army!" The unicorn's thin pink lips seemed to mock me.

I avoided his eyes and caught a glimpse of gold behind him and focused in on a bottle. A pretty yellow and red bottle filled to the rim with golden liquid. Cuervo golden liquid; a souvenir from my step-father's military travels. The word 'military' tangled itself together with the words in the manila file and danced around my head to the staccato rhythm of my fear. And then a howling laughter rose up in me -a strange, seductively uncontrollable laughter. It rushed up from my gut like vomit and poured through my throat like puke – uncontrollable and ugly.

It hung in the air and the sound scratched at the still surface of the room. I reached for the bottle and watched in amazement as the worm spun around the bottom of it. Suddenly, there was one single solitary thought invading every corner of my mind the worm: If I could just get to the worm. I cracked the virgin seal and plopped back down on the couch before bringing the cool bottle to my lips. The taste permeated my mouth with satisfaction and I sank into the warmth of it.

A soft caress slowly began to reach into me like a fine gossamer thread. It slipped over my tongue and weaved its' way across the pounding of my chest and finally cooled the searing thoughts in my mind. I wrapped my mind around the thread until I was safe and comfortable in my cocoon. I looked again at the petrified body of the worm and shrugged. I knew that by the time I reached it, I would not care how it tasted.

17

Hole in the Wall

One Bedroom, One Bathroom Kitchenette. Utilities Included. $150 a month.

I dialed the number nervously. I was not sure how long it had been posted on the grocery store bulletin board but I hoped the apartment offered in the newspaper wasn't rented yet. The ad also said that it had a separate entry and was located on a mature property. It had to be rented already. Still, I listened to the phone ring for the third time and hoped to get an answer. I didn't care if 'mature' meant dilapidated – I needed someplace I could afford to stay.

Sgt. House was always kind and understanding, but he was as mad as I had ever seen him when I told him I changed my mind about going into the army. I got the "You need to do something with your life" speech, but took it in stride. I would rather for him to be disappointed in me for being lazy than to know what the man at the MEPS had told me. To my delight, a deep-voiced man named Charles picked up the line and interrupted my tortured worry.

"Yes," he said flooding my mind with relief, "the apartment was still vacant."

"Yes, I could come by today and take a look at it."

I gathered my quarters for the cab ride and tucked the $150 deposit deep into my pockets and headed across town. I knew I was not coming to just look at the place. After my blowout with Sgt. House he put all my things in the outdoor storage room and I spent nights on the street at the bowling alley hiding out from the cold. No matter what state the apartment was in, I needed someplace to be.

The meeting was quick and fruitful. Charles Middlebrooks turned out to be an older man who lived with his mother on a large hilltop property near Marietta Square. He was tall, kindly and had the purest, loveliest Native American features I had ever seen. He said his mother was not in good health and he needed to cut his work hours to be at home with her more.

He said that renting out the garage apartment would help cover the missing hours in his budget. I was glad he did not ask me a lot of questions and seemed to be satisfied with the story I gave him about just wanting to get out of my father's house and on my own for the first time. He said he respected my independent spirit and seeing him so easily assured by it I felt badly for the lie. He offered to help bring my things over in his pickup truck and I moved in with a smile.

Over the next few weeks I sat on the tiny cot tucked in the corner of the cramped dark apartment and looked for potential. Every week when I got paid, I bought something new that helped bring life back to the place. A gallon of paint brightened the walls and a cheap, but snazzy yellow and blue colored rug hid the stained concrete floor.

A pair of lovely blue curtains hid the rusted garden tools leaning against the outside of back window and matched the rug impeccably. Crisp white sheets with lacy blue trim dressed up the old rusty cot and hid the shoes I had tucked beneath it. With every frilly new item I brought into the place, I left thoughts of where I had been behind.

By the time I was able to afford a new set of dishes and matching glasses the army doctor's words began to fade and I pretended his voice was from a distant dream. But as I allowed my gaze to meet with the wall, I reluctantly understood. I followed a thin crack at the corner of the window down to the center of the wall. It had spread into a hole the size of my fist. Plaster spilled from its' edges like guts - and I knew that my life needed more than a fresh coat of paint to fill the hole that had formed smack dab in the middle of it.

18

Ghetto Knights

Randy took my hand and guided me through the crowded dance floor towards the exit. I protested only slightly because the beer and brandy were swirling in my head so loudly that I couldn't hear the music anyway. We stepped outside the small, run-down nightclub and stood on the dirt parking lot. My friend, Randy was looking around wildly for someone named Pluto. I laughed and swayed in the night while mimicking him, "Hey Pluto! Where the hell you at Pluto? Tell Mickey and Minnie we leaving!"

I giggled and rocked back and forth on my feet: emphasis on back – way back. Fortunately, Randy reached out and grabbed my shoulder just as I was heading for the ground. I had lost count of how many drinks I had but guessed from the angle of the earth that it must have been a lot. Much to my surprise, I seldom drank sociably or with any kind of restraint.

Ever since I had come home from the army processing station and found my stepfather's souvenir tequila I drank solely for the purpose of getting as drunk as fast as I could. The nights I spent hanging around sleazy hole-in-the-wall nightclubs were especially inebriating. Often, I would have four or five drinks promised to me before I even found a place to sit down. The only thing that seemed to make my life bearable was the absence of pain I felt when I was drunk. I was trying to forget something ... something un-mentionable. I couldn't believe I hadn't spilled my secret yet, especially once I'd had enough to drink to loosen my inhibitions – and my tongue. I suppose it only went to prove how deeply unmentionable this particular secret was; even stone cold drunk I wouldn't release it carelessly into the world.

A car rounded the corner and skidded to a stop in front of us in the dirt and gravel parking lot. Randy ushered me into Pluto's shiny black Regal and I felt like a movie star being wielded away from an overly-zealous crowd. I blew kisses to the wind while ducking ungracefully into the car and the three of us sped away from the club all crunched into the front seat.

I glanced at my comrades for the night as the car maneuvered the now familiar streets of Rose Garden. I quickly learned that everyone in the Garden had a nickname and aside from the chums I knew from Wills High School it was unspeakable to ask the aliases be broken. Most of the guys who hung out at the clubs were criminals of one kind or another, but mostly drug dealers.

I never paid much attention to the specifics of what they did or with whom as long as the brandy kept flowing. Charles Middlebrooks expressed his concern to me about where I hung out on more than one occasion, but I was all right as long as I stayed drunk and somebody dropped me home. For now, it was Randy by way of Pluto – since Randy didn't actually have a car.

I shifted back and forth between Randy and Pluto as the car took corners much faster than I thought it should so I shot the driver a mock angry look. He glanced down at my thighs peeking out from beneath my mini-skirt and let out a long high-pitched whistle. Then, he punched the gas and took the next corner so swiftly that I almost feel over into his lap. He smiled widely and I pinched his arm in drunken disgust.

Pluto looked me up and down and proclaimed loudly, "Damn. Randy I don't think we should take all of this to Rod's crib. I think I want to marry her myself man!" Blind to the grimmer implications of his statement I merely giggled and wondered who the hell Rod was.

"Man I already tried to make her my girl, but she shot me down." Randy laughed as I winked at him. Randy and Pluto went on babbling about this and that, but the radio had my attention. Janet Jackson spit her Nasty Boys groove out of the speakers and I snapped my fingers not quite to the beat. The deep rich sound of the bass was singing lullabies to me as the car headed toward heaven.

In a moment of modesty, I looked down at myself to see if what the fuss from Pluto was all about. My shirt was thin and partially unbuttoned.

Did I do that? I couldn't remember. As I tugged at the bottom hem of my miniskirt trying to get at least another inch out of it, we pulled up into the parking lot of some luxurious apartment homes.

In a flurry of activity, the guys helped me from the car and for the moment I forgot all about my clothes. Surprised at the cold wind that whipped at my legs, I was slightly sobered as we headed up the stairs. Hell bent on not stumbling, I concentrated on my feet and sung the *"Weebles wobble but they don't fall down"* song in my head. I carefully placed one white pump in front of the other until I stood at the top of the stairs. With the most immediate danger behind me, my thoughts bounced back to my clothes. I vaguely wondered how I managed to keep my white blouse and skirt free of beer stains.

Randy looked me up and down with a sly grin and rang the doorbell. I shoved him boyishly and a tall dark man opened the door just as Randy went tumbling toward it.

"Wooah man - you drunk?" a deep voice asked. "Come on in before you pass out for all of my neighbors to see."

Randy stepped aside and I entered the doorway and found myself surrounded by luxury. The carpet was white and so were the leather sofa and marble tables. I feasted my eyes on glass and statues that surely belonged in an exhibit hall and not some guy's living room. I was so busy looking around that I did not realize I was being spoken to. The liquor in my head swirled again and I look up into the handsomest face I had seen in all my life. His eyes were fierce, but intriguing.

His chin was squared and softly shaven. He had thick, unruly eyebrows that made me want to brush them down. I said "hello" softly as my eyes greedily took in his broad shoulders and powerful chest. With his shirt open, I glanced at his nipples but quickly averted my gaze as I realized that I was staring. As if he had felt my eyes, he quickly brushed a hand across his chest.

His voice was soothing as he spoke. "If I had known an angel was going to visit me tonight, I would have dressed more appropriately." I tried not to, but I blushed at his corny flattery. Suddenly, he shifted his attention to Randy and Pluto and I felt strangely abandoned. The new sense of drunkenness I felt must have been a delayed reaction from all the beer I had earlier.

Our polite host seated us and offered more drinks. Against my already impaired judgment, I accepted a Courvoisier. I was impressed when he served us in chilled crystal snifters. I had found that in the Rose Garden juke joint I frequented, very few of my new drinking buddies spent money on good liqueur and crystal and no one cared for the elegance of Fendi or Gucci. Having lived in both excess and in hard times, I easily accepted my associates' lack of appreciation for the finer things. But it only dawned on me that moment how much I missed the rest of the world in the small circle my life had become.

I graciously thanked the handsome stranger and watched closely as he sat elegantly in a nearby chair. He crossed his legs and his long fingers held the hip glass gingerly to his lips. He spoke to Randy and Pluto briefly about the weather and the latest sports scores. I was content just to listen at the moment so I said nothing. But I did make note of his passion for the Lakers. His eyes lit up when he described how Magic Johnson whipped Byrd's ass.

"Yeah, they thought they were going to pull some more of that back-to-back shit, but the sixties was the end of the Celtic reign. The Lakers bout to eighty-six all that shit." He went on and on. Just as I was building interest in the basketball battle, Rod surprised me buy turning his attention my way. I laughed when he threw me a tired line about my height. He grinned and tried again,

"So tell me, did your mother have the good sense to name you Angel?" he asked.

"No, I'm afraid not," I said matter-of-factly "she chose Denise instead."

"Well, Denise – that's just as beautiful."

He glanced at Randy. "What are you doing hanging out with a dangerous cat like this?"

I laughed. "I went to school with his brother Clay– so he's practically like family to me. Besides," I added, "Randy's harmless."

Randy looked at my ankles while whistling through his teeth.

He grinned mischievously. "Yeah man, slim is just like my sister."

"Hey brother man - above the neckline please." I gave him a look of mock indignation as I met his eyes. We all laughed. I joined in the guy talk and swayed the conversation to a more neutral area. Rod kept looking into my eyes as if he were trying to read some hidden meaning. I giggled to myself and blamed it on the brandy.

I could not seem to hide the crush I was quickly developing for him. I was impressed as he followed my chatter from politics to literature to economics. I scanned the walls for some hint of where he had attended college; nothing. Degree or not, he had me wrapped around his lovely brown finger before the clock could strike twelve.

As if he just remembered why we came, Randy cut the chitchat short.

"Hey man, let me holler at you a minute before we get out of here."

Rod and Randy disappeared to the back of the apartment while Pluto and I finished the last of our drinks. Pluto looked at me and laughed.

"What's so funny?" I asked. "You had too much to drink or something?"

"No baby girl" he said cryptically. "I was laughing at you."

I glanced down at myself to see if I had finally spilled something on my clothes. Seeing nothing, I looked back up at Pluto laughing.

"Damn! What's so funny? You don't know me well enough to be laughing at me like that."

"Oh, I'm not being rude - but slim - you glowing like a mother-fucking firecracker. Rod done got to you with the quickness!" he accused with a grin.

I blushed at his open accusation - but did not deny it.

"See? I knew I was right." He smiled.

I swished the last of my brandy around the bottom of my oversized glass like a grownup and smiled widely. I decided to cut to the chase. After all, he probably knew Rod just as well as Randy did.

"Hey Ploo - you think he's interested in me?"

"You damn right he is." Rod himself boomed from the doorway.

I almost dropped my glass.

"Oh ... I ... uhm ... I didn't hear you guys come back in." My thin skin turned a hot shade of pink as I fumbled with my words. Randy roared with laughter, obviously enjoying my discomfort.

"So slim, this long black spider got you in his web huh?" Pluto doubled over while Rod smiled at him.

"Ok boys that's enough, can I have a little bit of my pride back now?" I begged. But they laughed even harder at my expense. I set my glass on the cocktail table and rose from my chair. Rod's eyes swept from my ankles to my eyes and I could swear I felt him on my skin.

"S-so," I stammered, "it was very nice to meet you Rod - thank you for the drinks - and for the laugh."

Pluto, still laughing, reached for his keys. Randy joined him heading toward the door. Suddenly, Rod scrambled in front of them and offered us another drink. It was the first un-cool thing I had seen him do all night. I smiled broadly out of spite. He ignored his embarrassment and made one last effort to get us to hang around a little longer.

"Look man, on the real, we gotta to roll out. I got some people to meet at the after hour joint."

My ears perked up and I stared Randy down.

"I thought this was the only stop – then you were gonna drop me off at home?" I asked suddenly impatiently.

"Oh baby girl, I'm sorry, but I gotta make one more run - then I'll get you in."

I rolled my eyes and looked at Pluto for help. Nothing.

"I'm kinda tired Randy," I tried valiantly, "another club isn't what I had in mind. Besides, I thought this was the quick stop."

"Hey look," Rod interrupted with a polite smile. "I know you just met me and all, but I'd be more than happy to take you home."

Before I could dismiss the offer, Randy chimed in, "He's good people Denise; I swear. If you don't feel like going to the joint with us, this man here - he'll make sure you get home safe. My word is my bond."

I looked him square in the eye and saw he was for real. I hesitated for a minute more and looked from Rod to Randy. I was unsure of what to do. Caution told me to go with Randy and dream about Rod when I got back to Middlebrooks' garage. But the burning on my skin told me not to let him out of my sight. Seeing my hesitation, Rod took over. He stepped aside and ushered Randy and Pluto to the front porch.

"Hey," he insisted, "I got her man. Go ahead and make your money run - you know she gon' be all right." Randy looked at me for an answer.

"I guess I'm cool." I said softly giving in. He grinned widely and I blushed.

"Bye Randy." I said dismissively.

"Ha-Ha. All right slim - check you out later."

Pluto and Randy left and Rod secured the front door. My nerves pulsed as I heard the dead bolt connect. Suddenly I wondered if I should have gone with Randy after all.

"You all right baby; I don't bite." Rod smiled at me and it was even more dazzling than earlier.

"So, you ready to head out right this second or would you like to have another brandy with me?" I looked at the twinkle in his eye and knew I wanted nothing less than his undivided attention. I smiled and let him lead me back to my seat. He poured another set of drinks and eased himself into a chair directly in front of me.

His legs were so long that they almost brushed mine as he stretched them out. We were silent for a brief moment then we feel into a soft flow of conversation that swept us both up in its' undeniable current. Just the sound of his voice was enough to move me, but it was much more than that; he was interesting too. Looking at him, he didn't strike me as the type that liked to golf, but it was his secret passion. He didn't discuss it with any of the guys from the club because they didn't even understand the game. I smiled and admitted that I didn't either.

"If I have the pleasure of seeing you again, I'll take you with me one day -my dad and I go a lot."

My stomach fluttered at the thought of seeing him again. All of a sudden, I wanted to know everything about him all at once.

"Where is your dad? Were you raised here in Georgia? Do you have any brothers or sisters? What do your lips taste like?" I caught myself before I let the last question slip out. I heard a lot of my guy friends talk about lusting for a girl as soon as they laid eyes on her, so I always thought it was a guy thing. But as, I drifted on the sound of his voice, I knew that Rod had indeed tangled me in his web - a luxurious, silken web that convinced me not to struggle.

I let all the worries of the garage apartment and work fall away from me. Even the dark truth that danced on the outskirts of my mind was not so sharp in the magic of the night. And I didn't want it to stop. No matter what happened, I wanted the evening to keep on going. As if reading my mind, Rod brushed his ankle against mine and electricity shot up my leg. He leaned forward in his seat and looked into my face.

"My God, you are absolutely beautiful," he said, as if astounded.

Feeling much bolder, I leaned forward and returned the compliment. A wild energy was growing in me that I had never felt before, but I liked it. I didn't care about modesty or protocol. I just wanted to climb out of my chair and curl up in his lap.

"Yeah: he said smiling, "we gon' be tight girl"

He reached out and slipped my glass from between my fingers. His hand lingered along with his eyes. My heart raced wildly, half hoping that he would pull me to him.

Instead, he rose from his chair and opened an overhead cabinet at the bar. He reached in and brought out a silver tray covered with powder and a tightly rolled hundred dollar bill in the middle.

"You don't mind do you?" he asked calmly. I

hesitated only slightly. I hadn't sniffed cocaine before, but I had seen people do it.

"No," I said casually, "knock your-self out." I smiled trying to be sophisticated. I knew that things were moving out of my league, quickly escalating, but there was something about him that just made me relax regardless of the flags that were waving in my mind. His warm smile and reassuring looks made me feel instantly safe.

My curiosity peaked as he sat the tray down on the glass table top and joined me on the couch. He kept chatting while he picked up the bill and sniffed a cleanly formed line from the tray. He leaned his head back and moaned. I found the whole thing strangely intoxicating. His moan sent butterflies through my stomach.

I watched him take a card from the table and form two more perfect white lines on his silver tray. I sipped my brandy and he sniffed yet another line. All the time, his warm voice kept me wanting him. I tingled as I watched the tiny flakes of white dust fall onto his full lips. He slid the tray over to me and extended the money tube. At first I declined with the shake of my head, but his eyes were so mellow. It intrigued me. The liquor warmed my senses and I was easily convinced to give it a try.

Rod's shoulders were relaxed and his long legs spilled carelessly over the edge of the sofa.

The whole scene was just right. I looked at the white lines and wondered where they would take me, never wondering if it was someplace I should go. I held the rolled bill between my thumb and forefinger as he had done and bowed my head into the tray. My hair spilled over into my face but just before it could fill the tray, Rod gracefully swept it across my forehead and tucked the falling the lock behind my ears. I smiled. I connected my nose with the tip of the money and inhaled deeply.

The sting of the cocaine slammed into me like a freight train. The burning was horrible. I dropped the tube and grabbed my face. My eyes filled with tears as the white powder assaulted my nose. Alarmed, Rod reached over and put his arm around my shoulder. He seemed very concerned as tears flooded my face.

"Damn baby, why didn't you tell me you had never done this before?" he asked.

"I... don't know... it didn't look that hard," I stammered embarrassed, "I didn't want you to think I was a square either."

He spoke with deep concern. "Sweetness, this shit ain't been stepped on and I don't want anything to happen you; not when you gonna be with me."

"What's 'stepped on?'" I asked innocently. He looked into my eyes as if to see if I was for real.

Somehow satisfied, he shook his head and laughed.

"Well, you should have told me you was green, girl." He looked down into my eyes and wiped the tears away from my cheeks. Did he just say I was gonna be with him? I was torn between fear and fantasy as butterfly fingers moved through my groin again. I felt the cocaine leave a numb trail as it drained into the back of my throat. It seemed natural to lean my head back as

I had seen him do.

A soft-hot feeling was quickly spreading through my body. It was unlike the mellow high I knew all too well from brandy. Or the awful sick dizziness of weed. This was so soft that I could fall into it. He noticed the look on my face and relaxed his grip on my shoulder. Before I was aware of it, he had started to caress me. My skin burned wherever he touched me.

"Oh, baby you're all right." he cooed. His long, slender finger traced my neck and he gazed deeply into my eyes. I tried to fight the feeling, but I was flooded with everything at once. The warm touch of the brandy, the soft whisper of the white lines, the hot waves of pleasure his fingers left on my skin. Suddenly free of embarrassment, I found myself whispering his name aloud.

I could hear his own desire, soft like another language, he answered me. "Yes baby... what do you want? I'll give you anything. Just tell me..."

I leaned into his arms and rested my head on his chest. My lips brushed against his nipple through the open buttons of his shirt and I felt his heart pound harder. Before I could change my mind I let go. The fire between my legs was too much to ignore. I ran my tongue down the deep crevice in the middle of his chest and he moaned.

He pushed his weight against me and looked down into my eyes again.

"Girl, I could love you," he moaned. "I could really love you."

Desire was so thick in his voice that my nipples hardened too. His lips closed over mine and I did not realize just how thirsty I was for him until that very moment. His lips tasted like brandy and passion. His tongue wrapped around mine and pulled at me greedily. Breathless, I kissed him back without abandon.

My clothes were suddenly heavy against my skin. I undid the last buttons on my blouse and let my breasts spill out. The cocaine rushed in my head as I stood in front of him and unzipped my skirt. He grabbed at his crotch as I let it slide silently to the floor. His eyes traced the curves of my legs until they rested on my panties. I floated on the air as his long arms reached out and pulled my hips to his face. His breath was hot as he whispered passionately into my crotch.

His hand squeezed at my thighs as his tongue dove into my belly button. I sighed while he peeled my panties down around my hips. His tongue pushed its' way between the gap in my thighs and teased me endlessly. I was so hot and wet that I grabbed his head and pulled him deeper into me. I swayed to his rhythm as he tasted me. I stood there until my knees gave way. He gently lifted me from the floor and placed me onto the couch. I swallowed the lump in my throat as I glanced at the hardness through his pants. He whispered my name as he unzipped his pants and freed himself.

He whispered how good he was going to love me. How long he was going to love me. I yearned for his promises as he slipped out of his slacks. To my astonishment, he reached for the silver tray and put some of the white powder on the head of his hardened penis. I knew that I was moving a hundred miles an hour but it flowed so seamlessly I did not want it to stop. A warning tried to go off in my head but I was so drunk with lust that I could not heed to the brewing fear. I grabbed his hips and pulled him to me as I slid my tongue along the head of his penis.

The white powder did not sting as it had before. It was bitter, but it soon numbed my tongue. Suddenly his taste was in my mouth. He was sweet and hard. I pulled at his hips greedily. I slid my lips around him until he was moaning and rocking fiercely. I felt his manhood throb wildly and I did not want to stop. I could taste him forever. His finger traced lines of poetry onto my body and I sank my lips around him more urgently with every verse.

We were becoming one flesh; tangled and spilled onto each other. He eased me back onto the couch and brought his body down over mine, gently parting my legs. I watched wide-eyed as he held himself over me and paused as if to ask permission. He was so beautiful, glistening in the soft light of the room. I fidgeted against the pressure of the moment and the spell almost broke.

Still holding himself over me, Rod gently pressed his finger against my lips to prevent the objection then let his hand slide down to something against the side of the couch. He expertly retrieved a rubber from the end table and looked at me again as if to ask if it was okay now. I couldn't wait another second. I let my head fall back over the edge of the couch and opened my legs wider, letting him almost touch me.

He moved swiftly. No sooner than I heard the rubber wrapper rattling to the floor, a long moan escaped his lips. I could not help but raise my head to meet his eyes as he pressed urgently against me. With a flood, I granted him passage and moaned along with him. He was so hard he was already throbbing as he entered me and I felt him so deeply that my moans became cries.

He paused as if to savor the moment then started to move inside me. My hips found his rhythm instantly and I swayed until I was frenzied. My back arched up into his body and I came again and again. With every stroke, I called his name louder and louder. His name was the only word I ever wanted to come from my lips. I called his name with such passion that I think the sheer sound of it made him release.

He spilled into me so violently that I could feel the hotness against the rubber and I had to grab his waist to take it. I felt christened by him. He thrust one last time and fell onto me and held me tightly. We kissed and gazed into each other's eyes without a sound. With him still inside me, we lay in each other's arms.

I felt waves of his lovemaking still moving me, calmly drifting me out to a peaceful sea. It was so still in the soft glow of the moonlight I drifted with him to a place of abandon. I prayed silently to myself that he would keep his promises and love me. Neither of us dared to move.

Instead, we slept together and dreamed the same dream.

19

Once Upon a Time

Something dark troubled my thoughts but just before I could grasp it fully the sunlight stirred me from sleep and I drew in a long breath and stretched. My mouth began to water as the warm scent of coffee and syrup tickled my nose. I looked down at myself to find that a mink blanket had been tucked around me to secure me to the couch where I fell asleep last night.

As nice as it all felt against my skin, I longed to feel his arms and searched the room for any sight of Rod. If it were not for the sound of breakfast being cooked and the soft white hues of leather and marble, I would have dismissed the fluttering in my stomach to a lovely dream. I pulled the soft blanket from the folds of the couch and grabbed the robe that was tossed thoughtfully over the arm of the couch. I wrapped it around my naked body and shuffled toward the smells.

"Hmmm good morning sleepy." Rod called seductively from the stove.

"Hi..." I moaned softly.

"I hope you're hungry, because I was in the mood to cook."

"I don't usually eat breakfast, but how could I resist this?"

"Well, I don't usually cook breakfast, but a man has to keep his strength up for a woman like you."

I blushed and seated myself at the elegant black lacquer dinette just off the kitchen and watched the handsome stranger cook breakfast for me. My face flushed as I remembered the love we had made into the wee hours of the night. I smiled as I remembered myself returning his passion without shame or abandon.

It had not been that way with Richard. Instead, I had always been unsure of my movements and let him take the lead. I sniffed back the slight drain still in my head from the cocaine. So, that's why people were so crazy about it - it made you an animal! I giggled out loud as Rod laid out his lavish breakfast spread and joined me at the table.

We chatted easily over the delicious food. Although it should have seemed strange to me, I accepted that we had made love first and then only began to know each other the morning after. I thought of Mr. Middlebrooks and his constant urging. Well, I was sure that I had gone far beyond his recommended "interest in dating again", but as I looked into Rod's eyes and wrapped my mind around his fascinating conversation, I had no regrets.

Even to tell him I had recently dropped out of high school did not bring the usual dry lump to my throat. At least I was able to add that I had left the fast food industry and snagged a comfy clerical position in an office. Of course, I was still trying to figure out how I was going to have a career as a writer without a degree, but I did know that I had gone as far as I could go at McDonald's. He received my spoken resume without judgment and my smile grew even wider.

He was so different from everything Richard was; I clung fiercely to those differences. I watched his wrists and noted that they were strong and decisive in their movements. His eyes were dark and clear. His shoulders were muscular and broad. His voice was seductive, but not dreamy as Rich's had been. There was masculinity oozing from every pore of him. And the ferocity just beneath the surface of his smooth face assured me that this man would not betray me as my first love had done. I knew that nothing less than a woman would ever crawl beneath his sheets to comfort him.

Against his wishes, I helped him to clear away the table and clean the kitchen before showering and preparing to peel myself away from him to finally head home. We left his place arm in arm and floated across town in his Mercedes. He placed one hand on my thigh as he drove and it made me feel safe and pampered. I had felt on top of the world all night, but my heart sank as we rounded the last corner and pulled up in front of the dingy garage apartment. I tried to smile over the shame, but it could not be hidden.

"This is your place?" he asked

"Y-y-yes," I stammered, quickly adding, "for now."

"Hey girl," he quickly assured me. "You know there is no need to be embarrassed, right?"

I was actually grateful for the place and quite proud that I had been able to pay my rent on time every month since I moved in. It just felt like such a stark difference after leaving the luxury of his apartment. I looked over at the handsome, kind soul I was so fortunate to meet and thanked him for his encouragement.

He smiled and asked if he could stop by the following day after I left work so we could spend some quality time together. I thought of his beautiful apartment and how all the improvements I made to my garage apartment would still pale in comparison to such extravagant luxury. Then I thought of his kind words and agreed with a smile. I walked, or should I say floated, up the driveway and closed the door behind me – unable to stop smiling.

"Hghmm" Charles cleared his throat from a chair in the corner of my apartment.

"Charles – what are you doing in here?" I asked only partly irritated.

"I was worried; I didn't hear you come in last night."

I smiled. Charles had been something of an uncle to me since I moved in six months earlier. He was kind with his advice, but not too protective. Just the right mix I thought. With sincerity, I apologized and told him I should have called knowing he would worry. I was so excited about my encounter with Rod, I couldn't wait to tell him about it. So, neatly editing out the cocaine and the sex part, I described the perfect gentleman to "uncle" Middlebrooks. His face was happy and dark all at once and I knew that despite my attempt to assure him he was still worried.

"Don't worry, Rod is a really nice guy – you'll like him."

"Hmm – so I guess that means you're expecting company?" Charles asked.

A little worried that we had not discussed the rules of visitors, I grew suddenly quiet.

"Oh no, don't be concerned kiddo. Its' fine for you to have a gentleman caller." he said sounding outright old–fashioned. "I'm just surprised that's all." he went on. "You went from not talking to guys at all to being in love overnight!" he exclaimed.

"In love?" I muttered dumbfounded. "I'm not in love, Mr. Middlebrooks." I denied

But as I went about my day dusting and sweeping all I could think about was seeing Rod again...

The next two months flew by like they were days. Rod came to see me almost every day after work. Charles ran into him a couple of times and seemed to start to steer clear, but I did not care. Charles didn't have to be crazy about him, because I was.

We had long lunches, deep conversation and heavenly weekends at his place until it seemed unbearable to be without him. He started to hint that maybe I should move in with him, but despite his otherwise impenetrable magnetism my independence was unscathed. I worked and saved money and spent every free moment with him until it began to dawn on me that maybe I was silly for struggling with my garage apartment when such a fine man wanted me to be with him.

One evening, after a not so subtle hint, I pushed away all the concern I had for independence and was ready to be "Mrs. Rod". In true thoroughbred form, Rod sent for me - complete with truck and movers to gather my hard earned belongings. Charles was happy for me, but I noted, still somewhat worried.

I reassured him with a wide infectious smile and proudly handed him two month's rent before taking one last look around. It was not fancy, but I had done it on my own for almost a year. I had escaped the dark thoughts that kept threatening to catch up with me and found someone to start my own 'Once upon a time' with. I hugged Charles and skipped down the driveway to enjoy my very own piece of good luck.

20

The Game

If heaven had a waiting room on earth, it seemed to me that it was at Rod's place. Although I had feared moving in would cause him to change towards me, I took a chance anyway. If it did not work out, I reasoned, I was almost sure I could move back into the garage. But the other shoe did not drop; nothing changed. His charm and sweet attention did not falter. His polite conversations did not cease after seeing me day in and day out.

My fear that he would quickly bore of a girl so much younger than him was slowly laid to rest. He seemed to admire my drive to have something, but more often than not he still discouraged me from pursuing a better job. I did not mind waking up early to walk to the small office in Smyrna, but he insisted on giving me a ride.

All the way there he would tell me how much more it would please him if I just let him take care of me. I had never heard the concept of not having to work – but the more he described to me the way a "good man" was supposed to care for his woman, the more sense it seemed to make. His arguments were very sound.

"I make enough money to take care of you."

"I need you at home with me."

"You can take a few months off to relax then get into college instead of working a dead end job."

The more I listened, the more right he sounded. Finally, I put in a two week notice at work and waited to see how I felt about it. At first, I didn't know what to do with myself. I had worked since I was 15 and not going just made me uneasy. I would soon be 18 and I knew I could take a college entry exam with my GED and finally go to school like Rod said, but shouldn't I be trying to do that now instead of just sitting around the house?

"How's your math?" Rod inquired as I sat around trying to figure out what to do.

"Excellent" I proclaimed proudly, proudly, glad for the chance to finally use my brain.

"Well then," Rod announced, "you're my accountant.

I said nothing but wondered why a drug dealer needed an accountant. He watched the puzzled look on my face and, true to his form, explained it to me so that it made sense. He needed me to be his right hand when he went to do business because a man of his position needed a good woman to watch his back and count his money.

He needed to keep receipts for all of his credit purchases and a separate log of all his cash purchases. He needed the monies to be judiciously divided between his account, his father's account and his grandfather's account. There could never be more than 15% more money going through his or his father's accounts than could be proven on paper and all excess funds were deposited into his grandfather's account since he was retired with real-estate income. There could be no large single deposits all money had to split into two batches: one to reinvest in product and one to break down into smaller weekly sums for deposit.

At first, it was overwhelming. The massive sums of money that he dumped on the dining room table scared me. But I was a quick study and felt grateful that he had enough trust in me to give me such an important job. Unaware of just how much trouble I could get into for my savvy math I was meticulous and painstaking in my division, book keeping and with my deposit slips. Moreover, I was glad to have something meaningful to do with my time. I didn't know there was a name for what I was doing. I just knew that Rod needed me to help and I was more than happy to do so.

Life in our pleasant but criminal household played out like the good times in the second act of a movie. He lavished me with nice things and spent quality time with me between his obligations. Like other happy, well-adjusted couples in the 80's we had friends over and drank brandy and sniffed lines.

We got dressed up and went to parties with other people who seemed to be doing well. Some of them were obviously in the same profession as Rod, but a few were afforded their lifestyles through more legitimate occupations, like sports and music. So I danced and floated and sniffed with Rod, never once thinking again about the college entry exams.

My 18th birthday was nearing and Rod kept promising something "spectacular." I could not imagine what it would be! He began to talk about us long term and whenever he did my eyes always got deep and dreamy. I knew that he was serious too because his father, Flavor, spent more and more time with us. He called me "daughter-in-law" and I basked in the glory of it.

It was not uncommon for Rod and I to meet his father at a party - where he flaunted me around for a few hours while he did business – before heading back to our place for drinks and lines as a team. It was on one of these superstar nights that I finally got a glimpse of what might lie on the other side of Rod's always cool demeanor.

The other shoe, it turned out, had been waiting to drop all along. Rod and his dad, or 'Butter and Flavor' as they were known, sat at the dining room table discussing business in low hushed tones and I propped my feet on the coffee table watching the very same guy we had just partied with two nights before play baseball on TV.

"Come here daughter-in-law." Flavor's voice beckoned me from my cozy spot.

"Yes Pop?" I stepped up to the table.

"C'mon try some of this new shit we got."

"Pop..." Rod started, but his father quickly cut him off.

"Butter," he announced authoritatively "I taught you the game and I'm telling you it's time to take this Philly to the next level, playa."

Unsure of exactly what he meant by going to "the next level," I looked uncertainly at Rod and waited for him to decide what I should do.

His father noted my action with a gold-toothed grin.

"See," he teased, "she prime baby."

Not sure of what I had done so right, I followed Rod's gesture to sit down at the table.

"Now," Rod sniffed a lot more than usual as he talked, "go easy baby. This shit just came in." He slid me the silver tray.

I followed his suit and sniffed a short line while I waited for him to finish talking.

The powder flew into my nose and immediately drained everything in its path. I pushed the tray away, realizing that Rod's warning was an understatement. His father noted my reaction and pulled the tray to him and began building another series of short lines.

I focused on Rod's face as the drug took immediate effect.

"Baby," Rod announced, "we getting ready to take this operation to a whole new level." Interested, I perked up in my chair.

"It's a whole lot more money out there that we ain't even started to take a stab at, but we a team – and we going for broke now – you understand,

baby, what you gotta do for your man?" Rod asked me.

I did not, but nodded anyway.

"That's my girl," Rod said, winking at me.

His father slid the tray back over to me and motioned for me to take a toot. I grabbed the brandy I had brought over from the coffee table with me and shook my head no.

"C'mon girl," he urged, "them just lil' baby lines – and tonight you graduate to a big girl."

I bent over the tray and felt my head rush with the movement. I counted out the lines he had built and began at one. I don't think I ever made six because the lines started to crisscross on the tray as I alternated nostrils like Rod had showed me. The rush was overwhelming. I backed away from the table and widened my eyes to keep the spots from taking over my vision. My face and neck were on fire so I grabbed at my silk blouse for some relief. Rod stood and reached out to assist me in my struggle. I was grateful and leaned back into his arms as he undid my buttons from behind. Then, as if I had imagined him there behind me, I leaned against the solid wall behind me and watched him rise again from the table to help me with my slacks. His voice was soft but fiery in my ear. He used a tone I was not sure I had heard before.

"Bed?" I questioned.

"Yeah baby," I agreed, "let's go to bed."

"Goodnight Pop," I called to the empty couch.

My whole body was hot so I stopped just long enough to come out of the panties that seemed to be trapping heat between my thighs. Rod's hands were on my back stabilizing me then it seemed at the same time they were in front of me making sure I did not trip over my panties. My head rushed and drained and my heart beat dangerously fast.

It felt like all the veins in my body were throbbing, instantly sending a pulsing sensation everywhere I was touched; and it seemed like I was being touched everywhere, all at once. So I kept touching a different place, fascinated that the blood beneath my skin was responding that way. Rod helped me touch the places I could not reach and the feeling became more intensified. I giggled and moaned and watched other hands take over what I had started.

They moved so fast I could not focus on them, so I fixed my eyes on the pretty chandelier hanging from the bedroom ceiling. The light danced through the crystals like tiny fairies fluttering to and fro. The heat from my body seemed to rise to the ceiling in vapors and dance along with the fairies. Strong lips engulfed the hollow in my neck and I sang the tune they strummed against me. The bed seemed to take on a hardness all its' own and it pressed against my buttocks as Rod's body finally covered the dancing light above me.

His voice sounded like it had doubled and I fell forward and backward to the sound of it coming from all directions. I floated and swayed and rocked against hardness in the bed until it formed hands that reached around my back and covered my breasts. Rod's chest pressed into the grasp – sandwiching the feeling between us until I floated clean away between the rock beneath me and the hard place on top of me. Finally, the room spun so quickly that I closed my eyes and sunk into the soft part of the bed drifting off into a deep, intoxicated sleep.

Morning crept in through the thin linen curtains and spilled across my body. I tried to take a deep breath but my nose was completely clogged. I opened my mouth and sucked in the clean morning air through my throat and tried to stir from my position. I leaned to one side and almost rolled on top of Rod from the middle of the high, king sized bed. Not wanting to wake him, I slowly rolled to the other side and came in contact with…another sleeping body. I slowly focused my eyes in the intrusive early morning light and took in the almost identical body of his father lying naked next to us.

My mind reeled and I closed my eyes and opened them again thinking the high was still fogging my brain. But he was still there. Frozen, I looked to one side then the other and let my mind put the pieces of my dream back together more clearly in the harsh light of day. I slid myself from between them to exit at the foot of the bed and stumbled back slightly as I turned to look at the two men I was pressed between all night.

They were both naked and sleeping soundly.

My eyes scanned the floor next to bed and saw two empty condom wrappers discarded in plain sight. I leaned my head back and cocaine from the night before drained down my throat, numbing what little feeling was left there.

I stumbled the short distance to the bathroom and bent over the sink – coughing up a mixture of blood and still translucent white powder. I glanced quickly in the mirror at my disheveled hair knowing I did not want to look too long or, for that matter, too closely.

"Indeed," I thought woefully, "I was a big girl now."

The numbing drain continued as I cleared my nose and brushed the tangles out of my hair.

Deliberately and without tears, I walked naked back through the bedroom and seated myself at the marble and glass dining room table. I pulled the silver tray toward me and formed lines of reasoning in the dirty white snow. My trembling fingers managed to roll the unraveled bill back into a tight tube and I leaned forward to take a long sniff….

21

The House That Hell Built

The doorbell sounded and Mack rose from his chair in the hallway to answer it. His towering black frame moved with authority. I heard the sound of the dead bolts giving way to his large hands and listened to the muffled chatter that followed. I looked nervously across the living room to see who would enter. I inspected myself quickly and fussed a bit with the lace of my camisole. As the last ruffle politely fell into place, two men rounded the corner. The clatter of the beads hanging in the doorway announced them noisily.

Mack looked at them suspiciously (as usual). His already beady red eyes squinted even more so reminding me of a fierce predator watching his prey from the shadows. Suddenly he seemed satisfied and broke into a wide yellow grin as they entered.

I looked up and batted my eyelids invitingly as I had been taught (although I secretly hoped that the neither of them would choose me). I only wanted this day to end - with or without another well tipping customer. I nervously tugged at a lock of hair that had fallen into my face and wondered how I had gotten myself into this.

My mind slowly drifted away from the approaching men...

I remembered the day I left Atlanta to come to the house in Queens, New York. Rod enticed me from a deep sleep with the smells of hot maple and coffee - much like he had the day we met – only by now I knew him well enough to know that he wanted something this time. He fed me tenderly and with a wide grin, slid a plane ticket across the table to me. To celebrate my 18th birthday, he was sending me to New York to have a good time – and to help him with business.

I was unsure how going to New York was going to help him, so I looked into his eyes for a deeper meaning to this "noble" gesture. He smiled and told me how beautiful I was. He said modeling new intimate fashions was popular in New York and that a young, pretty southern girl like me would do well. I would be working with old friends of the family who had been in business for years. He assured me that within six weeks, the money I wired him would be so good that he could finally make an investment that would expand his business to the next level.

When he mentioned lingerie, my mind tried to warn me of danger and settled back on the scene of him and his father lying naked in our bed. But I would not listen. Instead, I let the shame of what happened drive me to silence and numbly agreed to Rod's request. I dismissed my hesitation and packed all of my laciest things to take to New York with me. But when Mack and his wife Cozetta met my airplane at LaGuardia, I knew the incident with Rod's father was much more than a one-time, drunken aberration. It was, instead, a carefully orchestrated tactic designed specifically to strip me of the last bit of dignity I had left and, of course, to prove my loyalty to the game.

I was obviously being primed to master the oldest profession known to woman and could not bring myself to admit it. I was naked to Rod's will and afraid to question him. So I remained calm when Mack gave me the rundown of the house. I listened intently as the rules were read off to me. I did not lower my head when I met the other working girls. I swallowed my fear and stifled my desire to run. I looked each of the women in the eye and shook their hands. Rod called as soon as I arrived and told me to check my suitcase.

Deep in the interior pocket was a large plastic bag of white powder labeled with a note that said 'For the hard times". In a sick way, I thought it was sweet. I thought that maybe I was being "*green*" again and forced myself to do what I was told to do. I wanted to do whatever it took to make him happy. What was six weeks anyway? Time inched by from that day forward.

The sounds of moans filled the room and broke my reverie. The VCR displayed blue movies to set an enticing atmosphere. I looked over at my new co-workers. Cassie was an older blonde woman who wore far too much make-up. But she did things with her tongue and hands that let the customers know her experience would make up for her lack of youth. Sherri was a statuesque Puerto-Rican girl with the silkiest long black hair I had ever seen. She stroked it slowly as she crossed and uncrossed her legs often. According to Cozetta, I was supposed to learn how to fish – but was not happy to be the bait - so I just sat hoping to go unnoticed.

I wondered why Cassie and Sherri were allowed to come and go from the house as they pleased, but Mack always escorted me everywhere I went. I only went down the block to the Western Union to send Rod money and to the corner drug store for condoms anyway- but still, I was always escorted. I took a little comfort in knowing that even though the other girls could move freely in the day, we were all locked in at night.

Mack and Cozetta did not want money being transacted in their absence because they would not get their share. I always laughed when they locked the front door from the outside in the wee morning hours. If they thought I was going to spend a minute more than I had to taking poker chips for sex, they were mistaken. As if hearing my thoughts, the two men moved to either side of me, sandwiching me on the couch. I became aware of them staring at my long brown legs stretched out before me and tried to tuck them beneath me before they noticed but it was too late. I sighed as both of the men slipped me the blue chips they had purchased from Mack at the door. The blue ones meant they had paid more money for more time and included a big tip. In return, I was supposed to be "very nice" to them. I silently cursed myself as I rose from the sofa and strolled across the room. I heard the breath escape the lips of the older man as I stood to my full height and they followed me anxiously. I hated threesomes.

I entered my private room and the smell of soap and sex immediately assaulted me. I closed the door behind the last man and the routine began. I was taught to wash them from the fresh water that was drawn into the porcelain bowl on the dresser. I was taught to check them as I washed them. I did not know what to look for, but Cassie and Sherri said I would know if I saw. I saw nothing strange so I handed them condoms - a sign that we could now proceed. I silently wished the girls would've taught me to ignore the empty feeling I had along with all the other little tricks they had taught me.

I stood in the middle of the room and began to slowly remove my teddy. Their eyes greedily drank me in - like I was sweet warm cocoa on a chilly evening. A pile of black lace lay discarded on the floor as I freed my breasts from bondage. My stomach began to sink when I thought of them touching me. My teeth gnashed together but I smiled politely to keep the hatred from seeping through. I was beautiful one of the men said.

My head began to fill with the sound of my own thoughts as I escaped the room quickly filling with their pleasant insults. "This is for Rod," my mind whispered, over and over again as if to block out the sights, sounds and feelings I was experiencing. "Do this for Rod," it urged.

The conversation carried on without me and I climbed silently into the middle of the bed. A cold hand caressed my thigh and I shuddered. My heart broke loudly as one of the men took my breast to his mouth. I lowered my head and let my long black curls shade my face. I tried not to wince when they moved their hands down my legs to my inner thighs. They clawed and moaned and brought themselves pleasure with little help from me. I watched from far away as they gripped me and took turns pushing themselves into me. I felt the anger rising up in me again and gnashed my teeth to try and push it back.

I turned my head so they could not touch my face - or see the fury in my eyes. They danced until their bodies were spent and collapsed onto the bed. They lay there with smiles and watched me move away from them. I floated across the room to wash away the evidence from my body. Their self-satisfied laughter rose and fell like the crackle of a dancing flame. I smiled politely once more and saw them to the door. I was exhausted. The sacrifice had lasted far too long.

I closed the door behind me and leaned against it for support. My knees were weak with emotion. I tried not to feel the emptiness that gnawed at me. I tried to toughen my heart against the pain that assaulted me. I slid open the dressing table drawer and filled my pinky nail with hard time powder and waited. It was not working. I sniffed another nail full hoping for relief but my thoughts became clouded with memories of the last four or five weeks. Fine porcelain skin slipped out of well-tailored European suits to brush against my body.

Taxi's delivered me to beasts with strange accents at fancy hotels who padded Mack's pockets for my services. It seemed like someone else's life had taken over my own and I cringed to admit the lack of control. I sat dazed in the middle of my Merrick Avenue prison and wondered, were there two men just here? Why did I let them touch me? If Rod loved me, how could he know I was here with them touching me and not come get me?

My mind reeled as it searched for an escape. It was eating me up and the drinks and cocaine weren't keeping the pain at bay anymore. Didn't Rod know that I could die in this place with strange hands grabbing at me? I had my doubts that he knew what it was like for me, or if he knew that he even cared. The last time he called, I'm sure I heard a girl giggling in the background. Was she with him now? Was he kissing and holding her? Did she see the sun rise in his eyes like I did?

I plopped my body down onto the bed and thought about Rod's father. I just wanted to fit into his warm family. He knew I was high out of my mind that night. How could he let his father sleep with me? The tears finally came as I remembered with a sob how violated I felt when I woke up that next morning to the revolting reality. Sickness washed over me as my eyes danced around the frame of the wicked picture seared in my mind. I was stupid to make excuses for Rod... for myself... for his father. The shock was so strong that the full pain of it had scattered into the far recesses of my mind. In the middle of the bed on Merrick Ave, the shock wore off and I buckled under the weight of remembrance.

I walked weakly to the mirror and dared to glance into it. Wild, wounded eyes stared back at me; the feral and injured eyes of a stranger. My wavy locks were tousled around my head and shoulders. I reached toward the mirror to see if it was real – if I was really there. Behind me, I saw a small pile of money on the wrinkled covers of the bed.

It wasn't enough.

There was nothing I could buy to make me feel better. The little green gods were more important to Rod than they were to me. I could not love him again tomorrow. I could not drown in the tears that would flood my pillow tonight. My pain would not be silent anymore. The thought of his voice could not comfort me. The pain screamed and deafened any reasoning he could come up with. His words would never soothe me again.

I turned and stepped over the used lace in the middle of the floor and reached into the closet. I found the pants that I wore in the daytime. The slim black ones I went to the Western Union in. I slid them onto my sore frame and grabbed the blouse that I wore to wire the money to Rod. I would not wire money today. Mack would not escort me again; not now, not ever.

I thought briefly of Rod's sweet smile, but it was quickly erased by the faces of the men who had just been in the room. My stomach churned and I rushed to the porcelain bowl and threw up violently. I felt a hot flash of fear when I thought about the locked front door. I had to get away but I would not be able to fool Mack into letting me go down the boulevard by myself. I had to find another way. I walked over to the window and stared at the fire escape.

After some struggle, it raised with a whoosh. I stood silently for a second to see if Mack heard the window clatter open. He would surely clasp his powerful hands on my neck if he had. Would he let go before he finished the job? I couldn't take that chance, no matter how tempting the thought of sweet release might be at this moment. I heard nothing but the quickening of my own heart so I ducked my head outside and the wind welcomed me. It brushed my face invitingly. I stepped out onto the grates and looked down at the three stories below. They didn't seem as high as they should.

What if I slipped and broke something? What if I died? I looked back at the bed and knew that I would die if I stayed; at least this way there was a choice – a possibility. I had to get to the street and follow it to the end of my tears. I pushed against the stubborn ladder and it finally gave way with a loud creek. Just as it delivered me to the second floor, I heard the door of the room fly open. I fell awkwardly down the inclined ladder to the landing below me and leapt from the metal balcony– barely avoiding the cactus on the ledge.

I heard the wind applaud as it passed my ears. I felt the sharp pain rip through my legs as they found the concrete below. I tumbled dizzily for about a second. A lady glanced at me then hurried her step when she looked up to the window I had come from. The sound of Mack's voice being hurled down frightened me.

"Hey bitch! he called. Get'cho ass back here!"

Fear made the pain in my legs disappear and I found my feet to stand. I was half broken and quite mad, but I could not let Mack cage me again. I could not let Rod's love bury me. With the streets of New York laid out before me, I spread my wings and desperately flew down the block - away from the blue poker chips and clattering beads.

22

Say Uncle

I tried not to think of Rod as I walked down the streets of New York into the wave of heat rising from the asphalt so I focused on the people filing along the sidewalks. They looked like they were on a mission much more important than daily errands. Every face I passed was pinched or contorted into a scowl and every set of eyes was glazed over with drudgery. No one looked around and no one looked back.

I thought of the movie "Invasion of the Body Snatchers" and became afraid my curious glances would give away the fact that I was a lost stranger in this surreal subterranean world. I tried to look straight ahead the way they did, but my eyes were magnetically drawn back to the barrage of hostile nonchalance passing me. I tucked my arms tighter to my body to avoid bumping into anyone and pressed onward through the sea of anonymity.

Strange smells assaulted my nostrils and the roar of traffic and sharp-tongued foreign languages cut through the thick hot air like lightning. I wasn't sure exactly where Hell's Kitchen was but imagined it was concocting its' latest witches brew and I floated on the surface of the pot with the flesh and spices unsure of how I fit into the recipe.

I didn't know which direction to head or what to do I allowed myself to be swept along with the crowd and tried to think of a plan as the human wave surge pushed me where it would. I jammed my hands into my pockets and stopped abruptly causing the woman behind me to spit nasty Spanish words at me for almost making her crash her two-wheeled grocery cart into me. I retrieved the paper from my pocket to confirm that it was in fact a wrinkled wad of money. Performing what must have been a ridiculously foolish act I pulled the money out and counted it in public before realizing my mistake. Then, I ducked out of the crowd into a diner I was passing.

When I left Mack's I had been too crazed and too ashamed to think clearly, so I left all of my money in the middle of the bed. I had no way of getting home to Georgia, no place to sleep and no money to even make a phone call. I felt lucky for having found the remnants of what must have been left over from my last trip to the Western Union. My legs were aching from the impact of my jump to the concrete and I was exhausted from the adrenaline rush that had now receded to a dull, thumping ache. The sound of clanking dishes being set onto the counter caught my attention and my stomach growled as if on cue. I shuffled toward the sounds and found a seat facing the menu board. Eighty-two dollars would not last long, but a hot meal seemed like a better idea than anything else I could think of at the moment, so I ordered.

It took everything in my power not to cry while I waited on the waitress to bring my soup and sandwich. I was afraid of being alone in New York, but more afraid of calling Rod and begging for his help. I wasn't sure what his reaction would be, but if the whorehouse was what happened when he was happy, I was sure I didn't want to know what happened when he was upset. I didn't have any ID to prove that I was 18 and I was sure no hotel clerk in their right mind would rent me a room. Against my will the thought of sleeping on the hard streets of the city filled my eyes with fear and I hung my head so that the tears would fall cleanly away from my face.

I had not noticed the man sitting at the table beside me until he rose and approached my table. Almost in slow motion he strode up next to me and seated himself. For the few hours I was wandering around no one had even looked at me. Suddenly I found myself eye-locked with his strange face only inches away from mine. His skin had a deep olive tone to it and his nose was long and hawk-like. I recoiled away from him instinctively as his Italian-Jersey twang grated my ears.

"Hiya, doll... what'cha doing?" He flashed me a greasy smile then immediately reached across the table to try and touch my hand. I drew away from him and began gathering the un-eaten half of my sandwich to take with me.

He went on smugly as if I had responded favorably to him. "Well, seeing as how yous had your grub, whaddaya say you let me get'cha an ice cream?"

Then his eyes left my face and grazed over my breasts before traveling downward to my waist and thighs. Mustering as much attitude as I could, I tried to brush him off by scoffing and turning my nose up at him.

Undaunted, he reached into his pocket and pulled out a crisp hundred-dollar bill.

"It ain't like I can't afford it ya know." He scoffed, "Geez, you high class types really bust my balls."

The crisp bill stared up at me from the dingy white tablecloth and I almost choked. I wished I had a hundred more - it might be just enough to get me a bus or train ticket home. But the last thing I wanted to see at that precise moment was some strange guy putting his money on the table. He might have just been showing me he could afford to take me out – but my gut said he was fishing to see if I was for sale.

Could he tell that easily that I was a whore? The thought attacked me like a rabid dog and my shoulders slumped. My backbone softened and I lowered my eyes. I was not a lady – I could not even pretend to be a lady and everybody knew it. I could almost hear the sickening clank of the beads in the doorway at Mack & Cozetta's place.

The sound had followed me over the balcony and across city the streets to this very diner. Even when I was free the chains of my history clung to me so visibly, so blatantly that even this small-time hustler could sniff me out in the time it took for me to order lunch. I couldn't run fast enough - or far enough - to escape it. I got up quickly, almost knocking my chair over. I was determined to outrun that seedy third floor apartment. I hit the door with a gust of wind behind me and made a path for myself through the maze of bodies.

I ran a few blocks before I saw a subway entrance. I took to the underground and rode the train through the bowels of the city still trying to figure out what to do. Then it hit me. I could call for help. I was born in Manhattan. With some help, I could probably get my birth certificate and some ID! Upstate was where half of my mother's family was from – and although I did not know them all, I could think of one person who stood out: Uncle Jerry.

Granddaddy lived in the Bronx and had always been loving towards me, still, there was little conversation between elders and children in my family. But Uncle Jerry was good for at least a whole days' worth of chatter every time I saw him. He always asked about school and about sports and listened carefully to every exaggerated answer I gave him. New York was not an easy place to find a man but it was a cinch to find a man whose name and address you knew.

After all, he had written my mother so many letters over the years that the address was seared into my head. So, as the train pulled into the next stop I exited and came up to the street to find a phone book. It wasn't easy since most of them were either ripped to shreds or missing altogether but since my two choices were find my uncle or spend a night on the streets, I was diligent. I went block to block until finally I found one phone book in legible condition. I rummaged down the massive list of names until I laid eyes on one that was familiar. It had to be my uncle. I pumped coins into the slot and, sure enough, his voice filled the receiver with sound and filled my heart with relief. I dug deep into my imagination until I fished up a story about saving my money to celebrate turning 18 with a trip to New York – and how I lost my purse at a club.

Instantly, my uncle flooded me with questions: Did I ask the manger to see if he had found the bag? What club? Why didn't I call to tell him I would be in town? I bumbled through his questions until it seemed he was convinced. Where was I now? I looked at the building across from the phone booth and gave him the address. Then I crossed the street and sat on the stoop of the building holding my breath. My body shook against the fear of Mack finding me and from the shame of where I had just come from. To keep from crying, I recited TS

Eliot's "Macavity" to be the best of my recollection and within an hour, Uncle Jerry pulled up smiling. We rode across city blocks in happy chatter about this and that and it seemed that I had pulled off a major coup. Still, I silently hoped he would send me home without calling my mother.

I looked up and recognized the street as the very same one listed on Uncle Jerry's letters. We pulled up at a lovely brownstone in the middle of the block and my heart skipped a beat as he swung the door of the building open and ushered me upstairs. It was hard for me to believe that all I had to do was make a phone call and the dreaded decision to trust Rod could be instantly, irrevocably reversed.

"Girl, you have grown miles," he whistled appreciatively as I climbed the stairway. I smiled because he said the same thing every time he saw me. I relaxed and let the cool brick of the building's insides welcome me. He walked ahead of me and opened the door of his apartment to reveal a large room. A couch sat against the wall with a coffee table and chair neatly completing the living room ensemble. Not five steps away was a bed tucked neatly onto the far wall and made nicely with an old blue spread like the one Grandma used to throw on her bed.

There was a desk by the window with a Commodore Amiga and fax machine hard at work atop it. Across the carpeted gray floor an entertainment center had been placed against the far wall to complete the main living space. An office, bedroom and living room all in one... how crafty! I stepped across the threshold and saw that there was another area to the left of the front door that led to a tiny kitchen. It was humble, but it seemed like a mansion compared to the hostile flat I had just left behind on Merrick Boulevard, not to mention the mean, hungry streets beyond.

We plopped right down on the cozy brown couch and chatted for hours. Although he was quite curious about my night in New York, I avoided talking about my "birthday celebration" as much as possible, so we eventually moved on.

We talked only briefly about my mother, but there was no denying that he was her favorite brother. It would have been useless to try and explain where the disagreements in our relationship came from and how difficult it was for me to deal with her. So with respect for his sister, I also avoided talking too much about mama. He was very understanding but it was obvious to both of us that if we didn't limit the topic of our conversation the atmosphere would shift from delightful and polite to strained and uncomfortable.

As if reading my thoughts, he reached out and patted my head.

"Why don't you stay here and visit with me a few days, he suggested, and I'll put you on a bus back to Atlanta."

I almost could not believe that he cut to the chase so quickly and said the words I wanted to hear to so badly. It was as if after all the heartache, the strain, the anxiety and stress the clouds had lifted and the very voice of God spoke those very words. My body sunk deeper into the chair from the relief that I felt and I sighed loudly.

That's what I liked about Uncle Jerry... he knew how to deal with things without making a big deal out of them. He was one of the few adults I knew who had not forgotten what it was like to mess up. He let me be as adult as I could without expecting too much out of someone who was still, after all, just a kid. And just when I got in over my head, he would remember that I was a kid and take care of me. Obviously my Uncle Jerry was very wise and I felt blessed for having looked him up.

Relieved, I walked around the small space that was his home and began investigating as we chatted. Piles and piles of book were stacked up against the legs of the coffee table and I looked closer at their spines to see what he was so interested in; *Accounting 101, The MS/DOS Handbook, The Basic Principles of Accounting, Understanding Money*. Working for a bank fit him quite nicely. I laughed and thumbed through one of the well-worn book and joked, "I see you're into foreign languages."

I looked at the large schoolboy glasses propped on his nose and giggled even louder. He was short and had the good looks of my mother's bloodline, but he had plenty of "geek" in him too. Just like me, I thought quietly, realizing at that moment just how far I had come from the bookish schoolgirl of only a few short years ago. I was suddenly very grateful to have him as my uncle. I could be more open with him than anybody else in the family and, at the moment, I needed that more than anything.

Soon, we both crossed the floor to his office area and began fiddling with his computer. He punched a few keys and green letters floated across the black screen on cue. I listened to him talk of motherboards and megahertz and of the future of the personal computer. I enjoyed listening to him because he was so smart. He knew everything.

I was surprised when he abruptly stopped talking techno-slang and suggested that we go to a nightclub to celebrate my late birthday properly before I left New York. Even though I was comfortable enough with him to go just about anywhere, I would never have thought of night clubbing with my uncle! He just didn't seem like the type. When he visited us in Savannah, he would always go to the club with my mother when she had to DJ. I thought it was only because she had to work and he wanted to spend as much time with her as he could. As if reading my thoughts, he asked incredulously, "You think I can't dance?!"

I giggled and shook my head "no."

"Well," he explained," standing up abruptly, "I have to run a few errands but I'll be back around 9:30. There are a few dollars in the jar on the table and some shops if you go right out of the building two blocks then three blocks left. Be ready when I get back and I'll show you who can't dance!" He ruffled the top of my head again and grabbed his keys and headed for the door. Before I could protest, he was gone.

Feeling more light-hearted than I had in months, I cleaned up what little there was out of place and grabbed the spare key from where he left it. Still afraid Mack would find me I cautiously headed to the shopping area to find something to wear. I was going out to party with my uncle... how cool! Immediately, I laid eyes on a little black skirt and classic white blouse. I grabbed my size from the rack and headed for the shoe rack. I felt funny about spending my uncle's money on clothes – especially when I was in such a jam. Since he was going to pay to send me home I just depleted most of my own money and headed back to the apartment.

I found the bathroom right down the hall where he said it was and took a quick bath and brushed my long black hair into a pile atop my head with my fingers. I fastened it with an extra ribbon I pulled out of my new blouse and let few a strands fall loose to frame my long narrow face. I slid into the skirt and blouse and slipped my bare legs into the new black heels. Perfect! I swished vigorously with his mouthwash, glossed my lips with a dab of Vaseline and finally looked at myself in the mirror with a smile. The haunted look of the last few weeks was starting to go away and I could see a little bit of myself again. With immaculate timing, Uncle Jerry burst through the door just then and whistled.

"So you are a girl!" he said with a smile. I blushed and took his elbow as we headed for the city lights.

The club was huge. I had never seen anything like it. A million lights were flashing in time with the music and smoke pummeled from the dance floor as if straight out of a music video. Both sides of the dance floor had wrought iron railings and real train tracks just beyond them. It appeared to be sitting right in the middle of a subway track! Nobody in Atlanta would believe me if I told them about it!

The music was loud but clear - not like the muffled bass of the clubs I had been to down south. We headed straight for the dance floor and grooved up a storm. I watched in amazement as Uncle Jerry hit every twist of every new dance I could think of. He wasn't just as good, he was better than me! I laughed in delight and secretly hoped to pick up a few moves along the way. In the safe company of my uncle and with each beat of the music, my woes slipped further and further away.

I didn't think about Rod or about the house on Merrick. I just danced and glowed in the safe light of my uncle's watchful eye. When the dance floor got crowded, lights appeared at the end of the tunnels and it looked like a train was coming both ways! It was a nice relief from the panic I was feeling just a few short hours before the Tunnel worked its magic on me.

We worked up a sweat and headed for the bar with the crowd. Uncle Jerry ordered a brandy for himself and a margarita for me. I was a little uneasy drinking around him, but he quickly reminded me that I was 18 now. I smiled assuredly and sipped at the bitter-sweet concoction in bliss. The night floated on without borders as we danced and drank for hours. I noticed a few men staring at me when we went to the bar, but I ignored them. Uncle Jerry noticed too and said that it was because I was so beautiful.

"Only a relative would say such a thing," I laughed, unaware of his seriousness at that moment. The margaritas were singing a song of their own and I spun my body to their tune. We danced until the music began to seem too loud and decided to call it a night. I wanted to get up early the next morning and find out how much a train ticket to Georgia would be.

The short distance through the parking lot was crooked and unsteady, at least according to my head full of margaritas so Uncle Jerry placed his arm around my waist to steady me. I plopped down in the car and struggled with my seat belt. As if he hadn't had one drink the whole night, Uncle Jerry smoothly seated himself behind the wheel and leaned over and clicked my belt without effort. It must have been my imagination, but the hairs on my arm stood up as I felt a finger brush against my chest.

I quickly dismissed the misguided thought and leaned my head back drunkenly. Maybe I shouldn't drink so much, I thought. When did I even start drinking so much? Thoughts of Merrick Boulevard tried to creep their way through my alcohol fog, but I dismissed them too. I did not have the energy to hold the pieces of my heart together any longer.

I felt the roar of the car cranking up and we wheeled away from the pounding bass and flashing lights, leaving the nightclub far behind. We floated through the city as if on a magic carpet. Street signs whizzed by my window like ancient knight sentries keeping the scowling faces at bay. The smooth, easy jazz pouring from the car radio wrapped itself around me and I drifted into a trance.

After what seemed like eons of flying through space, we came to a slow crawl and then stopped in front of the lovely brownstone. I sighed happily and tugged at my door. I felt like I had been on a marvelous circus ride and I did not want it to end. Uncle Jerry came around and helped me from the car and into the building. I laughed when I realized I was a lot drunker than I thought. I stumbled up the stairs with Uncle Jerry close behind.

Without turning on the lights, he led me to the bed and sat me down. Then, he crossed the room and began to pull out the couch to make his bed. I did not want to put him out of his own bed and tried to insist that I take the couch, but the liquor just made my head swim. I slurred a blurry "thank-you" and kicked my shoes off. I focused on the desk as my eyes adjusted to the dim streetlight glowing through the curtains.

"You've got to have a night-cap," he called from the couch.

"Oh... no way," I moaned. "I couldn't drink another sip of anything." Eighteen or not, I'm nauseous." He rose from the couch and headed for the kitchen.

"Your head is going to be nasty in the morning if you don't. Brandy will make you feel better now and you won't have a hangover in the morning." I thought of having a hangover on a long train ride and cradled my head. He appeared before the bed glass in hand. I accepted it gratefully and as I sipped, I thought of Uncle Jerry's infinite wisdom. He suddenly plopped down on the bed beside me and blurted unexpectedly,

"So, what are you really doing in New York?"

Caught off guard, I said in a limp voice,

"I fell for a stupid line from my stupid boyfriend." I hung my head and sipped the warming drink before continuing,

"It wasn't lingerie modeling."

"Here, let me get you another one kid, you've had a rough time huh?" he asked rhetorically. I was thankful for his understanding and, despite my earlier resolution to drink less, gladly accepted another glass of liquid sympathy.

I thought about Rod's twilight promises and gulped pitifully from the glass until the bottom stared back at me. Uncle Jerry quietly rose from the bed and sat in the chair by the couch. I sat there a long while and contemplated the house on Merrick, then blinked to find myself staring at an empty chair. The room began to fuzz over and then I didn't know where I was. A low whispering voice was consoling me and kind hands urged me to finish my drink.

"B-but I thought I did," I slurred.

"No, finish it... you'll feel better." Unable to balance anymore, I slumped on the headboard to steady myself. I brought the glass to my lips and took another sip or two. The liquid slid down my lip and doused the front of my new blouse.

"Let me help you with that," a kind voice said from the darkness. My head floated in and out of the tiny apartment and began to rock back and forth. I tried to speak, but I had forgotten how to form words or even use my lips. My tongue seemed far heavier that it should. I wondered how the few drinks could have had such an effect on me so quickly, but thinking was difficult and the headboard began to feel crooked, so I lay back on the bed to keep from falling forward.

Bits and pieces of Rod floated past me as I tried to focus on the pattern in the ceiling. Every time I had it figured out, it shifted and I had to start all over again. I thought that Uncle Jerry was talking to me, but it could have simply been the drone of the stereo. When did the stereo come on? I reached for my head to stop it from swimming and was suddenly aware of my naked shoulders. I tried to sit up, but felt a firm hand pressing me back against the bed. "Ssshh," the soft voice whispered to me. "Don't try to get up, baby."

Fingers brushed against my chest and then I felt the warm softness of lips against mine. My stomach churned with tension and my head grappled to understand the sensations. Wasn't I in my Uncle Jerry's bed? No, I thought through the alcohol haze as hands floated down the lower part of my stomach, I must be in Rod's bed. The music danced in and out of my ears; first close, then far away.

"Doesn't this feel nice?" the voice whispered urgently.

I felt panic and liquor rise in my throat as I struggled to concentrate. The hairs were standing up on my arms again and I knew I was in danger, but I couldn't quite place where the danger was coming from. I looked up into Uncle Jerry's eyes and felt the panic start to subside. Then my mind locked onto the warmth of another body bearing down on me and I squeezed my eyes shut and opened them again. Something seemed oddly out of place. The room rocked and faded in and out but I managed to look up into his face again. His eyes were closed with his brows furrowed together. As I read the intensity on his face, my mind fell over the edge of panic again.

Uncle Jerry was on top of me!

Oh nooo," I moaned. My lips still seemed too reluctant to form words but I struggled to be heard. I protested until I could hear my voice over the stereo. His body pressed more urgently into mine with every objection. Soon, his hand sealed my lips and his eyes stared intently into mine. My head swam as I pushed against him to free myself. I felt the cold air on my thighs and realized that my skirt had been discarded as well as my blouse.

He breathed into my ear harshly and I could not escape his hot breath. Then like a clap of thunder, he had his way. My mind raced a million miles away as my body went limp. I couldn't struggle anymore... I was too tired. My tongue had a strange bitter taste as I tried to form a prayer on my lips. I could not hear myself, but I was sure that I called the name of God. I looked up into the eyes of my mother's brother and knew that God had no mercy for a soulless creature like me. I fell through the bed and back into the thick of the jungle. The claws of the animals devoured me and my eyes spilled brandy laced tears onto sex tangled sheets...

23

Sherri

I woke the next morning with a start. The sun peeped through the thin curtains with urgency. I jumped from the bed and quickly gathered my things. They looked so oddly out of place with the light of day illuminating them. My head echoed with the sound of Uncle Jerry's voice and my stomach heaved at the taste of stale liquor on my breath. I looked around the empty apartment in disbelief. Was this the safe-haven I had found just yesterday? What a difference the setting of the sun could make.

I thought about Granddaddy and wondered if I should call him. The thought quickly left me when I remembered the war stories Mama often told him about me. He must already think I'm a monster. I shuffled down the hall to look in the mirror as I rinsed the foul taste from my mouth. I saw that the familiar hollow in my eyes had returned.

Did it really happen? Could it have really happened with my own uncle? The sick feeling did not come and go in waves any more. It had settled in to stay. I turned off the water and grabbed a gym bag that was lying in the corner of the small bathroom. No one would believe me. I wasn't sure if I believed myself. I knew my mother would curse me for trying to tarnish her baby brother's good name. The police would ask me what I was doing in New York alone and where had I been staying before I came to my uncle's place. They would find out that I was a whore - and tell me that you couldn't rape a whore. They would say I wanted it; that I was drunk and I deserved it. Or worse yet, that it never really happened. I cursed the empty air and damned myself.

My mind clicked loudly as I walked back up the hall and into the apartment. I almost didn't hear the front door open. Uncle Jerry strolled in like he had been on a long peaceful walk in the park. He looked fresh and un-bothered.

"You up sleepy-head?" he asked almost gleefully. His school-boy frames reflected in the sunlight and his smile made me sick to look at. I turned my head away from him - afraid to let his eyes touch mine. His voice slithered through the air and made the hairs on my neck stand on end as it reached my ears.

"You headed somewhere?" he asked innocently. I turned the nasty words over in my head in disbelief. He was acting like nothing happened! I hardened myself to the shame and confusion that was swelling up in me. I didn't trust my voice so I kept my words to a minimum. I wouldn't let it tremble under the weight of the hurt I felt. He would not see my head bowed or my eyes swell with tears. I drew my shoulders back and daringly looked into his eyes anyway. To my surprise, they didn't scorch me as I had feared.They were soft and shapeless and without the character that dwells in the eyes of decent men.

"I just need to go," I hissed.

"Sure. Did you call the train station to get a ticket price yet?" he asked indifferently. The shape of his face began to blur and his features melted with every man who had ever walked through the door of Merrick Boulevard. I couldn't get away from them. I was marked "whore" from the first nasty blue poker chip they had pushed into my unsure hands weeks earlier. Now I was going to be paid in a ticket instead of cash. I finally bowed my head in shame and threw the gym bag over my shoulder not caring what he thought of me taking it.

"I'm good," I mumbled under my breath.Without pausing, I pushed past him and tackled each step down and away from his apartment door as if the floor would suddenly open up to swallow me back into hell if I did not place my foot firmly on it. I opened the door to the building and turned to look again at the lovely brownstone. The door closed behind me with a slow, gushing "hussssh." He would not come after me and the building would keep my secret and all the secrets it had been told before mine.

Grand Master Flash had said there were eight million stories in New York. Now there were eight million and one and nobidy cared to know the details. I gritted my teeth together and connected my feet to the pavement. Anger threatened to take over and send me rushing back upstairs to scream at him so I swallowed until it was lodged firmly in the back of my throat. Before I knew it, I had put enough blocks between me and Uncle Jerry's street so that nothing – and no one - looked familiar. The sounds of the city assaulted my ears and I tried to put together a clear thought.

Where could I go? How would I get home? I reached into my pocket and pulled out a few crumpled bills and a couple of coins. I cursed myself for spending my money on the stupid black skirt and blouse. How could I be so stupid? I should've just taken the money in the jar and run to the Amtrak station before Uncle Jerry came back. I should have known that a man was a man – relative or not. Still unsure of where to go, I followed the signs to the subway and climbed back into the bowels of the city to think for a while.

The train jerked unkindly against the underground tracks and I wondered why it did not jostle the other passengers as violently as it did me. Before I could stop myself, I laid my head against the window and cried. I did not care that the lady with the Macy's bag shook her head at me or that the boys wearing Polos and Lee jeans perked up to get a closer look. I did not care that snot smeared against the thick plastic and made the stranger's initials permanently etched there shine against the light in the train. I just needed to let some of the pressure in my chest come out of me. The train stopped and started to collect new bodies but I could not stop the tears. I was only able to catch my breath when I felt an arm brush against mine. I looked up into the crowded train but did not have the energy to feel embarrassed. The old man who had taken the set next to me looked at me with concern.

"You okay?" he asked genuinely.

I glanced at his face and it reminded me of the kindly old men who sat on my grandmother's porch to chat from time to time. The thought of Georgia brought the tears down my face in force – although somehow I managed not to sob. The man continued to look at me waiting for an answer. Finally ashamed, I wiped at my face and sat up from against the window. I did not know how to answer his question, but I knew that I was not okay.

"I'm lost," I muttered.

He smiled in relief and asked, "Well, where are you trying to go?"

I wanted to tell him where home was. I wanted to beg him to get me out of this city that swallowed lost little girls, but I knew he could not save me. Without a good reason, I told him,

"Merrick... I'm going to Merrick Boulevard."

He nodded and leaned over me to point at the map on the train wall. He traced the yellow and blue and red lines until he had described a route for me and I smiled at his kindness. He got off the train at the next stop and I retraced his route – carefully taking the stops he told me to take until I came up out of the earth a few blocks from the Western Union I knew so well. Slightly dazed, I walked down the street until I came face to face with the prison I had just escaped. Suddenly terrified that Mack would see me and snatch me back up, I darted into the building across the street and waited. Maybe Sherri would come out soon. Maybe she would know what I should do.

Hours passed and the only activity I saw were a few men coming to and from the building. I wondered how many of them had been to the third floor. Just as I was about to leave the building and wander back to the subway, Sherri came hustling out of the building. She did not stroll or meander the way we often did at home. She had what I was learning to be a signature New York City stride. Quick – certain – unwavering – uninterruptible.

I waited for her to get halfway down the block then sprinted from my hiding place. Afraid that she would pummel me for rushing up behind her, I called out to her before I reached striking distance. At first, she continued to walk – even seeming to quicken her step. Then as soon as she swung the corner, she stopped abruptly and motioned for me to catch up.

"What the hell girl?" she exclaimed, grabbing my arm to walk with her. "You know yo man looking for you?" I thought of Mack but she quickly filled me in.

"Shit – Rod was here first thing this morning raising hell with Mack for losing track of you. I just can't believe you fuckin' jumped outta the window 'B'!!" she said almost admiringly.

"Sherri, I don't know what to do. I need to go home," I whined in desperation. "I just... I..." I tried to explain but something in her face quieted me.

"So what'chu wanna do?" she inquired level-headedly.

"I don't know," I said near tears again. "I don't have any money and I can't go back to Rod, Sherri, I just can't do it."

"Damn this shit is a trip yo." She shook her head.

"I mean on the real, I like the money and I make good dough too – but'chu ain't the first one I seen that just ain't cut out for this shit right?" She schooled me while smacking her gum for emphasis before stopping abruptly in the middle of the sidewalk to face me.

"Why you can't just do a few more tricks and hustle your money back?"

I hung my head afraid to tell her no, but terrified to say yes.

"Das cool 'B'– I got someplace you can crash till you get it together. I used to have a man and we still cool. He no like your man though – he a'ight if you ain't down – plus, I still be giving him money sometime on the strength. He'll look out for you while I'm on my hustle."

She picked up her stride again and motioned me on.

Desperate and out of options, I followed behind her like a stray puppy. I didn't know who her man was or if he would really help me, but I knew that I was lost and afraid. And had nowhere else to go. Wherever Sherri was taking me had to be better than Uncle Jerry's and it had to be better than the hell house on Merrick Boulevard.

24

Wolf in Sheep's Clothing

I wrung my hands nervously as Sherri walked up the sidewalk of Linden Boulevard. Her shiny black curls bounced with each step. Afraid to ask too many questions I just followed behind hoping that my next stop would get me home. I thought about Rod and was unable to help fretting about the guy she was taking me to meet. I slowed my step and she turned to urge me on.

I froze in the middle of sidewalk and looked squarely in the face.

"Sherri, I confessed, "I'm serious. I can't do it no more."

I waited for her to respond. She popped her gum animatedly and reached into her pocket pulling out a knot of money.

"Like I said – I get it that 'chu ain't down. Umma look out for you – but I just can't do nufin right now cause this money is debted. But I'm telling you – lay low for a couple of days and I got'chu – word to my motha." she consoled.

I nodded numbly hoping that somebody would be able to help me get home. I followed Sherri down the main street until we turned on a residential street just past the VA lined with looming three-story houses. We turned into a small front yard with a dented chain link fence. The house looked like it was nice at one time, but was no longer well-kept. The deep blue paint was peeling in places revealing its' past life of dull white. The porch was small but had a bench and two chairs lined against the house. Sherri took her gum out of her mouth and tossed it over the side of the porch before knocking on the door. A light skinned black woman wearing an old flowered robe answered the door. Her graying hair was rolled in a bun with long strands brushing against her neck and her glasses were steamed. The familiar smell of collard greens drifted out the door and greeted us on the porch.

"Hey darling!" she drawled, reaching for Sherri and planting a friendly kiss on her cheek.

"You here for dinner or for that son of mine?" she chuckled.

"We came to see Robert," Sherri sang sweetly – all of the grit suddenly gone from her voice.

"Oh dear – who is your friend?" the lady inquired looking at me with a smile.

I fiddled with the hem of my shirt making sure it was pulled down snugly over my waistband.

"This is Dee – she my home girl from down south," Sherri offered without missing a beat.

"Oh – nice to see you love." The older woman said sweetly. She turned away from us and yelled up the staircase behind her, "Rob – your girl is here to see you!"

With that, she opened the door wide and disappeared back in the direction the smell of home cooking was coming from. Sherri motioned for me to follow her as she stepped into the house and took two steps at a time up the nearby staircase. I closed the door behind and followed her – still unsure of what to expect.

"What up girl?" the voice came from a huge high yellow man wearing only a bath towel. My heart pounded at his stature and deep voice.

"Hey Dave, is Rob here?" Sherri kept climbing until she reached the top of the first stair landing. Relieved the giant man was not Robert, I followed closely behind Sherri as she rounded the hallway and took the second flight of stairs leading to the attic. I fidgeted with my hem as she reached for the door knob.

"Yep – he up there chillin'." Dave offered as he called up the stairs behind us before shuffling across the hall to another room.

Sherri opened the door into a small, cluttered attic room. It was bare of furniture except for a small desk by the window covered with brown paper bags and a bed tucked into the corner. Along each wall and well out into the middle of the floor, clothes and shoes were strewn about in piles making it difficult to find a place to stand without stepping into the piles. I had never seen so many Adidas. I navigated myself against the wall into one of the few bare spots on the floor and watched Sherri as she approached the man asleep on top of the tangled bed spread. She plopped down next to him and leaned over planting a kiss on his sleeping face. The tall lean man stretched and turned toward us groggily. His hair was like Sherri's – stark black and wavy. His skin was soft beige and his face was accented by pouty pink lips.

"Wake up babe – I got somebody I want you to meet." Sherri announced.

Robert opened his eyes revealing deep green irises surrounded by blood shot red. If his lips were not so boyish, the combination would have been threatening. Either way I eased closer to the wall while he inspected me through half-closed eyes.

"Daaaam!" he exclaimed, still sleepy. "She fine as hell."

"Yeah, don't get no ideas though – she just my home girl." Sherri teased his hair with affection. Robert rose from the bed stretching his legs out over the edge and leaned against her still looking at me.

"Damn," He sighed

"Look – she got jacked yo ," Sherri launched into an explanation-slash-request. "Can she crash here for a few days Umma hook her up, but I'm short right now. I'm headed out to Far Rocakway for the weekend 'cause you know I owe Pratt all that money. I'll be straight when I get back this way though."

"C'mon girl – that shit played. Won't you come on and let your man work it out for you?" Robert pleaded rubbing her thigh seductively.

I looked away as they interacted.

"C'mon Rob – I got dis. Just look out for me ok?" Sherri waited for his response and I held my breath.

"You got me?" Robert perked up taking on a more serious demeanor.

Sherri reached into her pocket and peeled off some of her cash wad.

"I got'chu." She rose from the bed and headed toward the window dresser. In one motion she grabbed one of the small brown paper bags and crossed the room to approach me.

"He cool, Dee. Just chill 'til I get back and I'll look out for you." She said pressing a crumpled twenty-dollar-bill into my hand.

Unsure of exactly what had taken place between them, I looked from Sherri to Robert and back again afraid to react.

"Um telling you – he good people." Sherri turned to Robert as if urging him to say something. He smiled in a sweet boyish way and cocked his head to the side to address me for the first time.

"I'm good people. You a'ight here for a few days, slim."

I nodded and Sherri motioned for me to follow her outside the room after giving Robert another quick peck on the cheek. She pulled the room door closed behind her and whispered to me in hushed tones.

"You'll be alright – I'm telling you Rob is like – harmless a'ight. You won't have to do nothin' girl – just chill and when I get my cash right I'll drop back by and hook you up." Then she looked intently at me to make sure I was okay with her plan as I understood it.

Gratefully, I thanked her for her kindness and relaxed for the first time since we entered the house. I was "okay," I assured her. Sherri would help me get home in a few days and Robert couldn't be any worse than the guys I just got away from. His mother was right downstairs cooking and it made me feel safe. I watched Sherri bounce back down the stairs and call out a quick goodbye to Robert's mother before slamming the door. I turned and slipped back into the small room before I ran into Dave again. Robert made polite chatter as he searched through the piles of clothes for something to put on over his boxer shorts and T-shirt. Seeing his frustration, I helped him tackle the piles of clothes separating shirts from pants from shoes.

He smiled sweetly and nodded his head with approval.

"We gon' be cool 'til your girl get back."

With that, we settled into a polite friendliness while I waited for Sherri.

The days had stretched into weeks of waiting. Robert had reluctantly filled me in on the whole story as the Monday rounded the passing weekend and Sherri had still not called or come back by. He explained that she was a good-hearted person, but she was caught up. Seeing the question in my face, he explained that "caught up" meant she was on dope and seldom kept her word about anything. He said she had probably made her money and spent it two or three times over by now. I looked at him uneasily as he explained her habit while sniffing a powder too dark to be cocaine. He said it was "boy", and that I should never try it because that's what Sherri was so fucked up on. I watched him nod while talking to me and took heed. Between nods he offered to pay me $10 a day to keep the attic rooms clean for him and his four brothers.

I gladly accepted any means of putting together what funds I needed to make it back home. Dave brought in a small love seat and pushed it in the corner next to Robert's bed so at least I had a place to lay my head. I ate Jamaican patties from the corner store because they were the cheapest food I could find. Then I counted the dollars I had left wondering exactly how much I needed to get home. I was in strange, unfamiliar surroundings, but as long as there were no men coming to see me with poker chips, I accepted my temporary circumstance without too many tears.

Robert indeed proved to be a sweet person – never making a pass at me and always chatting politely with me when he was at home. He often left in the evenings and did not come back until the wee hours of the morning. I would stay in the room to avoid his brothers and any questions from his mother but I quickly learned that she never came up to the third floor.

Occasionally, Robert would let me ride with him to get fast food or to run errands but I stuck closely to the attic room where it felt safe. I fell into the habit of cleaning the four small rooms and staying out of the way when the brothers got together and became boisterous. Making $10 a day and spending five or six on food was not going to get me to Georgia anytime soon...

25

Dragon's Lair

Robert pulled his pick-up truck to a stop alongside the curb and I glanced at the house. It was just like all of the other houses on the block... tall, dark and gloomy. Unlike the pretty little country homes in Georgia, they didn't have frilly curtains peeking from their windows or cheery petunia's bedded in dainty window boxes. These houses were dulled by years of winter snow. They looked positively grim and unloved. I looked past the chain-linked fence into the small yard and saw that the porch light was flickering as if it would go out any minute. I scanned the rest of the small, bare yard, but my eyes were drawn back to the porch light competing with the afternoon sun - it seemed misplaced.

New York was a strange city with strange ways and I tried not to feel so lonely and lost - but with each passing day my hope dwindled. Sherri never came back to make good on her promise to help me and Robert told me he couldn't afford to pay me the $10 to straighten up anymore after my second week with him. I had only saved $45 so I got on the subway to look for work. Everyone I spoke to brushed me off when I explained how I lost my wallet and just needed work. So I visited the social security office and the hall of records – but with no ID to start with, getting anything official was just an endless loop of people behind thick glassed windows telling me they couldn't help me.

Robert watched me come with no good news for two weeks in a row. I was so desperate, I was almost ready to hit the highway and hitch a ride back to Georgia. Every night I thought about it though, I always saw the bloodied T-shirt scene in the movie, Hitchhiker so I stayed put. Robert finally said that if I gave him a little time to hustle his money up, he could give me the rest of what I needed to get home. It was beginning to sound like a familiar lie, but with few other choices, I waited and hoped.

Then Robert came in one evening excited about a chance he had for making a lot of money and said it would really help the deal if I rode along to meet the guys with him. I agreed unenthusiastically. What choice did I have at that point?

As I watched the porch light flicker, I hoped this was finally the big score that would send me home. Robert and I got along fine and even seemed to be becoming buddies, but living in a stranger's attic in a city that could destroy me at will was not where I wanted to be. Each day, I just tried to live in the moment until fate made a way for me to reach the safety of the south.

I followed Robert's lead and got out of the truck. We hastily made our way across the street and through the creaky gate.

"Take your hands outta your pockets." Robert instructed urgently.

Sensing his nervousness, I did so without hassling him. The door swung open and I found myself staring into the dark gaping hole of the doorway. Seeing that I would not move on my own, Robert pushed me at my elbow. A hand reached out from the blackness and assisted him. My heart began pounding in my chest so loudly that I almost didn't hear the door slam behind us. Standing in the middle of a dark abyss I wondered what the hell kind of a place we were in. Just as I was about to object, I heard a hollow authoritative clicking. My skin crawled as I recognized the sound of guns being cocked.

Click-Clack! Click-Clack! Click-Clack!

The sound of semi-automatics came from every direction - caging us in. Not knowing which way to run, I froze and braced myself. I gritted my teeth and dug my fingers into my palms. Suddenly, light flooded the room as if our captors were anxious to see what they had snared. My eyes slowly began to adjust to a bare bulb swinging from its' chain - revealing the contents of the room. In a macabre dance, the movement of the light grew and shrank shadowy figures against the walls. I noticed a long bar in the darkness of the far left corner of the room. Upon closer inspection, I saw that there was a man sitting motionless behind it.

His eyes stood out from the darkness and looked sharply at me. Fixated, I tried to make out his face. Distracted by the heat of bodies around me, I reluctantly peeled my eyes to see where all the clacking had come from. Robert was opening his jacket to reveal the insides to a circle of men. They were tucked into every corner like a pack of urban wolves. Instinctively, I slowly placed the hand-me-down purse Robert loaned me from his mother's things onto the floor in front of me and took a small, careful step away from it.

One of the men lowered his weapon and examined the bag. The others did not move. They just stared at us through the barrels of their guns ready to react. I looked to Robert in the dim light. He shot me a quick little smile but I could sense that he too was unnerved by the hostility in the room. I could not find words so I just looked at him wide-eyed. My bag was handed back to me and the men slowly began to leave their positions. I looked again at the man sitting behind the bar. He nodded his head slightly and we were allowed passage deeper into the room. Terrified, I followed closely at Robert's heels.

"These are my partners baby," Robert oozed with false confidence as we each took a barstool. "Don't worry about 'em."

I wanted to ask him why he called me "baby", but I was shaken from the sound of the clacking guns still reverberating in my head. The man behind the bar reached over and shook Robert's hand. Without speaking he turned to me and extended the same courtesy. Though his eyes were still fierce, his expression was soft and pleasant. His skin was dark and smooth but his hair was rolled into his head and chin as if in shame. Unable to accept the fact that he had just stopped combing his hair, I assumed that he was in the process of growing dreadlocks. I smiled nervously and gently took his hand.

"This is my girl, Denise." Robert announced with pride.

Unable to stop myself, I shot Robert a questioning look and it did not go unnoticed. The man stared through the center of my eyes and I felt violated. It felt as if he were looking for something deep inside my head. I lowered my eyes and fiddled with my fingers, unwilling to allow him such intimacy.

"They call me M.O. love, said the man, "but you can call me whatever you want to."

I glanced up again and he broke into a wide grin full of gold teeth. My cousin, Patricia had a cold cap with a Playboy bunny on it, but I had never seen so much jewelry in a man's mouth before. Still unnerved by the hostile environment I did not address Robert's newfound ownership of me.

In an instant, Robert took a dope sack from his jeans and began making a line on the bar. He pre-warned me he would toot a line or two when we got there so the guys would know that he wasn't an undercover agent, but I still wondered how he could get high in such an unwelcoming environment. M.O. shifted his attention from me and looked at the line Robert was perfecting. He casually swept his large diamond studded hand across the counter and wiped the heroine to the floor. Shocked by the blunt gesture, I looked to see what Robert would do.

His face reddened, but he kept his cool.

"What's up with you man?" he asked nervously. "You squared up on me?"

If there was any doubt before that second, I knew now that this man was the kind of heavy weight I had never seen before – even in my days of watching Rod do deals. In the time I had hung out with Robert and his brothers, I had not seen him back down to anyone – even when he was indulging in his favorite pastime of sniffing heroine he would jump straight up from a nod to set someone straight if they offended him. But he remained gracious under this man's fire. M.O. dusted the powder from his fingertips and spoke slowly as he made his way back behind the bar.

"I just don't allow outside shit in my spot man." he grinned.

Robert dropped the empty plastic sack along with another full one into the ashtray next to him. Concern rose up my spine making me sit up straight. I wonder how much the dope cost he was throwing away. I wondered if the people in the basement were going to hurt us and why Robert would bring me to a meeting with people who were so unstable? Unable to hide my feelings, my eyes flashed angrily from Robert to the tall gold-laden man.

"You have a problem with that slim-goody?" he inquired.

Fear was threatening to make me panic so I masked it with bravado.

Before I could stop myself, I spoke, "Well, you're rude."

He looked at me as if to see if I was joking. I held my ground and did not smile. He reached under the bar without taking his eyes away from me. I thought he might be reaching for a gun, but instead of flinching, I held my chin a little higher. It might have been the dumbest thing I had done in a while, but I was so scared, I had little control over how I reacted. To my relief, M.O.'s hand emerged with an over-sized zip-lock bag full of dingy powder. He broke the seal and dumped a hefty portion onto the bar in front of us. I relaxed my shoulders. I could have been killed. As the danger passed I expelled the breath I did not know I was holding. The two men looked at me.

Robert's face might have been tinged with red but M.O.'s expression did not change. He nodded his head and addressed Robert, "She green as hell, man, but she all right." MO finally laughed, seeming pleased. Robert relaxed the pinched expression he had assumed and joined the laughter, if only in relief. The tension in the room dissipated as if on cue and one of the men came from his corner chair and opened a refrigerator behind the bar. He passed cold beers around and the tops popped with the same succession as the cocking of the guns had just a few minutes ago. Still shaking from my experience I accepted one of the icy cans and waited for a glass. The laughter rose higher as M.O. looked at me in disbelief.

"Man, you got to be shitting me?!" he laughed while Robert slapped high five with him.

"Come on kid, you know I always go first class. Now get the young lady a glass man." Rob said in his most respectable ghetto voice. Knowing it was best to deal with Robert later I ignored the comment and poured my beer, still thankful that I wasn't shot.

With the introductions made and the air lighter, I sat back and quietly listened to the guys talk about ounces and keys. It was strange talk to me, because Rod always did his negotiating behind closed doors – leaving me only to count the money. But in the drone of their voices I forgot all about the cold reception. Whatever we were here for at least it would not be another boring night in the attic and I enjoyed the first drink I'd had in weeks. Still, I wished Robert would do whatever he had to so we could get out of the dark, cold room.

After we had been sitting for a while, the beer made its way through me and I squirmed on my seat. I tried to catch Robert's eye, but he was too busy bragging about money he didn't have.

"The bathroom is through that door and to the left," M.O. offered smoothly.

My face reddened and I looked at him. How did he know? He was staring through me again. My face tightened and I wondered how long he had been examining me. I silently wished Robert didn't need his money and without a response, I gladly left my hot seat and followed his directions. The furniture I passed seemed to be black like everything else in the room - it was hard to tell in this dim light, though. The single bulb cast just as many shadows as it did light. I could tell the men in the basement had been there for some time without the touch of a woman's hand. There were beer cans scattered here and there and a thick layer of dust on everything. I saw movement in the corner of my eye and realized that the man who passed the beers around was following me to the bathroom - brandishing his pistol.

I started to turn around and just hold it - but my bladder would not allow me the luxury. Still, my pulse quickened as I maneuvered through the narrow dark hallway. I stepped into the bathroom and relieved myself in the rust colored bowl. I washed my hands without the benefit of soap and turned off the creaky faucet. When I opened the door the man stood there waiting. He stood with his arms folded with his gun cradled in the folds. People in New York didn't know much about smiling. Feeling more relaxed with my beer buzz kicking in I ignored his grim expression and smiled brightly at him anyway.

"Thank you for your protection, My Lord," I said in a mock English accent. "I will be sure to tell the King how nice you were to me."

I batted my eyelashes at him and broke into a giggle. To my surprise he chuckled with me as he led me back to the bar. I slipped back through the maze of chairs and bodies and found my seat next to Robert again.

While I was gone, more piles of dope had been laid onto the bar. One tightly bundled package sat in front of Robert and he guarded it with his elbows as if M.O. would change his mind and take it back. Two men scooped seeds from a pile of weed in the center of the bar and rolled fat joints. The thick smoke slammed into my nostrils forcing me to scoot my stool back from the bar to avoid a contact high. Damn! I hated reefer smoke. Somebody to my left passed me a joint and I took it and passed it to Robert.

"Oh, you don't smoke?" M.O. asked in suspicious surprise.

Robert answered for me. "Naah man, she mostly a good girl. I been trying to get her to loosen up, though. Just give my girl some of that good liquor, man - you know she like that fancy shit."

Robert winked at me and I shook my head in disbelief. He was quite the actor when he wanted to be. They cracked the seal on a bottle of Hennessey and poured generous glasses all around. I sipped slowly and the conversation around me picked up again. The rest of the men began to join in and before long boisterous laughter had filled the room. After a while, and despite my best efforts to avoid it at all costs, the reefer smoke seeped into my head anyway. I got up and found a safe haven in one of the black chairs I had passed going to the bathroom.

"Hey! If it isn't My Lord," I giggled, recognizing the man who had escorted me to the bathroom.

It's Gino," he said, smiling, and tucked his gun further into the belt of his pants.

"Well Gino, thank you" I said looking at the place where the gun had poked through, "but weapons make me very uncomfortable you know."

"That's what they supposed to do." he said seriously

I swirled my glass letting the liquor get dangerously close to the rim.

"Want some?" I tempted.

"Sure, why not?" He took a long sip from my glass and, before long we had picked up a pleasant conversation. In contrast to the now rowdy atmosphere just across the room, we quietly chatted as if we were at a jazz club. Still, I found myself gazing at Robert wishing he would pack up so we could leave.

"You in love huh?" Gino asked watching Robert's animated conversation at the bar.

Remembering the lie Robert told I tried to stick with it without feeling like a fraud.

"I suppose you have to be somewhere," I answered almost wistfully. "Why not be in love?"

"Not only is she gorgeous, but she's also witty." M.O. called from the edge of the bar. My mouth dropped open and I stared at him. How the hell could he hear what we were talking about through all of that clatter? I shook my head and looked at Gino in disbelief. He shrugged his shoulders and smiled. I giggled uncomfortably.

"Come here, baby," Robert urged happily. "I got something for you."

I headed to the bar again.

"Don't forget your glass," M.O. reminded me.

"You know," I began on my way across the room, "you're really starting to give me the creeps." I pointed my glass at him beginning to feel the liquor.

"Good. I was wondering when you were going to recognize."

He steadied my waving hand and poured more liquor into my glass. Feeling the buzz come down, I did not object. I shrugged off his comments and turned to Robert.

"Come on girl - stop being such a prude and celebrate with your man," Robert said in slow motion. I had never seen anyone do heroine before Robert, but quickly learned not to be concerned when it made him move in slow motion. But I was still uncomfortable at the idea of having to act like his girlfriend. Why did he have to lie about it?

I shrugged and scooted a little closer to him knowing we would be able to leave in a few minutes. Besides, it looked like he had finally hit the lick he was talking about I could already imagine myself on my way back to Georgia. M.O. began placing more bags of dope than I had ever seen in front of Robert. My eyes widened and I wondered what kind of deal Robert struck to get all of that stuff.

"You gonna turn all of that Robert?" I asked in shock unable to contain my disbelief.

"Yeah, thanks to my new partner here."

M.O. looked at me intensely and I decided I didn't want to know what it was the partnership rules were.

"Well, I see why you celebrating now." I laughed and sipped my drink. M.O. plopped down on a bar stool sandwiching me between him and Rob.

"You sniff baby?" he asked with a sly smile.

Before I could answer, M.O. raised his diamond clad finger to my lips.

"Don't talk," he said, "just sniff."

He opened one of the bags of cocaine and used a measuring cup to dump a pile on a magazine.

"Daaang! That's too much!" I warned.

"Don't even worry about it - your man got your back." He glanced at Robert before plunging his pinkie into the middle of the pile and bringing it to my nose. Uncomfortable with his closeness, I turned my head and looked at Robert. He was on the down swing of a heavy nod - but still managed to mumble to me, "Go on girl; just take a little toot so the man knows you're not the fuzz."

I shrugged my shoulders and turned my attention back to the tall, strange man. He was hard to figure out. One second I thought he was a nice guy, the very next... who knows? I delicately steadied his hand with mine and sniffed as deeply as I could, but still didn't get it all. I leaned my head back and let the rush flood my brain. The warmth started to grow in my stomach and sent mellow waves through my legs and toes. My fingers tingled with excitement as the drain hit the back of my throat.

"Yeah girl! That's it," Robert cajoled.

Unable to help myself, I giggled at Robert's slurred encouragement. Sherri was probably right – even when he was up to no good, Robert was a nice enough guy. I was sure he lied to M.O. for a good reason. I fidgeted with the buttons of my blouse as the rush of the drug hurled me into fast gear. I looked again at Robert and felt like a jet taking off from the runway... leaving my slow moving friend behind.

His head lay on the edge of the bar and I knew that from now on he would be privy to only half of the conversation. By the time the drain in my throat slowed to a drip I was blanketed in a soft coat of confidence and easiness. I sipped at my drink and allowed M.O. to feed me more cocaine than I had ever sniffed in my life.

Everything was so smooth. I kicked my shoes off my throbbing feet and rode with it. M.O. and I chatted about things I couldn't quite remember. I would open my mouth to say something and brightly colored words fell out like alphabet blocks. We laughed at them and kept sniffing while Robert nodded. I reached for my glass but it was already at my lips. I looked at Gino and giggled while he tried to hold it steadily to my lips. I returned the favor by sliding my finger into the pile of powder and bringing a nail full of cocaine to his face. He smiled and pushed by hand away.

"Crew don't sniff," Gino said. Giggling I taunted him.

"Well, what does crew do?"

"We murderers, baby."

Only slightly chilled by his words, a testament to how high I was, I mocked his gruff voice, "Ha-ha-ha – murderers!"

I leaned forward for fear I would fall off of my stool. A hand brushed my chin and lifted it slightly. I sniffed in and felt the soft burn spread through my chest again. I reached out and placed my hand on Robert's. Perplexed at the size of them, I looked up to see that I had grabbed M.O.'s hand instead.

His diamonds were gleaming so brightly in the direct light of the bare bulb that they dazzled me. I laughed and announced that there would now be a fireworks display at the bar. I lifted his hand up in the air and rocked it back and forth catching the light of the bare bulb. Sure enough, it gleamed bright rays of blue and pink with every angle. He smiled broadly playing along with me.

Robert stirred from his nod and laughed at me.

"You blasted girl!" he accused.

"Well, you told me to get blasted," I teased in mock indignation. I could tell from his eyes that his high was just about mellowed out. I smiled as he left his barstool and stood behind me.

"Robert, are you ready to go yet?" I asked.

"No, you're too high to even walk across the street. Come on; sit over here a while... then we'll go."

He ushered me from the bar back to the big black chair where I had chatted with Gino. Robert knelt before me and looked at me with the same sweetness in his face I saw the first time I met him rousing from a sleep.

"You know you a sweet girl?"

"Robert, stop" I whined- surprised that I was blushing but reassuring myself it was probably from the cocaine.

"No seriously," he went on. "You so damned sweet and innocent."

I rolled my eyes and leaned up to the edge of the chair. I thought about the clattering beads on Merrick Blvd and started to tell him just how wrong he was.

Before I could, M.O. interrupted, Yo man," he called out to Robert, "you need to save that. She'll be here after you make that run."

My face fell in disappointment as I figured out we were not about to leave together after all. I started to object but Robert pressed his lips to my ear.

Sssshh," he assured me, "I'll be back before you know it."

The liquor swirled in my head and added rhythm to his words. I decided not to fuss.

"It's okay Rob. I'm okay. Just hurry up, okay?" I mumbled through my high.

He leaned back from me and looked into my eyes in a way he never had before. Sorrow filled his face and it unsettled me.

Had he started to really believe that I was his girlfriend? He brushed his thumb across my lips leaving my question unanswered. When he rose, it sent shivers through me; it felt so final. I felt more cocaine drain in my head and knew I was wasted. I brushed off the uneasy feeling and leaned back in the comfort of the chair.

Before I closed my eyes, I watched Robert cross the room and gather his bundles of dope. He shook M.O.'s hand and walked toward the dark frame of the door. The strong orange glow of the evening sun flooded my eyes and gathered Robert into its' center. It faded back to black as the door closed.

POOF!

He was gone.

26

Belly of the Beast

I sat watching the closed basement door warily until my eyes began to get heavy. Robert sure was taking a long time. I tried to keep chatting politely so I wouldn't get nervous, but one by one most of the men had left – leaving only M.O., Gino and two other men relaxing against the bar. Conversation had dried up and all I could think to do at this point was watch the door. Something in the mood was changing and, instinctively, I didn't want to focus on it. Gino stirred from a hushed conversation he was having with M.O. and shot a strange look in my direction before stepping aside for M.O. to pass. He approached me in what looked like a death march. More suspicious than ever, I struggled to sit up in the low chair to receive him.

Afraid of what he was going to say, I spoke first,

"I – uh", I stuttered uncomfortably. "I should go. Robert must have gotten caught up. I-I'll just take the train and wait for him."

M.O.'s face did not change as he motioned to the two men standing at the bar. I tried to read something in Gino's face but he lowered his head in a shocking move not to meet my eyes. I watched in horror as the two men approached me from either side as if on cue. My head swirled with liquor and cocaine and I unwillingly reached for the arm closest to me to keep from falling.

Finally, M.O. broke into a wide, gleaming grin. His words were chilling, "You can't leave yet, slim - you debted."

"Debted?" I asked afraid to know the answer.

"Wake up baby – you're man debted you to me until he turn my package and bring my money back."

He paused and looked into my eyes as if he were going to ask for my hand in marriage. His long, diamond fingered hand reached out to caress my face in a chilling display of open affection.

"It's a'ight, Slim. I gotchu" he crooned. "Red don't know what to do with a high-post girl like you anyway – and I need a stunner"

His eyes flickered dangerously and as quickly as the charm poured from beneath his cold surface it came to a grinding halt. "But," he hissed, "I gotta break you before I can build you, baby."

With my nervous fears becoming real I instantly I found a burst of energy and tried to dodge the space closing between the men but the liquor would not let my body respond to my command. I only managed to wedge myself in tighter.

"B-but – M.O. you don't understand…" I began before he interrupted my plea.

"There is nothing to explain or understand love. Man or no man, knowledge or no knowledge – you got a debt baby. We big boys and these are big rules." He motioned his finger and the men began to drag me towards the back of the basement oblivious to my kicking and screaming.

I lay in the grips of a restless sleep in a small filthy bed. My legs were so cramped that they ached even in sleep. The haunting images of two men having their way with me came to me throughout the night in white hot flashes.

"Hey man, is she still knocked out?" I heard someone say from the other side of the door.

The sound of the voice roused me from a torturous sleep. I shifted in the bed and looked shakily at the door. They were coming back! I shuffled in the bed until I was able to sit up. A draft rushed across my bare thighs with the sudden movement and I knew I had not been dreaming. I reached for the dark object on the rickety nightstand and gripped it in anticipation. The door swung open and I lunged toward it. My hand was met with force mid-swing and I fell against the body pushing its way into the room.

"Chill, slim," Gino warned as he wedged the empty bottle from my hand while pushing the door closed with his foot. Before he could close it another man I had not seen before jammed it open thrusting his arm through the opening. He flung a thick rope onto the floor unceremoniously.

"Tie that bitch up man – M.O. gon' be gone three/four days and I don't want no more shit on my shift." He paused to drink in my nakedness before continuing, "I see why they did it, but them niggas gon have hell to pay when M.O. find out they cracked the seal on his new shit."

Gino gazed at the rope with what looked like genuine sorrow on his face and I ceased my vane struggle against him. The sound of the rope thudding to the floor had calmed my agitated state. I looked into his eyes and though they seemed kind, there were no answers to be found there. Without words I turned and sat on the bed.

Seeing my submission the man turned to exit back out to the hallway leaving only his unsettling words, "Well, the shit done now. We might as well let the crew go on and wild out." As Gino bent over to pick up the rope, his gun pressed against the blue Members Only jacket he was wearing. I wondered if I should rush him again and go for the gun. He had a small stature and maybe if I was quick...

As if he sensed my thoughts he tucked the gun deeper into his jeans and shook his head.

"Don't struggle, Slim."

"Gino – why?" I asked honestly trying to understand why I was being held like an animal. The rope shifting in his hand made me shiver in the bed.

"You got caught in the cross baby – that's all. I ain't slow – I know Robert aint'cha man for real but you gotta be careful who you fuck wit'." He shook his head again.

Understanding that no matter what I said I was not going to be allowed to leave the basement, I just spoke my mind freely.

"Don't act like you care – I don't see you letting me go. So go ahead – do what you gotta do to me – your boys sure did last night."

His hooded eyes followed mine to the discarded condom wrappers on the bare floor. My words seemed to affect him, but not enough to disobey the man in the hallway. Gino motioned for me to lie back in the bed and so I did without a fight.

"I'm not gon' touch you – but yeah, Slim, my word is my bond. I gotta take care of my business." He half apologized while looping knots in the rope for my hands and feet. He tied me securely to the metal bed frame and quietly left the room as I stared up at the water stained ceiling. Sobs racked my chest and I turned my head to the side to keep from choking on my own tears. I cried as quietly as I could for fear that someone other than Gino would come into the room if I made too much noise.

My heart thudded in my chest as the door whooshed open a few minutes later. I stopped mid-sob and watched Gino cross the room again with a bottle of Hennessy in hand. All the air left me as the understanding of his gesture settled in my bones with a chill. He tossed a handful of condoms on the nightstand and loosened the liquor cap without looking at me. Partners in a sick game, I lifted my head for him to feed me the anesthesia I would need to get through the night.

There were no windows. I lost track of time listening to the voices floating under the door like a macabre choir - chanting to some unknown God. Had they already come to take me to the bathroom again? I couldn't remember. It hurt to pee because I was sore down there. I pulled my thighs as closely together as the ropes would allow and focused on holding my bladder steady until the door opened again.

I flexed and un-flexed the muscles in my calves so maybe I would be strong enough to run the next time they took the ropes off. My leg began to cramp so I stopped and tried to relax it out. I turned my head back to the side in exhaustion. There was a bloodstain smeared in the mattress next to my head and a salty taste on my lips. I tried to make out the shape of the stain as my weakened body fell backwards into the dream again...

The door opened to reveal a tall, shadowy figure. He stepped closer to the bed and his face became clear. A lump fixed itself in my throat as my eyes locked with his. They were cold and red.

"Get'cho ass up" he growled.

"Nooo!" I moaned in weak defiance. I choked out before I could stop myself. He closed the rest of the distance of the small room and struck my face in one swift motion.

"You don't tell me no - bitch! You can '86 that shit if you know what's good for you."

I shook my head numbly as reality tumbled from where it had hidden itself and fell into my lap. I looked down at my naked body wishing I could hide it from him. The man followed my eyes and looking down in disgust. He tugged the ropes free and grabbed my arm roughly dragging me from the bed and through the door to the bathroom. He shoved me toward the shower.

"Clean up." he growled fiercely. My hands shook as I reached for the faucet. My legs almost flew out from under me with relief when he closed the door and left me alone to clean myself up. I steadied my wobbly legs and splashed the water gratefully against my skin trying to soothe the indignities of the last 48 hours. I ached even through the numbness and the mirror over the sink revealed the abstract of purple bruises where the pain radiated from within. I thought about Roger's drunken fit that had left me wounded in Steve's bed.

Though it was harsh at the time, I now found myself longing for the brevity of the attack. Only tiny bits of reality were able to slip through the waves of pain and disbelief that washed over me, but it was painfully clear – this was no dream; everything happening to me was real! Robert was gone for good and I had been turned over to a crew of murderers like commissary.

No one knew where I was and no one was coming for me. I trembled and grappled to find some sane thought to hold onto. I began to wonder if I would die in this place with the long bar in the corner and a urine-stained mattress in my holding cell. I could not find one happy thought to cling to so I reached for the only thing I could. I gazed into the mirror unable to stop myself, and in my head letters formed words and words formed thoughts of a former self:

The death of a poet
is a haunting thing.
A song of silence
my soul must sing.
A futile attempt
to play a melody
That has long since
faded from my memory.
Thoughts without a voice,
an ink-stained dream.
Whispers of beauty
drowned by a desperate scream.
The yellowed memoirs
that reek of age.
The lonely pain
of a still blank page.
Yes, the death of a poet.
So swift. So sure.
And the birds of freedom
shall sing no more.

A loud banging interrupted my thoughts and the door swung open slamming against the back of the bathroom wall. Gino stood in doorway watching me stare into nothing. His shoulders slumped from the rigid position I had become used to seeing them in and he moved toward me slowly. He grabbed my hand and pulled me toward the bedroom again. Unable to struggle, I leaned against him and let him guide me to the position dictated by the ropes. I looked up into his face and studied the furrows on his forehead.

"Hey Gino," I began. His eyes met mine and he waited for me to finish this time.

"If I ever get out of here again you know what I'm going to do?" I leaned my head as close to his as I could get and whispered in his ear, "I'm going to be a writer Gino. I'm not going to drink anymore and I'm going to be a good writer."

I let my head fall back against the nasty mattress and stared at the patterns the stains made. He left me examining the artwork and suddenly I wondered whatever had happened to the poetry book I used to carry with me.

27

Escape from New York

I swallowed the fowl taste of fear that had settled on my tongue in a pasty film. I strained to lift my weak head from the mattress hoping to relieve some of the sweltering heat radiating down the back of my neck. My hair tumbled away from the back of my shoulders and I was glad for the slight stir of air it created.

I cursed Robert for being so cruel and cursed myself for being so stupid; suddenly I began to shiver again. I hated Rod and Uncle Jerry – but even deeper than the hatred, I despised myself for just being so stupid. I looked into my mind's eye and saw the faces that had looked down into mine in the filthy bed and my stomach tightened. It was becoming clearer to me that I would soon have to choose death over the torture they did not seem to be tiring of.

The door opened and my heart pounded dangerously. I hoped it was only shower time. It was too early to be anything else just yet; the men did not come until they were drunk and I heard no rowdy laughter in the hall that told me they were drinking. I strained against the confining limits of my ropes trying to get a glimpse of who was coming.

Two pair of legs moved toward me and I knew they were not there to take me to the bathroom. Only one man came for that. They were coming to touch me again. Tears stung my eyes and I thrashed violently against the bed to discourage them. One of the men slipped his hand under my head and held it up to him. I tried to pull away, but my neck was not strong enough to turn in his grasp. I looked into his face and stopped thrashing. It was M.O. My eyes widened as he looked down into my face. Had he come to shoot me? I prayed silently as he examined me. Maybe death was not such a good idea.

"She done yo." Gino announced

"Man, what the fuck?" M.O. asked with surprise in his voice.

M.O. loosened his grip on my neck and looked into the center of his eyes. I had never seen eyes so cold and I wondered if he had just announced me dead.

Terrified, I choked out in desperate plea to the kindest of my captors, "Gino - pleeease?!

Oblivious to my cries for mercy, M.O. shook his head and stormed out of the room in disgust. I tried to cover myself by turning my knees to the side. Gino took the ropes off with a somber face and when he realized I was too weak to get up, he lifted me up from the mattress himself. I suddenly became aware of the fact that Gino was not taking me to the bathroom but my ropes were off.

"Oh God Gino – you're not really gonna kill me are you? You were just saying that stuff about being a murderer right?" I asked in a hopeful voice.

He shook his head vigorously. "No, Slim this shit real – but I can't let 'em do it no more." He paused and looked at my shaking body "Motherfuckers!" he suddenly exclaimed

He stormed out of the room and I heard his angry voice in the hall. "God damn man! I leave and ya'll can't follow instructions? I said hold on to her – not run no damn express train. What the hell was you niggas thinking?"

I jumped at the sound of a loud crashing noise and looked into M.O.'s face. It was not a dream. M.O. was mean as a snake, but he seemed genuinely angry that his men had not done what he told them. I didn't understand the kindness mixed with the cruelty in him, but it at least gave me hope of leaving. Maybe they would drop me off now that M.O. was back and raising hell.

Relief came too suddenly and all of the tension left my body leaving me unable to sit up on my own. The breath that I expelled was the last one I had in me and my lungs felt flat.

M.O. turned and knelt on the mattress in front of me helping to support my tortured body. Full of emotion and not sure what was happening, I reached up to him and wrapped my arms around his neck to plead my case,

"Let me go... please let me go." I cried and held onto him for dear life. My mind raced, but I was only able to grasp one thought.

"Please God, let me go. Gino will tell you – I wasn't no trouble."

He let me hang onto him and sob until my voice was hoarse and my head was light. Then, he wrenched my arms away and silently left the room. I rubbed at the red whelps on my wrists and ankles while trying to listen carefully to the commotion in the hallway. The voices were angry and no one wanted to back down.

"This ain't just about you and Gino man. She know where we at and what we look like. I ain't doing time for no bitch." One voice barked.

"Man look, she just got caught up. She aint even a round-the-way girl. Just let her walk - and she's outta here - back to the fucking South or wherever she from. We ain't never gonna hear from slim again." Another voice seemed to plead for reasoning.

A full scale coup d'état was unfolding and M.O.'s typically iron fist was molting under the pressure from his crew. Back and forth the argument went until it sounded more and more like I would never walk out of the basement again. Finally, there was silence and the door swung open again. Gino entered the room with his head hung. He had brought me another bottle of liquor and plopped on the side of the bed next to me and took a long swallow. Without looking at me, he passed me the bottle and, emotionless, I mimicked him. My terror soon turned to a more familiar numbness and I waited resolutely for the other shoe to drop.

M.O. opened the door and led me to the middle of the hallway where a few of the men had gathered. The faces were familiar - even vertically. I wanted nothing more than to be lead back to the bed that had held me for those dreadful days.

As many horrors as it had seen, wondering what was going to happen in the hallway made my whole body shake.

The three or four men who stood grouped at the other end of the small corridor talked amongst themselves while Gino and M.O. stood with me. Gino pushed me at my shoulders, propelling me toward the entry into the front room. I leaned against the wall and hung my head, waiting. M.O. slipped past me and out of the corner of my eye, I saw him go to the door let a sliver of light into the room before slipping back behind the bar. As I watched curiously, Gino whispered to me urgently,

"Run like hell and don't look back, Slim."

My heart jumped in my chest as his words sent a volt of electricity straight to it. I tried to confirm in my head what I had just heard. I looked into his face and his eyes twinkled with excitement as he stepped between me and the men at the other end of the hall. He smiled briefly and turned his back to me. M.O. came back into the hallway and pressed his body against mine while maneuvering in the narrow passage leading from the hallway to the living room. Almost inaudibly he too whispered to me as he passed, "Run, Slim!"

I let my hand brush against his chest in a gesture of gratitude and waited until he had passed me. He reached into his coat in slow motion and pulled out his gun. I realized that he was positioning himself to look as if he were ready to shoot me. I glanced quickly at the men at the other end of the hallway. They were still enthralled in animated conversation. I slid my back against the wall into the living room then, in one swift motion, turned and bolted for the door.

"Oh shit! Get that bitch man - she's tearing ass!" One of the men yelled.

With only a split-second head start, I prayed the outside gate would open easily. I heard the clatter of M.O.'s gun hit the floor in the excitement. My heart pounded in my ears as I reached out for the door that had been left only slightly ajar. It swung open and I flew through its mouth and up to the gate as if the house had regurgitated me. Thankfully, the gate opened with only a little tug.

My feet pumped with an energy I had not known was still in me after my long ordeal. My bare toes made contact with the concrete of the sidewalk and I heard angry voices erupt behind me. Icy tentacles of fear grabbed at the back of my neck and propelled me forward. My naked body sliced through the opposing wind as the fear greedily consumed my fingertips. It washed over me until it had frozen my voice and glazed over my eyes. I ran into nothing - thinking nothing - and nothing had ever felt so safe to me.

28

Crack-Head

Damn, they kept the building cold. People filled every corner of the Atlanta airport, barely leaving room for me to stand in the midst of them. I shuddered as their bustling bodies reminded me too much of the crowded sidewalks of New York. I prayed for Charles Middlebrooks to hurry up and get me but then cursed myself for being ungrateful.

It was a wonder that anybody was coming at all.

I wrapped the little blue sweater tightly around my shoulders and wondered where it had come from. The last memory I had of New York was being dropped off at the airport by some faceless person.

It seemed I was coming out of a fog as the voice had asked, "Do you have anyone at home who can send you a plane ticket?" My mind was so numb I could not distinguish if the voice was male or female. They must have found me naked in the streets and put some clothes on me. When the voice asked me about home again, I could only answer in a series of tortured sobs. After taking a deep breath I had then managed to nod my head and tell them that I had a friend named Charles who would help me.

It had taken every ounce of concentration I had to recall his last name and call information for his number. I called collect and like a Christmas miracle in September, he had answered my call and listened to my distress without judgment. His kind fatherly voice told me not to worry – he would send me a ticket. The faceless stranger gave me a Nathan's hot dog and fries. I ate the warm food and tried to keep from shuddering. Finally, I checked the counter and a ticket had been purchased for me. I kept trying to remember something about the kind stranger, but I could not. I silently thanked God for whoever it was – and thanked God that Charles was coming to pick me up in Atlanta.

I scanned the crowd again and saw one head sticking up above the rest. As it moved toward me, I recognized the kind eyes and soft, leathery skin.

"Charles!" I exploded with relief and rushed into his arms, giving him a huge grandpa hug.

"My God girl, you look awful." He scowled down at me.

"Yeah, I know but…"

He held his hand up to interrupt me. "No need to explain. It's just good to see you again."

I smiled thankfully and stayed close behind him as we headed for the exit.

"Well, where are your bags?" he asked looking around for the claims area.

I tilted my head in mock defiance to hide the shame. "I'm wearing my luggage."

His eyes grew a deeper shade of sad and we silently continued across the airport and to his car. Once safely inside, I relaxed my shoulders and tilted my head back onto the old musty plastic seat. I thought of all the smells I had just left behind. The smell of black smog oozing from city busses – the smell of thick reefer smoke in dark basements - and the smell of anonymity in a city where no one cares what your story is. I opened my nostrils and filled my lungs with the slow, musty smells of the South.

"So, where to?" he asked cranking the old bomber up.

Surprised I asked in return, "What happened - did the basement blow up?"

"Denise…" he hesitated as if to search for the right words. "…I rented that place months ago. I can't just put him out." He finished apologetically.

I looked at the dilemma unfolding on his face and felt badly for assuming that he was just holding the basement apartment for me - of course he had rented it. Of course life had gone on for most people. It had only stopped to torture me.

"Charles, it's okay." I smiled and placed my hand on his. "Don't worry, there's a place I can rent in Rose Garden." I said, trying to lie. He still looked skeptical. "You know, getting robbed for your plane ticket and purse is stressful. I just wanted to hang out and unwind a few days." I added a layer to the shoddy lie to sound more convincing.

"Are you sure?" he examined my face for some sign of deception. I gave him the poker-faced smile Rod had taught me so well and nodded my head enthusiastically. Seeming satisfied, he smiled back at me and rustled my hair affectionately.

We pressed on through the old familiar streets and I was glad to see the Georgia red clay again. Unable to help myself, I thought again of the bustling city that had just spit me out and shuddered. Then I let the monsters subside in my head before they took over my poker face. I studied a lovely stand of Magnolia trees instead. They dominated the landscape with their deep, glossy leaves.

Although their branches held no blossoms yet, I recalled how one of the buttery white dollops would scent my entire room as a child. Each day I would leave the third grade and head for the nearest Magnolia tree so I could present my mother with a fresh blossom. I would be oblivious to the scrapes my knees and elbows would sustain during my quest and the tiny yellow bugs who tried to guard their treasures. It was all worth the kind smile Mama gave me when I got home cradling my gift. I looked down at the angry whelps the ropes had left on my wrists and wondered where all the time had gone.

The lovely magnolias gave way to mighty oaks and Charles maneuvered his large blue car through the seemingly narrow passage into the sub-division. The same rusty black sign hung from a meager post welcoming all who dared to enter. I smiled at its' wasted persistence. Nothing was welcoming about this place.

When I first visited here, the houses seemed normal – almost cheery. I once admired the handsome yards and fancied myself a part of one of the surely happy families who lived here. Now, I could see the sharp teeth that waited just beyond the gates and the smiling curtains. It had not been so evident to me before. I swallowed the regret that welled up in my throat. I was back in Rose Garden where not a single rose lived. No one dared set such precious roots in the foul soil that was only useful for burying dreams.

The car slowed and I realized that Charles was waiting for me to give him directions. Thinking quickly I motioned him towards the dirt road the led to The Hole.

"You know what? There are a lot of folks I just can't wait to see. I'm gonna stop off and have a few drinks with the natives so I can get reacquainted."

The skepticism returned to his eyes but I found it easier to brush it off now.

"Now you know, you're the last one to be looking cross-eyed about a harmless glass of whiskey." I giggled and it brought a broad smile to his face. I almost choked. Instead, I pressed my lips closed before I could stumble over my guilt. I scooted over in the seat and wrapped my arms around his huge waist and hugged him tightly.

"Thanks Chief... for everything."

He hugged me back and winked as I swung the door open and walked away from the car. It chugged up the street and headed out of the Garden. He was such a sweet old guy. I pledged I wouldn't bother him again with any of my tragedies.

As the sound of the familiar engine died into the distance I began to hear the dull thud of Miami bass music coming from the rinky-dink club at the end of the dirt path. I set one foot in front of the other slowly heading toward it. I slipped the baby-blue sweater off my shoulders deciding that the white T-shirt would draw fewer stares in the southern heat. I needed my clothes and stuff from Rod's place ... and I wasn't going to wait. Determined, I marched against my fear.

My heart began to pound as loudly as the bass at the thought of seeing him again. Maybe it was too soon. I could hear the crunch of the gravel under my feet so I concentrated on it to drown out the sound of my pounding heart. It didn't make sense for me to be scared to face Rod. Not after all the changes I'd just gone through in New York. The energy I exerted trying to reassure myself made my palms sweat. Still, I needed my things from his apartment so I could go find a job and take care of myself.

As I neared the bottom of the path I laid eyes on the group of guys gathered on the stoop. Did they know where I had been? Was Rod going around bragging about how he turned me out? I turned over the brand new fear in my head as I came within speaking distance of the group.

"Slim! Is that you girl?" I struggled to recognize the face that went with the enthusiastic greeting. Oh yeah, Ray Brown. I didn't really know him – but we had some mutual friends. I was relieved because despite my brave face, I wasn't quite ready to see anybody that I really knew … like Rod.

"What the fuck is up, girl?" He asked with an almost toothless smile.

"Nothing much. How you doing? I asked, uninterested.

Looking closely at my face he went on, "Well, things might just be looking up for a poor-hustling nigga like me." Unaware of just what he meant I shrugged. One of the guys on the stoop passed him the joint they had been smoking and he stood up and crossed the distance between us with a twinkle in his eye.

"No thanks Ray, I don't smoke." He studied me for a second as if to see if I was lying. Apparently satisfied he shrugged. I continued towards the door of the club and I heard him deliver the last word to his audience.

"Humph – she don't smoke... but she will when she see what's in there." I opened the door and let the loud music out just in time to cover their rude laughter.

The club hadn't changed a bit. Still dank and dark – and busy no matter what time of day you came in. I scanned the crowd looking for Rod's tall broad shoulders. My heart raced even faster as I remembered how good it used to feel to wake up in the mornings and roll over in bed and snuggle myself into his comforting chest. I was still stunned at how quickly things could change.

Just as the fear was about to take me over again, I spotted him. His back was turned to me, but there was no mistaking that regal frame. I drew a deep breath and walked towards the tiny booth where he was huddled engrossed in conversation with someone I couldn't see. His animated hands punctuated every point me made. Still Rod. As I got closer to the booth I realized why he was putting on his best show.

She was about my complexion but built a little more thickly. Her hair was pulled away from her face and her make-up was heavier than it should be – but still, she was pretty. The rhythm of my heart changed from fear to anger as his words rose up from the table and crossed the small space between us. "Baby you know I love you. Shit, I wouldn't be paying all this damn money to send you to New York if I didn't care something about you." My heart almost stopped as he reached across the table and took her hand. As if fate had decided to be kind enough to soften the blow, a deep voice called him to the bar area to answer a phone call.

I lowered myself into a nearby booth to avoid him as he strode up the pathway with decided assurance. I shifted my eyes back to her. She waited for him with anticipation. I could see it in her eyes. They darted to and fro trying to get a glimpse of him coming back. She was hungry for the sound of his voice again. I had to admit, he had that affect.

Her delicately manicured hands fiddled with the brandy glass in front of her. She raised it slowly to her lips and took a long sip then settled back into her seat so that she could be ready to hang on his every syllable upon his imminent return. I sat there, torn. Maybe I should run over to her booth and tell her what just happened to me. I looked down at the ill fitting khaki pants I was wearing and tugged at the collar of the thread bare T-shirt that covered my emaciated frame. Maybe I should forget my clothes and Rod and the girl and just run right back out the way I came.

The waitress stopped at my booth interrupting my self-torture. I sent for a double brandy. As she shuffled off to earn her tip I examined the girl again. She un-knotted the soft black scarf from her throat and eased it from around her shoulders. My mouth dropped open when my eyes ventured down below her neckline. It was the pink cashmere dress my cousin Sharon had given me. The expensive one with the careful stitching and meticulous detailing at the hem - the one that draped luxuriously over my hips and clung to my calves seductively. I wanted to scream when I saw that the deep pink of the dress cast the same warm blush over her face as it did mine. It was still exquisite. Dismayed, I rose from my booth and headed to the table after all.

The waitress returned with my brandy and I grabbed it from her tray and continued to Rod's booth. I plopped down into the seat where he had just been sitting and flinched when I felt that it was still warm from him. She looked puzzled. Silently, I brought my drink to my lips and emptied the glass. She looked around the club frantically for Rod but I knew him well enough to know that a business call took precedent over a woman any day of the week. Until he and his phantom caller settled on a place and a price, he would remain in the room behind the bar.

"Can I help you?" she asked with all the attitude she could muster up."

"You can tell me why you're wearing my dress." I asked smugly – all of the earlier compassion gone.

She glared at me taking time to notice my chipped fingernails and ill-fitting clothes. She was about to say something but I cut her off,

"Trust me, I didn't look like this before I took that trip to New York for Rod."

She gasped.

"No need to be shocked, honey. I may not look like much right now but I filled that dress out better than you a few months ago."

"Bitch- "she started but I cut her off again.

"Listen", my voice changed as the compassion for what she was about to go through came back to me, "I don't want Rod back and I can't even stop you from the mistake you are about to make. I just need my clothes from his apartment so I can move on with my life."

She still looked suspicious.

"You know - the white leather jacket and boots, the blue wool pant suit with the black piping, the red chenille bath robe I kept in the back of the closet for cold nights." I described my clothing items until she had been convinced.

215

Her face softened and formed a question at the same time. Just as we are getting the hostility out of the way and about to have a civil conversation, Rod abruptly broke in.

"I see you've met the girl I was telling you about."

He sneered at me, sliding next to her in the booth.

"Baby, I told you I tried to help her out, but she was gone on that dope. Just look at her." He mocked me.

In disbelief, I watched her face harden again and tried to stand up against his lies. I looked at the coldness in his eyes and knew that I could not. I tried to reach the girl one more time,

"Have you met Flava yet?"

Her eyes instantly lowered and she stammered, but answered defiantly, "As a matter of fact I have. He's a good father-in-law."

Rod looked pleased and I knew she was too far gone to save. Ashamed and defeated, I looked down at my own chipped nails and caught the waitress as she passed.

"My drink is on him." I motioned towards Rod snuggled next to his victim in the dimly lit booth.

Near tears, I headed for the door and began walking quickly up the dusty road away from the lion's den.

Before I could get too far, Ray caught up with me and offered a cold beer. I looked at him through glassed-over eyes. I felt a hole so deep inside me that I was afraid to face it. I had never felt so worthless.

Without a word, I accepted the beer from him and took a long swallow.

"Hey, how about that smoke now?" he offered.

I studied his sly, crooked grin and lying eyes. His skin was stark black and flowed without division into his hairline. I hated myself so deeply I did not care. He could not hurt me more than I had already hurt myself.

"Sure." I said without emotion and kept walking

He waved at the guys he left on the stoop at the club and smugly walked up the dirt road beside me.

29

Save Me Johnny

I waited still. I had been sitting on the bed for what seemed like years now, waiting. The heat was unbearable. It was making those little bugs crawl all over my skin. I stared at my forearm hoping to catch one of the little critters in action. I couldn't seem to spot one, but they were there. I could feel them moving. I glanced up into the old dresser mirror. My eyes had sunken into the back of my head in a narcissistic attempt to escape the view.

After almost digging a hole into my arm, I finally heard the creak of the old screen door. There were deep voices and laughter. My savior had arrived! I brushed at my once white T-shirt to try and relieve it of some of the dirt that had somehow collected there. I felt my trousers pockets to make sure that everything was in place. Feet shuffled toward the back of the house and a short, stocky frame appeared in the doorway. To my surprise it was not Ray, but Johnny.

"What's up, Slim?" he bellowed.

"Hey, not much," I said, peering past him to catch a glimpse of Ray.

"Your old man got caught in a road block at the top of Rose Garden," he sneered.

Immediately, my shoulders dropped and my hopes plummeted. I sought refuge on the rickety bed behind me. He took note of my reaction and smiled.

"You expecting something?"

"C'mon Johnny, you know what time it is," I said.

"Yeah, I know" he murmured with a distant look in his eyes.

I caught myself rubbing at my ankles with vigor and then began picking at the almost bald bed spread as an alternative. He studied me with that same distant look then reached into his pocket. My eyes widened in delight as he pulled out a large zip-lock bag full of crack.

"I didn't know you was slanging," I said, hardly able to contain my excitement.

"I ain't really, I just needed some extra cash-flow this week."

"You buying?" he asked after a long pause.

I licked my dry, cracked lips and spoke... too quickly

I-I-I'm busted, man. Y-you know – Ray – had all the money to re-up." I fumbled out the words vaguely wondering where the stuttering had come from.

He laughed and plopped down on the corner of the bed. He began to unravel the zip-lock and fish in the bag of goodies. I watched wide-eyed as he poured sack after sack onto the dresser.

"So... aah... you need anything other than money?" I asked.

"What'cu mean?" he asked.

"You know what I mean. I'm down for my crown," I said a little bolder.

He continued to arrange and re-arrange the sacks on the dresser. The pink and blue mini-sacks looked fat as hell. He watched me watch him for a minute then slid two blue sacks to the corner of the dresser. I smiled and rose from the bed to close the room door. When I turned around, he was reaching for his zipper. I knelt down on the cemented floor in front of him and waited for him to arrange his shorts. I thought about the "happy sacks" on the corner of the dresser and butterflies attacked my stomach.

I slid my hand over my pocket again to make sure that my tools were still in place. He noted this action with a grunt. He finally freed his shriveled penis from its' resting place and pushed it toward my lips. I ran my tongue over my lips again trying to soothe the stinging. I closed my eyes and took his entire shaft in my mouth, ignoring the fowl taste. With each stroke of my mouth, I recited the actions I would take when I was done. Stroke one, pull out the pipe. Stroke two, check the sacks. Stroke three, tighten the Brillo. Stroke four, he hardened. Stroke five - chop off a chunk of dope. He moaned and thrust himself deeper into my throat. Stroke, flick the lighter. Stroke - put the lighter to the pipe. He grabbed the back of my head and pulled it completely over him as he exploded in my mouth.

The warm fluid filled my mouth and slid to the back of my throat almost choking me. I controlled the urge to regurgitate and concentrated. Long stroke, long toke of the pipe. I felt him go limp and fiddled with him for another second. He backed away from me and I rose to see if the sacks were still there. They peered at me with urgency as I slipped my hand in my pocket and retrieved my tools. The glass was warm from my body heat. I reached for the grain alcohol that sat on the dresser and took a swig to wash his taste from my mouth. I hardly noticed that it was 181-proof as I prepared to smoke.

As I broke the seal of the first pack, I expected him to leave. Instead, he straightened his clothing and plopped back down on the bed and peered at me. I hurriedly finished preparation and lit the pipe. The smoke was thick and sweet. Immediately, the freeze hit my tongue and I felt my head zoning. He watched. I free floated in my chair, feeling the sweet high of the pipe. He waited until I had closed my eyes and took another long drag of the swirling white smoke.

Then, he asked in a low voice, "Where does it take you?"

I ignored his question and continued to hold the smoke in my lungs.

"I remember when we were in school together Denise."

Hearing my name, I looked up at him. His eyes were sad and serious.

"Do you remember the time we took pictures in front of the cafeteria?" he asked.

I felt my heart flutter with feeling. I struck the lighter again to ward off his words. But with the next rush I saw the picture in my head. Shit that seemed like so long ago. I was leaning on the cafeteria door with him standing in front of me. I could see the red Gucci sweatshirt I was wearing. Damn, I always had the freshest gear when I was in school. I inhaled deeper. The sounds of Gwen Guthrie flooded my ears. Man, that was the jam a few years ago.

He droned on, "What happened to you, Denise? You were so smart and pretty. Why you doing this shit?" he pleaded.

Tears threatened to fill my eyes. I searched the dresser through misty eyes and broke the seal on the second sack. I placed my pipe on the dresser and my hand trembled.

Suddenly he grabbed my wrist and looked into my eyes.

"Girl, do you know how long I waited to get with you? Do you know that every partner I got used to daydream about you when we was in school? Man, you could have been Freddy's girl; that nigga bout to finish law school and get his own shit. You could have been Brian's girl; he's playing NBA ball now. How the fuck you get to be dope-fiend Ray's girl? That rusty-assed nigga didn't even go to school with us." He shook his head in disgust and continued, "Denise, you don't have to do this... you need to get your life together. Sucking on a nigga's dick ain't what life is about."

His words continued but the shock of the blast had sent me to the radio in my head.

Gwen Guthrie's words echoed in a vain attempt to shut out his words...

No romance without finance
No romance without finance
Boy, nothin' in life is free
That's why I'm askin' you what
can you do for me
I've got responsibilities
So I'm lookin' for a man
whose got money in his hands...

Mangled images rushed into my head. Mack and Rod grinned at me with sharp teeth and I tucked my books tightly into my chest and tried to stay on the path to school. Was I screaming? Could Johnny hear me? Confused, I snatched my hand away from Johnny's and reached for my pipe. My eyes brimmed wide with tears so I stretched them even more to keep the tears from spilling over into my dope. He hung his head in defeat and quietly left the room. As he did, he threw two more sacks on the dresser and without looking at me again he growled,

"At least get paid bitch."

The tears finally rolled down my face and my heart fluttered ominously. I reached greedily for the other two sacks and loaded the pipe with both of them. I wondered what ever happened to that red Gucci sweatshirt as I struck the lighter. I glanced in the mirror at the stranger and brought the flame to my pipe. The smoke was thick and comforting. It swirled around my head in a gentle caress. It filled my lungs and soothed the heartache. I held my breath until the black spots came, blocking my view; clouding my eyes – shielding them.

As I inhaled deeply, one last searing thought fought its' way through the haze:

"Save me Johnny! Come back and save me from this shit..."

Part II

They ask me if I know what true happiness is
If I ever feel regret for all the things I did,
Hell no – I love the life I live
Cause I went from negative to positive
And it's all good...

~ Lil Kim

30

Sister Christian

The dingy cloth seats of the Greyhound bus had seen better days and could no longer hide traces of the passengers who had come before me. I scooted down into the high back seat ignoring the smells. I made sure to wedge the grocery store bag suitcase I carried tightly under my arm lest some desperate stranger decide they needed the clean T-shirts and underwear more than I did. The southern countryside stretched out beyond my view as I leaned my head against the cool glass of the large window to settle in for a nap. I-75 gave way to I-16 as I headed toward Savannah. A tiny spark of hope fluttered around my eyes as the hard living and lull of the road kept me dazing in and out of sleep.

Finally, the bus unceremoniously spat me out at the terminal. Unsure of who to call, I gathered my grocery bag and headed toward the east side. Unable to escape the gut-wrenching feeling of shame I responded to the first cat call that reached me and ducked into a rickety row house to lose myself in the smoke.

Moving in and out of traceable thoughts I smoked and chased clean places to bed down for weeks until Mama got word I was in town. Shocked that she was not still living it up in Miami, I dodged her like a stray bullet until finally she corned me at Mama Lula's house in West Savannah. She heard rumors that I was sick and forced me to go with her to Memorial Hospital emergency room.

I watched her cry and plead with the ER doctor like any "concerned" mother would – all the while taking pot shots at my character and spilling my business loudly enough for all the other patrons to hear. The long soliloquy began as she disclosed my early childhood mishaps then skipped to my pre-teen psychiatric visits before finally making sure the doctor knew that I was a dangerous "sex worker."

After years of being out of her house, she still had the ability to make me fidget with the hem of my shirt and my chin instinctively find its way to my neck. Seeing my humiliation, the merciful white-coated man told her that they could not treat me if I did not want to be treated. Gratefully, I told him I felt fine and left her to fight the lost battle under the "Quiet - Hospital" sign.

Reeling from the attack, I headed back to the east side to see if I could find something to get my head right. One month melded into the next until only the temperature outside gave me some clue as to what time of year it was.

Cars zoomed by at a harrowing pace, tearing up the already worn asphalt of Augusta Avenue. For as long as I had been walking around the streets of West Savannah I never figured out the fascination with flying down the street. Most of the dope boys who did it kept their cars in immaculate condition and their radios blasting. If the point was to be gawked at they had not yet figured out that doing 60 in a 35 would yield only a passing glance at best.

I tucked my non-existent curl behind my ear and licked my hand to try and tame some of my wild roots as I approached New Castle Street. The first thing Sabrina would do was look me up and down and her attitude would be determined by how homely I looked. It was no secret that her sister was turning tricks for crack. She heard it when she went to work and to the mall. She even heard it when she crossed the street to grab a cold soda from Tony's store.

Of course, I would always tell her that I was only smoking weed and defended the days on end that I disappeared by trying to get her to buy into my party-girl lies. Sure, I was at the club and we were having so much fun that we just took the party to my friend's house when the club closed. Shoot, we cooked and drank and played cards for days until we finally spun out.

She would look into my ever sinking eyes and smile as best she could to cover my embarrassment as my lie went crashing to the floor. She and I both knew that I had not seen the inside of a club in a while and that food was the last thing on my mind. Still, my sister was kind and always knew that if she just cooked me the right meal or took me to Fashion Bug and bought me the right little skirt set that I would straighten up and do right. It broke my heart to see her try and hide her shame and concern – but the call of the streets had long been louder than any propensity I had to straighten up.

I tucked the tiny T-shirt into my oversized pants and put one flip-flopped foot in front of the other one until I was standing at the door to Mama Lula's house. I knew that Sabrina didn't have much to give me since she was working hard to try and get her own place.

After she had Justin a few years ago, things got more difficult than she could imagine. Staying at home with Liz and her dad became impossible since (no matter how sweet her stepmother was) any new mother wanted a home of her own. Mama Lula's ever open door was as good a place as any to bundle her baby and look for a fresh start. Ignoring the guilty tug of the burden I was about to put on her I decided to knock anyway. Before I could ease the screen door open and tap she swung the door open wide-eyed.

"Where the hell have you been TooToo?" she exploded. "Me and Mama Lula been looking for you all week!"

I shuffled in stunned silence. Anger did not become her.

"Tell me what is going on Denise." She demanded.

"Every time I see you I try to get you to get a job and take you to church with me so you can stop running the streets like you do. I'll be damned if you don't just rest up and disappear again!"

She half hung her head as if to consider if she was fighting a lost cause before trying again.

"I'm sick of worrying and wondering if you are alive or dead. I'm tired of turning the news off every time they mention a woman's body was found. Every single time Denise – I just know that it's you!"

My sister's body trembled as she paused long enough to catch her breath and stifle a sob. She glanced over at Mrs. Brinson sitting on her porch next door shaking her head. A large red flush covered Sabrina's face and she opened the screen door to let me into the house before she continued,

"I can't do it anymore Denise, I can't. This is too much. Tracy is pregnant again and God only knows how she is even taking care of little Jerry. Patricia said she saw them downtown and the child look like he hadn't had a bath in days."

She finally inspected me head to toe.

"And you – look at you Denise! I can see the bones in your face. Oh Jesus! Why are you just throwing away your life like this?"

Her reddened face was swollen with frustration and sadness. I wanted to reach out and rub the smooth skin of her cheek but knew that it would only make her cry harder. Her tears had long been my Achilles heel and I would rather see her furious than broken and sobbing. I looked away from her unable to face the pain I was causing. She went on but I fiddled with the tuner in my head to find a more forgiving radio station.

The what-nots on Mama Lula's dining room shelves accused me with their beady porcelain eyes and I looked away only to come face to face with the 23rd Psalms sprawled open on the dining room table. This was too much. I could not bear the years of memories that kept trying to surface. I remembered long dinners after church – all three of us sisters munching happily on juicy chicken wings while eye-balling the sticky pound cake enticing us from the middle of the table.

The bustling Saturday afternoon playing hide-and-go-seek in the cool musty crevices of the house; the Kerosene heater smell ... something about the Kerosene heater smell that made me want to vomit.

No. Not the Kerosene heater. It reminded me of when my cousin spent the night and wandered over to my pallet in front of the Kerosene heater late in the night. His penis shoved in my face until it found passage in my throat. The God-awful taste of the thick white pee-pee he left there. And the whipping I got for throwing up too loudly in the bathroom when Mama Lula was trying to get her sleep. Shit! Every place I knew was haunted.

A cold beer - I needed a cold beer. Unable to handle my own, I focused back in on Sabrina's pain. She looked like she was going to have a nervous breakdown. My "Beanie," I wish I could make it all better. I wish I could be a better sister...

Catching the look in my eyes, she paused and calmed herself a bit before trying to reach me again,

"What happened to us Denise?" she moaned sadly. "Once upon a time, we were three little girls."

My sister is broken. I have finally broken the last good thing in my life. All the years I spent trying to protect her from mama's abrasiveness and kids teasing her about being chubby and how lost she felt when we moved and moved and moved... none of it mattered because here I was the one hurting her now. I had to leave this place of haunted memories and broken hearts.

"You got a dollar so I can get me a beer?" I asked oblivious to the insult.

Sabrina's hands snapped to her hips in an uncommon show of aggression. She was enraged.

"Get out!" she screamed at the top her lungs "Get out of this house!"

She unceremoniously ushered me to the front door and closed the screen behind me. I stood there in numbed silence. After only a moment, she cracked the screen door holding a phone book and the telephone.

"You can't come back here TooToo. You need to call somebody and get yourself some help." She slung the phone and phonebook into the green metal gliding chair and slammed the door leaving the phone cord protruding through the space at the bottom.

Out of the corner of my eye I saw Mrs. Brinson rise from her seat in silence and close her front screen. The sound of her voice boomed from her living room like God had forced open a door.

"Heeeeeey Glory, she bellowed. "Thank You Jesus! Touch her Lord Jesus. Command Satan to release her and touch her Lord Jesus! Save TooToo from hell and damnation Jesus!"

Her prayers went on and my soul fluttered against the wages of sin. I waited a moment to see if Jesus would touch me – but He did not. My eyes traced the cord from the finality of the closed door to the chair. There was nothing left to do but see if Jesus was in the phonebook...

31

Cemetery Road

The phone book did not have answers for my life but it did pose a question. Was I crazy? Flipping through the ads I had come across the section on hospitals and institutions and something about the way they were worded reached out to me and made me wonder if I belonged in one of them instead of out here wandering the streets.

Unable to make a decision I did what made me feel better when I didn't have any dope – I walked. I walked straight up Augusta Avenue and under the railroad bridge to Louisville Road. The rhythm of my footsteps soothed me so I kept pace down Styles Avenue headed toward Carver Village. At West Gwinnett the growl of one of the dope boy cars slowed behind me to investigate.

Yes, I needed a ride. No, I don't want a rock – but that pistol is something a girl could use walking the streets of the Village. All three of you? Okay but one at a time and I need some liquor if you want to make it good. Good, I'm glad dope boys travel with pistols, liquor, and condoms.

The brown liquor drowned out the sound of their insults as I earned my wages and before I could cringe I was on my way again. Ogeechee Road unfolded under my feet before ushering me onto Mills B Lane. As I passsed the Norwood house I wondered what the kids from school were up too – college I guessed. My 9th grade literature teacher danced around my thoughts and I got lost imagining all the A's I earned in his class landed me at Harvard. I smiled deeply not realizing the cars that passed did so quickly to avoid the crazy smiling lady wandering the curve of Mils B. Lane in flip-flops. Before I knew where my steps were ordering me, ACL Boulevard was before me and I knew what I had to do.

I rounded the curve and covered the last blocks with purpose. The cemetery welcomed me with silent disregard as I stepped over grave after grave looking for the one that was calling me.

Left, straight, round the bend in the dirt path. Slave grave. Straight, right, loop back around. Arthur Cummings left his loving wife to grieve him. Loop, long sip of liquor, straight, sit and get my bearings. Two small children dead within a month of each other. The weight of the pistol was pulling my big dusty pants down around my bony waste. A large gulp of liquor will fix them right up. Straight, slow, slow, there!

I crawled onto the cool concrete slab curling myself into a ball in my father's lap. Charles Edward Olav! Daddy, they spelled your name wrong. Daddy. Daddy. Do you know that I have never used the word Daddy in my life? Did you know that I messed up my life so bad that I can't fix it? Daddy, can you hear me?

I pulled the pistol from the overburdened pocket of my trousers and took all but one of the bullets out. Now, I'm going to ask you some questions and you better answer me the truth! Long gulp of liquor.

Did you know that I was waiting on you to come get me? Spin-Click. Why didn't you come for me? Spin-Click. Do you love me Daddy? Spin-Click. Do you love me daddy!? Spin-Click.

My questions echoed beyond the marble memories and into the gnarled oak trees but no answer came back through the dusk.

Afraid and defeated, I dropped the pistol and took a long swig from the almost empty bottle. I gathered the loose bullets, shoving them into my pocket with the cowardly pistol and lay flat against the concrete. Tears finally streamed down my face to form puddles in the concrete as I sobbed a long, deep, tired time. Daddy was not listening.

"Pleeeeeease hear me!" I screamed into the sandy brown dirt I had disturbed.

"Please – please- pleeeeease!" The tortured moans kept rising from me like vomit.

My body shook with frustration sending the liquor bottle crashing against the brushed metal marker that spelled his name wrong. Slightly sobered, I stared through tears at the shards of glass and liquid littering his resting place. Ashamed and tired I rose from my father's grave and collected the pieces of bottle to toss into the woods. I brushed the disturbed dirt off of his slab and stepped away to try and imagine his face. I could not.

"I'm sorry, Daddy" I offered into nothing. "I'm sorry that your little girl is just a pathetic psychopathic crack-ho." I slurred.

There were no answers on cemetery road so I dragged myself out of the cemetery and back onto ACL Boulevard, concentrating on the steady melodic sound of my dusty flip-flops.

In a stupor, I made my way through the charming southern parks and historical landmarks until I found myself at the feet of the Waving Lady at the river front. Though she had greeted me to hear my woes at the end of many benders, Savannah police patrol made sure she would not listen to me tonight.

Daunted, I walked through the night, resting only long enough for the throbbing in my toes to stop before setting off again. I looped through the bowels of the city under the cover of night until the sun began to break through the blue-black shroud over the sky.

Cars began their daily duty filling the streets around me with sound again. Tired and cold from the night air I slowed my pace to look for a place to sit and rest a while. As I crossed Abercorn Street I looked up into the building facing my path. The sign announced Tidelands Mental Health Center. I wondered if Jesus had taken control of my flip-flops and led to me to the very yellow pages ad I'd found back on Mama Lula's porch.

Determined not to step over the burning bush I approached the gutter at the curve and fished my pistol from its' loose pocket. Kaplunk! It found the sewer water at the bottom. I entered the building with only a few curious stares and followed the directory board to the third floor. As the elevator emptied me into the silent hallway I paused not sure of where to go next.

"May I help you?" a voice called out from some unknown source.

I scanned the floor in each direction unsure if someone had spoken or not.

"Ma'am, may I help you?" the voice called out again.

Taken aback, I scanned the hall one more time and finally saw the plate glass window the voice was being projected from. I approached the window to see a smiling, brown-skinned older woman sitting at a desk waiting for me to respond.

Relieved that the building was not speaking to me I spoke back to the kind face.

"Yes, I think I must be crazy, I announced decidedly.

Her face did not flinch and I knew I was somewhere I was supposed to be.

"Well, what makes you think that?" she asked genuinely.

"Have you ever been diagnosed with mental illness" she probed further in reposnse to my silent stare.

Shocked that she was still speaking to me I went on.

"I can't stop walking and I don't know where I am going." I offered as my only clear explanation.

"Well honey, you have come to the right place," she smiled. "I'll buzz you back."

I scanned the walls again and immediately saw the large grey door to the left of the window. Wondering only vaguely why I had not seen it before I grabbed the handle and just like that walked into the Hospitals and Institutions section of the yellow pages.

32

Jawbreaker

Heading up the main street of the dirty inner city projects, I was all too aware that the high had worn off long before daylight had shown its' ugly face. I stepped over empty beer bottles, looking closely at the ground. I wasn't looking for broken glass to avoid cutting my feet. Instead, I had high hopes of finding a fat sack of dope that someone might have dropped. I looked so intently at the ground that I stumbled over the curb as it came into my limited view too late. I looked around to see if anyone had noticed. No one had. I straightened my shoulders and held my head up when I realized I was already approaching Bankhead Highway.

The street was busy with bustling cars and school buses. People were on their way to work and school. When the cars with frosty windows whizzed past me, I tried to look dignified. I looked down at myself and swallowed the lump in my throat. My white pants were filthy with the dirt of getting high for days. My knees revealed grass stains from doing God-knows what for a hit last night. My T-shirt was torn and stank of cheap wine and hard liquor. I directed my attention to my shoes as I shuffled down the street. They too told a story of long dark alleyways and concrete gardens.

'How the hell did my life come to this?' I wondered seriously. I spent too much time trying not to think but finally, I didn't have a choice anymore. Tidelands had turned out to be a drug treatment facility so I stayed. Though it was foggy I completed the 7-day detox program and went to live in at

Hacienda House on 34th Street until I could find a place of my own. The people there were sweet and as long as I sat in the AA meetings and looked like I was listening, no one gave me any grief.

For a time, things seemed like they were finally looking up for me. In a few short months, I had secured my own poetry column in The Savannah Herald newspaper and got a job as radio DJ by night and an insurance debit agent during the day. I did not take long before I was one of the top debit agents at Atlanta Life and pegged to interview Big Daddy Kane for WSOK! I felt good.

As I shuffled across the trash-ridden parking lot I tried to understand what went wrong. Month after month, I did not drink or smoke any dope. I worked, I went to meetings and I shopped.

That's how I met Terry – at the Oglethorpe Mall.

He was a tall, handsome soldier on leave from the Navy. Something kind and gentle about him led me to tell him the truth about living in a halfway house and recovering from drugs. He thought it was "great" and after only a few dates could not wait to introduce me to his family. When my mother and Sabrina got wind of who his family was, it seemed our romance was on the fast track. Somewhat of a local tycoon, his family name meant respectable security and seeing how Terry felt about me, I was soon the victim of opinion.

I married Terry for two reasons; first, because no one had ever asked me before and second, because it seemed to make my family happy. Everyone applauded my Shug Avery impression as I sported my gleaming gold and diamond ring and smiled, "I's married now." It's no wonder that when he whisked his new bride off to Adak Alaska to be a new military wife, I lost my bearings and slowly slipped off the wagon. We were not there two months before I found myself overwhelmed by dark memories tryign to fight their way to the surface and began keeping company with the rowdy marines at the bar while nursing my own bottle of Tanqueray.

It all went to hell after that. I flew back to Savannah without my new husband and only had the courage to tell him I didn't want to be married anymore after I settled into the rooming house that would become headquarters for my crack runs. There was no pocket of anonymity to get lost in and the small fishbowl community in Savannah was not kind. Everyone knew whose daughter I was, whose wife I was and what I was doing cruising the projects at 3'o'clock in the morning. So, like a bulimic teenager, Savannah had once again digested me only to regurgitate me back toward Atlanta in my ongoing search to find ...something.

Not long after hitting the city limits Sgt. House turned me away but promised he would keep my things until I got my shit together. Still hell-bent on trying to show him I could be a good daughter, I wandered off the street and ended up in another detox place. One of the men behind the glass told me I was in the right place so I stayed awhile to see. It was foggy at best. I didn't understand how people talking in a circle would stop crack from dragging me back into the trap, so I absconded; eventually ending up back into the arms of Ray Brown.

I fidgeted against the awareness of the mistakes I kept making and longed for a way not to feel it. There was no dope within miles; nothing to pacify my aches. The Red Dog Narcotics Unit came through just before sunrise and scared everybody away. There wasn't even one poor-hustling dealer on the street I could beg a hit from. The same thing had happed in Rose Garden a few months ago. The police department was cleaning up the city, ridding it of trash like me. I wasn't lucky enough to get caught and locked up so when the dust cleared, I headed on down the road. For all the raiding the police did, they never did the one thing I hoped they could – stop me from hurting myself.

I continued shuffling across partially empty lots, wondering how much time they were going to give Ray – and if his mother could get him out this time. I didn't intend on ending up with him. Truth be told, I never loved him, but he grew on me. I hoped he wouldn't do hard time, but I could never tell when he was lying so I couldn't be sure if he had weight on him or not. I wasn't mad at him because he showed me how to smoke crack – I would have found it without him. I was just mad because he was stingy.

I hustled right along with him; checking traps and passing bags through the Cutlass window so Ray wouldn't have to handle them. I needed every high I could suck into my lungs. He must have known that because I couldn't hide the hopelessness that settled over me when I couldn't get my hands on something to put my mind at ease.

I sighed deeply, wondering if his brother took any cigarettes to the jail and accepting that I might never see Ray again. Still, while it lasted, I was glad to have someone to walk through all those dark alleys and abandoned buildings with. I was glad to have someone to fight about dope with – so maybe I wouldn't fight with myself so much.

I neared the McDonald's and the smell of food disturbed my tortured thoughts. It had been days since I had eaten. My bony frame made the announcement more clearly than I would have liked. The hunger that gripped my stomach was too much to ignore. I went inside the restaurant and was ashamed as women in business suits hurriedly wielded their trays of food away from me to the safety of tables by the window. I hung my head as I approached the counter. I reached into my pocket hoping to find at least a dollar, but I knew the liquor house had gladly taken my last 50 cents.

"May I help you?' the girl asked reluctantly.

I looked past her at the bin of food and silently moved away from the counter. Repulsed stares greeted me from the line of people nearby. My hand instinctively reached for my head of nappy hair and tried to smooth it down. Before I could stop them, the tears had fought their way to the surface of my eyes.

"Its' a goddamn shame" I heard someone proclaim disgustedly.

I headed for the door like a mangy dog. McDonald's bags littered the parking lot as I headed back to the street. I wiped the tears away and bumped along the highway headed for nowhere. My thoughts shifted back to the thoughts that tortured me. I was too smart to be out here like this. I guess it was a 'goddamned shame' after all.

I neared the K-Mart and followed my thoughts inside. I milled through the racks of clothes unnoticed by the K-mart girls in little red smocks. I had an idea. I would clean myself up and go get a job! That had to make things better. I could work and then get someplace to stay and then everything would be okay again. It would not take me long to save the money for a deposit. Hell, in a couple of months I could have a piece of car and everything! Then I wouldn't have to wander the streets hoping Ray got out of jail soon – or dodge the sneers of Rod when I showed up at The Hole begging for drinks.

I saw a pair of slacks on the rack in the girls department that looked like they were my current size; tiny with long legs. I swiped them from the hanger and rolled them tightly around my waistline, using the elastic to secure them. I turned to face a rack full of blouses and quickly secured the nearest one. I stepped over to a rack of summer jackets and slipped one right over my filthy clothes. Then, without guilt, I went to the beauty supply area and stocked up on things I would need to get a job. I stole a toothbrush, but decided that the toothpaste would take up too much precious space in my pockets. I would brush with soap instead. I swiped some lotion and a comb to see if I could do something with my nested naps. Suddenly aware that I wasn't wearing any, I went to the lingerie department and found a pair of panties and a bra.

Satisfied with my stash, I exited the store just as I had come, unnoticed. My heart was light with the prospect of getting cleaned up. I headed for a nearby gas station and dashed into the ladies room. I was glad that it was outside of the store because that way no one would rush me out. I locked the door behind me and happily emptied my goodies into a clean spot on the floor. I peeled my tired clothes off and the smell was sickening - I guess I was too high to smell it before. I stuffed the repulsive garments in the trash to put them out of their misery. I grabbed the bar of soap and a handful of the rough brown paper towels and went to work.

I glanced in the mirror at my naked frame. I was so tall that the lack of meat on my bones almost looked natural. But naked, my ribs stared back at me and the illusion of niceties vanished. My eyes sank far to the back of my head as if to escape their view of the world. My breasts had also shrunk from a lack of food. I thought of the starving children on television and quickly washed and hid my body under the new clothing. I brushed my teeth with the bitter soap until they shone brightly and styled my hair as best as I could. I examined the mirror closely as I applied the cheap make-up to my face. I could see a faint glimpse of who I used to be and longed for more. I was not white clad and beautiful like I was in a picture I had taken in one of Savannah's parks years ago, but it would do. Shit, if nothing else, I was clean.

I left the bathroom and headed for the bus stop. With no money to catch the bus, I was sure someone waiting there would buy the new lipstick tubes and earrings I swiped from the K-Mart. I felt good as the sun warmed the nice new shirt I was wearing. I was excited at the thought of getting a job at the mall and saving my money. I wouldn't need to smoke that shit anymore. What was I thinking, walking around the streets all that time? I could have tried to get a job months ago.

I sat at the bus stop with my new summer jacket swung carelessly over my shoulder and noted the schedule. The Ashby Street bus to The West End Mall would be along this route. I took a seat on the wooden bench and day dreamed as cars drove by. I thought of the simple pleasures that going to work every day would hold. I thought of my own little place tucked somewhere in Atlanta.

All I had to do was not take my money to the dope man. I knew if I tried hard enough, I could manage that. A car pulled up to the curb in front of me and interrupted my thoughts. I looked in to see a wild-eyed man motioning for me to come over, so I turned my head the other way ignoring him. He honked his horn and rolled down his window.

"Hey Slim, he yelled. "You need a ride, baby?" he yelled.

"No thanks," I said. "I'm waiting for the bus."

"Aaah come on girl... why you trying to be so hard?" he whined, irritated.

His insistence alerted me, so I rose from the bench. Instincts said stay away from this guy. I began walking away from the bus stop... and away from the car.

"Hey! Come back here bitch!" he yelled. I quickened my step as he opened his car door and began walking toward me with lightning speed.

"What's your problem?" I defended. "I said that I didn't need a ride," I yelled while moving quickly away from his approach. Before I realized the extent of the danger I was in, he had gotten close enough to reach out and grab my arm.

"Hey!!" I yelled while wresting my arm away from him.

"God Dam Slim... I'm gon' give you a ride baby." he said wildly.

"No!" I yelled. "Let me go you creep! Let me go." I said.

I looked around desperately. It was broad daylight. Surely someone was watching this nut. People walked along the sidewalk and only a couple of curious glances were shot my way. I began to panic as I realized that no one was going to help me. I pulled against him as he tried to maneuver me to his car but I was so weak from not eating that he was able to pull me along easily. I screamed and kicked at him.

"Bitch, you fucking kicked me," he roared. "Get in the motha' fuckin' car... umma take yo' ass for a ride alright," he threatened.

"Somebody help me!" I yelled, still struggling. "You can't do this... you don't want to do this." I struggled desperately.

I lost my footing and he was dragging me down the sidewalk toward his car. The concrete was scraping through the thin slacks I was wearing and my legs stung. Just a few more feet and I felt sure no one would ever see me again.

"NOOO!!!" I yelled again.

"Ugh Ughm, I'm gonna give you something good girl," he said feverishly. I looked into the blackness of his eyes and knew his soul was long gone. There was murder in his eyes and I was his fixation.

"No! Stop! Wait... I've got AIDS," I said desperately. "I've got AIDS!" I yelled at the top of my lungs. He loosened his grip on my forearm and I saw the hesitation in his face. I yelled up at him again,

"I've got AIDS and you're gonna get it." I could see the frustration in his face.

He snatched at me again roughly, then, as if it just hit him, he let my hand go and wiped it against his thigh. I was about to scramble to my feet and run when he looked down at me and hissed "You nasty bitch!"

The stream of sunlight behind his head blinded his face to me. As his foot swung back I knew he was going to strike me. I could not roll out of the way fast enough and his foot made contact with my jaw. The loud crunching sound it made as it broke made me sick to my stomach. My head reeled backwards to the ground and I caught a glimpse of his heel as he hurried to his car.

The sound of tires screeching told me he had left. I rolled over on my side and tried to get up. It took all of my strength to pull myself to my knees. My face was aching like it had never felt before. The pain made flashes of light dance in my eyes. I looked around, dazed. No one was there.

It was broad daylight, but as if some secret coded message had been delivered, everyone had deserted the sidewalk. I crawled a bit until I could finally climb to my feet. I thought I heard traffic, but I wasn't sure. I stumbled unsteadily toward the curb. I passed the discarded summer jacket on the bus stop bench and heard the honk of horns as I teetered into the street. I tried to wave cars down to stop, but they only honked and angrily swerved around me. Up the middle of the street I stumbled.

Isn't Charles Disco down this street? I vaguely remembered dancing under Charles' watchful eye until I had my fill and he made sure I made it back to my stepfather's house safely. Maybe Charles was there. I dragged my rubbery feet a half step at a time.

My head swung in circles and my neck was wet. I lifted my hand to wipe away the sweat from my neck and gasped in horror as I drew my hand away to find it red. Blood had soaked my shirt and as I looked down, was flowing freely onto the street. I stumbled into a yard on the other side of the street. I know I saw that curtain move. I looked closely to see an old woman draw the curtains closed with a resounding gesture of "No".

"Please ma'am... can you help me?" I managed to choke out.

"I... I need (cough) help." I moaned. "I need help!"

The curtain was closed. I stumbled away from her yard and back out into the street. I felt the blood running down the loose waist of my pants. I thought I saw the blue of a phone booth. I made my way to it but it seemed to swim farther away. The honking horns led me as my vision began to fade. Did André just kick me? Yep, that damned André had kicked me again. Well his ass was in trouble this time. When I make it to the principal's office, Andre is going to be in a world of trouble.

Those blue doors; that's where the office is. I fell to my knees. There was a white rope. A broken white rope. Someone was trying to throw me a rope. I grabbed at it to keep from falling, but it felt like concrete. I heard sirens in the distance as I choked on the blood in my mouth. I coughed to clear my lungs, but only heard gurgling. The pavement was cool as I lay my face against it. I would rest for a minute.

Then I would get up and try again.

33

The Dungeon

The ambulance scurried along the dirty streets of downtown Atlanta in a mad dash to deliver me to the emergency room. We arrived at the loading docks in a flurry of activity. Two uniformed men rolled me from the back of the ambulance and two other men moved me from their temporary cot to a gurney. Unable to maintain consciousness for very long, I peered up occasionally from where they parked me in the bustling hallway.

After what seemed like hours, the nurses finally came to see about me. They wanted to know who I was and what happened, but I had trouble telling them. My whole head throbbed and my lips were too thick to wrap around my words. One nurse poked around my head while the other impatiently scribbled my feeble half-answers on her clipboard. Appearing satisfied, they left on quiet heels.

I lay motionless in the hallway waiting for them to come back and help me. A burning sensation slowly crept through my groin and I foggily understood that I had to pee. With all the energy I could muster, I lifted myself from the gurney. My head seemed far heavier than it should be as I coaxed it from the flat pillow. Brown stains of blood marked the outline of my face and neck as I peeled myself from the sheets and painfully made my way up the grey hallway.

"Where ya going, hon?" a white clad nurse asked kindly.

"I gotta pee," I was barely able to mutter.

She seemed to understand.

"C'mon." She offered me her arm and I leaned against her gratefully as she ushered me into a wheelchair. I tried to thank her, but my lips still seemed very thick. We rolled through a narrow passageway with beds lining the walls. A few moans rose over the noisy bustling as we neared the bathroom sign. The wheelchair did not slow and I urgently motioned to the nurse to stop.

"No, we have to go to X-ray first," the nurse said apologetically.

I resigned myself to the woman's control and squeezed my thighs tightly. As we sped up the hall thoughts of the morning began to crash through; the bus stop, the strange car. We neared the X-ray room and I winced at the painful memory of a shoe connecting with my face.

We entered the room and I noticed the look the woman behind the desk gave me. As I watched the thinly disguised horror on her face I knew that there was something terribly wrong with me. I raised my hand to my face and was shocked when I came in contact with skin much sooner that I should have. It seemed to be larger. Seeing my reaction to the look on her face, the woman thinly disguised it and gently removed my hands from my face to stand me up.

It seemed like such a long time as she positioned me. She pressed my head against the cold white surface of the X-ray wall and it felt nice. My head bobbed to and fro as she tried to steady me.

Finally, it was over and we headed back to the long hallway. Safely back onto the thin white sheets I went with a plop. The nurse looked at me as if it were painful to do so. She hesitantly offered me some juice. I mumbled for the bathroom again but she seemed not to hear me. Without another word, she was off.

To my surprise a doctor finally came and stood over me silently with his eyes glued to a clipboard. He was a harried looking middle-aged white man with deep furrows in his forehead. His face was flushed and he fidgeted with his pen and papers for a long moment.

"You have multiple fractures of the lower mandible. The x-rays were not as clear as we would have liked, but that is due to the massive swelling," he finally spoke dryly. He did not look into my eyes as he spoke, so I concentrated on his pen. With its ebony resin barrel and cigar shape, it was unmistakably a Mont Blanc. They were nice, but the fussy gold bands aggravated my fingers. Personally, I liked the feel of a nice solid Waterman in my grip; reliable, classic simplicity with no bulky band to pinch my creativity.

I took the news as it was given to me; without emotion. I thought that someone should have asked me to make a police report by now, but it began to dawn on me: crack heads did not make police reports; they were police reports. And despite my efforts to find work, I was still just a drug addict. No job at the mall; no chance to save a few paychecks, no little rooming house to start over from; just a dirty, avoidable girl with 'multiple fractures of the lower mandible'. The doctor left as quietly as he had come and I eased myself heavily from bed in search of the bathroom I had seen earlier.

With much effort, my feet made their way down the hallway again. People stared at me from their beds as I plundered past them. I lowered my head and it seemed so heavy I thought I would fall forward. I took a brief moment to steady myself against a sleeping woman's cot. A few more shuffles rewarded me with the bathroom door. I pushed at it until it reluctantly gave way. My bladder was on fire and I gratefully squatted to relieve myself.

I looked at my bruised knees and calves as I sat there. My clothes had been stuffed in a plastic bag labeled "patient's belongings" and stuck at the foot of my rolling bed. I did not think I wanted them anymore, but this gown would not be enough when I got out of the hospital. I had never stayed in a hospital before, but there was a first time for everything. Maybe after they fixed my jaw, someone could direct me to a work program. Not that they cared, but to get rid of me, someone might actually end up helping. I concentrated on my newfound enthusiasm, trying desperately to nurture it.

I finished my business and lifted myself from the stool. I took the two short steps to the sink and turned on the water. As my hand reached for the soap, my eyes fixed themselves on the little plastic mirror mounted above the sink. Suddenly, breaking glass grinded in my head as my eyes made contact with a creature unknown to me. It must have been me because as my shock settled in place, the eyes in the mirror got larger as well.

"My head! Oh my God, my head is swollen to a pulp!" my brained seared

I had never seen such a grotesque sight. My face was not puffy, it was engorged! Flesh seemed to have multiplied, drowning out any bone structure beneath. Even my forehead was grossly disfigured. Like a failed attempt to put on lipstick, my lips were ragged and stained with dried blood. I thought of the pumpkin head monster in my childhood book and felt my knees begin to shake. My head wobbled back and forth ridiculously. I reached out to touch my face and screamed for mercy.

"Oooooh God!!!... Aaaagh God!" I slurred. "Wha' happened to me... Aaaarrrgh God!"

My voice was gurgling in my throat and the pain was like a bucket of cold water; shockingly real.

The bathroom door flew open and two men in light blue scrubs were reaching for me. I resisted only slightly, trying to burrow myself in the corner of the sink.

I reached for the mirror and screamed at it, "You lie! You lie!!"

My head exploded again and again, but I could not stop the sobs that racked my body. I was a monster; a complete monster. People would run from a face such as this. If it were not my own, I would run, too.

"Please Miss," one of the men said impatiently. "You are going to have to calm down."

He held my upper arm as if he wished he could restrain me without touching me. His white rubber gloves pinched the thin flesh of my arm and forced me to sit in the wheelchair they had brought with them. I plopped down without further objection and glanced up at the men. They looked disgusted, but more relaxed now. I was no longer a threat. They knew I would not be violent. I read relief in their faces as I sat in the chair and sobbed.

One of the men remained near me while the other one went to fetch a nurse. "They would bring me something for my pain," he came back to say. Something for my pain. I knew it was not for my pain; it could not relieve the pain I felt now. It was for their peace of mind. They would not have me screaming in their bathrooms. I coaxed the pills down with cool water and sobbed dejectedly, waiting for them to work.

"She can easily do runway, Mrs. Wright," the lady had gloated. "She has a rare quality that we don't often see here at the Barbizon School of Modeling. Oh, we get thousands of girls with notions of Paris and magazine covers, but Mrs. Wright, this one is a shoe-in. You bring her to me with papers in order. No worries about our fees – we will do whatever we have to. If you do that, I promise you, within 3 years she will send you to the Caribbean on your own yacht." The woman completed her plea with confidence.

She had laughed easily with my mother and looked at me again. She smiled broadly and lightly punched my chin. "Look dear, I don't sell hopes. I sell models. And you - I could sell you with a Polaroid portfolio…"

I woke from the light sleep and swallowed a tear of regret. What a bitter memory to have crept in to torture me. I looked down at myself and studied the little blue flowers in the hospital gown. They were upside down. The stems all pointed at me like little fingers. They seemed to want to know why the flowers were hung that way. They shook their angry little stems at me and accused me of disgracing those beautiful little blue petals.

I was roused from my lunacy by a woman touching my shoulder and smiling down at me. "Ms. Stokes?" she queried with a clipboard in hand.

I was sure she knew who I was already, but I mumbled "Yes?" anyway.

"My name is Linda; I'm a social worker here at Grady. If you don't mind, I'd like to see if we can't help you to decide how you would like to proceed at this point." She paused and glanced at me over her papers. "I hear that you have had quite a rough day."

Her words sounded a little sincere so I looked her in the eyes. She had a distant sort of gaze, but they did not dart quickly away from my eyes like the others. Cautiously, I responded to her. "What do you mean?" I asked my curiosity peaked.

"Well," she suggested, "why don't we first go to my office where we might be a little more comfortable?"

"Won't the doctors be coming for me soon?" I asked, perplexed. "Will they know where I've gone?"

"I don't follow you, Miss Stokes," she said sincerely.

"Well, my jaw is broken and I guess I'll have to have surgery or something," I mumbled through rubbery lips.

"I was not informed of any pending medical procedures," she said calmly, "but I was asked to offer my services to you before you were discharged."

"Discharged?!" I asked incredulously. "How can I be discharged? My jaw is broken and I was almost raped. Where are the police?" I demanded to know. "Don't they want my report – or can a strange guy just attack a girl without consequence these days?"

"Well, I am not a doctor and I have no control over the law, but I can try to help you with clothing and transportation. Also, if you haven't got a place to stay, we can look for some shelters in the area," she said seeming flustered.

She went on and on about the wonderful options she could offer to me, but my mind was beginning to shut down from confusion. For the moment, I dismissed the idea of the police. It was too much to deal with. But how could they release me without fixing my jaw? Were they mad? I stopped her in the middle of some self-important sentence she was singing and asked her to get the doctor that I had seen earlier.

"No, I don't know his name," I told her, "but some white coat pissed on me earlier and he sent you to tell me that it's rain."

She looked offended at my accusation – or perhaps just my language – and walked away.

To my surprise, she came back a few minutes later with a nurse. The discharge papers had been completed and were just waiting for my signature. I tried to barter with her, but I had no chips; no insurance, no address, no form of payment. Defeated, I signed the papers and like a stray dog followed Social Worker Suzy through cold corridors.

Each step I took was a testament to the wonders of narcotic pain killers. With its gray floors and halls that seemed to lead nowhere, it was like walking through a dungeon; a goddamned dungeon with demons chasing me. Even with all of the scurrying people around me I could still hear the shuffle of my own feet in hallowed halls.

We reached her chamber and she callously sized me up and handed me some shoes and clothes from a Goodwill box. She smiled with self gratification as I emerged from her bathroom dressed in charity. She handed me a brown bag and praised the nurses that were kind enough to take my pain medicine prescription to the pharmacy while I was being led to the gallows. They were thoughtful enough to give me liquid codeine so I could ingest it easily.

She gave a lovely parting speech as she prepared to finish her paperwork. She handed me some cute pamphlets, a number four bus schedule and a shiny bus token to use to get to the shelter. Fool's gold. Without a word, I took my little chest of treasures and headed for the dungeon doors. I wanted someone to fix my jaw but took my token to find the shelter. I was tired and sleep would do me good. Maybe tomorrow it would not be so hard to hold up the weight of my head and I could find a scarf to disguise the bruises.

Without regret, the doors swung open silently and released me back to the streets. I was sure they had already bid farewell to thousands before me and were now too tired to curtsy. In slow motion, I crossed the busy street and traffic seemed to halt as I passed. People cleared the sidewalk and I claimed it as my own. They did not want to walk with monsters. A little boy in a Falcon's jersey looked up at me as his mother fussed with her shopping bags.

"Mama! Mama! Whus wrong wit dat lady? Why she so ugly?" he whined disturbed.

His mother snatched at his shoulder and spit back at him, "Derek you know better than to..."

Her words trailed off as she shifted her eyes from her bags and settled them on my face. Her mouth formed a perfect "O" and suddenly she looked like the screaming Munch painting. I passed the speechless pair and found my place at the bus stop. I did not fear this bus stop. Unlike this morning, I knew strange cars would not insist that I ride with them. This bus stop was safe. I reached my hand into the pocket of my new hand-me-down pants and fingered the bus token mindlessly and leaned my heavy head against the cool brick wall and waited for the number four.

34

Drive-By

The bus driver roused me from my anguished nap and pointed to a large red-brick building on the corner.

"You wanted the women's shelter on Moreland Avenue right?"

I tried to smile at her patient words but I wasn't sure if my lips had been able to perform the daring feat or not.

"Thank you so much." I slurred to the best of my ability then slowly lowered myself down each of the three tricky bus steps and crossed the great divide to the corner.

Visible from the street, the large grey double doors of the shelter harbored a fading sign that welcomed me to Moreland High School. The front yard was mostly sparse grass and dirt, but the side was filled with newly constructed rows of swings and jungle gym equipment.

Children squealed in delight as they dashed through the maze of the shiny structures. Their excitement permeated the air, settling into everything within earshot. I was no exception.

Maybe the women's shelter would let me stay long enough to heal and go find a job.

I navigated the hallways plastered with posters about cancer, childcare, domestic violence, WIC, drugs, HIV and pampers; every burden that society squarely planted on the shoulders of women. Finally I came upon the makeshift office in the transformed teacher's lounge.

It did not take long for me to understand the Moreland Women's Shelter had no room at the inn, at least for me. My medical circumstance was too great and the priority was to women with children.

I gladly accepted a meal of mashed potatoes and milk, a warm shower and a good night's rest.

The next morning came much too soon and I reluctantly gathered my meager bounty of toiletries, t-shirts and tampons the closet clerk was so kind to give me the night before. I wanted to be gone before too many of the other women and children woke up. It would be painful to hear another child shriek in horror at the sight of my face.

An older lady with leathery skin and layers of ragged clothes peered at me from her cot full of bags. Though I tried to avoid her glare she would not disconnect her matronly eyes from me. I elevated my pace and scurried to quietly fold the brown sack with my goodies in it and clear my space.

"You gotta leave too huh?" She grunted.

"Yes ma'am." I confided cautiously.

"Where your people at, child?" she queried motherly.

My wobbly head drooped under the weight of the question. I looked at the white gray of her hairline peeking from beneath the Asante cloth scarf and knew I had to answer her out of respect.

"I had to leave them." I mumbled.

"Well go find 'em baby." She finally broke her glare and went fishing in a cracked patent leather purse she held closely to her. Her gnarled hands offered a shiny token like the one that got me to the shelter and I could not hold back the urge to hug her for her kindness.

Her half brown, half toothless grin sent me on my way with as close to a smile as I could muster.

I leaned my head against the back of the plastic Marta bus seat and let it chug me back through the city toward Bankhead Highway in search of the only place I might be able to find a place to sleep it off; Bowen Homes.

The project community accepted me without much ado. I suppose that in the naturally ambivalent atmosphere of the ghetto it was common to see a girl beat up, especially one who smoked dope. A few guys who I smoked with slowed their hustle long enough to hang around and chat with me. As close to chivalry as they could come, they offered me some of whatever they had to try and ease my obvious physical discomfort. The liquor was most welcome since it mellowed nicely with the liquid codeine I was given from the Grady pharmacy. After a few swigs of my self-prescribed concoction I was maneuvering my head as if it was weightless.

Thankful that Print-Up had shared two of his dope sacks with me I took them straight to Kathy's apartment to pay for the use of her couch for as long she would let me. For days I lay on her thread bare sofa listening to the sounds of the neighborhood regulars come and go. I was in excruciating pain and even Kathy's attempts to let me drag her straight shooter did not help ease the mad throbbing and stinging assaulting my head and neck. Seeing that I could neither keep the straight shooter between my lips nor inhale deeply enough not to waste the smoke we both gave up on the idea and she just let me sleep.

I could not tell if it was dawn or dusk but the beautiful blood orange light peering through the raggedy blinds mesmerized me. I shifted my weight against the pillows and was surprised when my movement was not accompanied by the now familiar lightning shot of pain. I gently raised myself to a sitting position and reached for the swollen bags under my chin I had taken to fiddling with. I was surprised when my fingers took longer than they should have to connect with the mass. Curious, I gingerly eased up the stairs and peered into Kathy's bathroom mirror. I closely examined the purple and green bruises that littered my face and neck marveled at how much the puffy mass had shrunk. The swelling was almost gone!

"Dang chick," Kathy joked on her way downstairs "you sho' is feeling yourself."

Unable to tear myself away just yet I gaped at the miracle for a long moment before I joined my gracious caretaker in the kitchen downstairs.

"Thank you for letting me crash, Kathy." I offered sincerely.

"Oh shit, it was cool." She muttered fussing with the Brillo in her straight shooter.

She cracked the seal of her dope sack and loaded her pipe. Then, in gesture that surprised me, she opted to let me light it before her. Unwilling to look a gift horse in the mouth I plopped down at the table and let the smoke transport me from the sticky plastic of the kitchen chair and beyond the littered sounds of children crying over the grinding bass of rap beyond Kathy's door. I passed the shooter back to Kathy and free-floated until the brief sanctity of the high began to elude me.

I watched Kathy begin to fidget with the stem trying to get one last puff from the Brillo before finally tossing it on the table unsatisfied. In her post-high silence she worked the corners of her mouth with her tongue until she could no longer sit still. The hunger chased her away from the blue-checkered kitchen table and out the back to door in search of the next ride.

Knowing that Kathy had a habit of tricking the most vile dope boys out of their goodies, I kept vigil in the kitchen often walking to the back stoop to catch sight of her or the sound of trouble that often followed her excursions.

Three young boys hanging at the corner of the building seemed increasingly amused as I ducked in and out of the apartment looking for Kathy. Their words floated past my ears unrecognizable in the after-fog of the dope. But there was no mistaking the cruel humor on their faces.

Unable to resist such an easy target, the smallest of the three stuffed his wad of money into his creased big jeans and loafed toward me dangling a sack of dope in his free hand.

"You looking for something, Slim?" he teased.

I ignored him with only a sideways glance still focusing most of my attention toward the top of the street trying to catch a glimpse of Kathy. I hoped no one had hurt her.

"You hear me, bitch." He proclaimed more boldly. "I said are you looking for something?"

His two friends doubled over in laughter while passing a joint between them. I finally shifted my focus to the boy standing in front of me and glared at him unappreciatively.

"I'm good, son." I spat nastily.

"Son?" he retorted. "Bitch, I ain't no damn son of yours. My mama aint no crack head." He spat back venomously.

Seeing the encounter escalating, the other two boys left their place at the end of the building and approached the unfolding drama to stand behind their friend.

"God'damn, man." one of them scoffed. "You can't argue with no damn dope fiend, them mothafuckers can't hear shit but that flame sizzling on the end of a shooter."

He mocked smokers by sucking in his cheeks and popping his eyes. The boys cracked up and pointed at me in ridicule.

I stood my ground but my knees shook from humiliation. The last remnants of the high floated away in the reality of the warm spring day.

I glared at the boys and before I could stop myself spat back some venom of my own,

"You know what? I began sternly. "I might be a crack head, but I wasn't always like this."

My mind danced over the tile roof tops of Germany and across the wide expanse of the lake at Mt. Scott, Oklahoma.

"I have been places in my life, and one day, I'm going to stop smoking and go back to my real life." I eyed the boys viciously before continuing;

"But you were born in these projects and you gonna die in these same damn projects."

My eyes flared with rage.

I glared at the faces of the boys whose smiles had been replaced with a deep somber glare. The laughter was gone and even the joint they were passing between them hung loosely from the tallest one's fingers before finally finding its' way to the concrete.

We stared at each other in silence, recognizing the pain in each other without shame. The look of sorrow in their eyes was too much to bear. They had called me what I was and it hurt. But I knew that my life could not be destined to end in a dark alley or an abandoned building. They did not seem so sure that their own lives would not end exactly the way I had said.

With the truth melting into a seething pile of rotten dreams between us I broke the stand-off and turned away from them. I pulled Kathy's screen door tight knowing that no one in the neighborhood would enter without her okay. Still feeling the sting of their words and the harm of my own, I walked past the boys and through the cut in the buildings to the curve in Chivers Street and rounded Yates without so much as a glance back. Once at the top of Bankhead Highway I steeled myself knowing that if looked behind me I might be caught in the brimstone and fire of Sodom and Gomorrah and never find out if I could, in fact, go back to my real life.

I allowed Bankhead Highway to take me where it would and turned at each invisible landmark as if following a map. The early spring day unfolded with passing street signs and shopping centers until it had spent all its' glory and was beginning to yield to the dark cover of night.

Unaware of why, I just walked until I found myself rounding the curve of Campbellton Road facing a choice of 285 North or 285 South. As I pondered my choice for the first time a car slowed to gawk at my indecision. I peered in at a short dark brown man and tried to focus on his words. Flashes of a large foot crashing into my face warned me but I did not care. If he was crazed, maybe he would be more precise than the bus stop man and stop my suffering for good this time.

I eased myself into the car looking straight ahead. I did not want to know what my next attacker looked like.

"Where are you headed?" he asked in a low but strong voice.

Oddly soothed by his tone I tried to give him a real answer.

"I wish I knew." I admitted honestly.

Ashamed and tired I hung my head and stared at the bruises on my wrists.

"Well, I'm going to get something to eat." He continued evenly. "You're welcome to come along."

Anger rose up in me from the place it had settled and I spat at him for no provoked reason, "I don't eat, dumb-ass, I smoke crack. I glared at him. "And all I want is $20 and a ride to Bowen Homes, okay!" I demanded insanely.

The man's tone did not change.

"Like I said, I'm going to get something to eat." He kept his eyes focused on the road and a slight smile on his face. "You're welcome to come along." His tone still did not change.

He slowly reached his hand down to turn the radio knob as if knowing a sudden movement would make me jump out of my skin. Even more ashamed than before I sat quietly tracing the amorphous shapes of the bruises on my wrists and arms. The city flew by in an unrecognizable blur as we rounded 285. The melodious jazz floated out of the speakers and soothed me until I stopped fidgeting.

We finally slowed at the South Cobb Parkway exit and took a left before ending up in the IHOP parking lot. Without looking at me he opened his door and began to walk toward the entry of the restaurant. I fumbled with my handle until the door swung free and followed his lead. To my surprise, he waited for me before extending his arm to open the door for me. With my head low I entered the restaurant and allowed the hostess to usher us to a cozy booth by the window.

As if to break the silence he opened his menu and began to talk about the delicious flavors of pancakes. Intrigued, I peeled my gaze away from his oddly calm demeanor to drink in the amazing assortment of hot delights the menu had to offer. Pictures of vivid red syrup and frothy white whipped cream jumped off the menu and made me salivate. I had not realized how hungry I was.

As the waitress approached the table I was too hungry to care what I would have to do for my meal so I followed his lead and ordered, "Two eggs over easy, dry, light wheat toast and tea; Early Grey if you have it."

Amusement danced around the man's eyes and for the first time I noticed how kind they were.

"Look, I'm really sorry that I was so mean to you before." I gushed apologetically. "I really didn't mean it."

He smiled and nodded his head in acceptance of my apology then resumed his now comforting silence as we waited for our food.

My jaw ached as I tried to stuff the toast edges into my mouth but the swelling would not allow me to bite hard enough so I dipped tiny pieces into the egg yolk until I could mash them through my lips. Though it was a struggle, he smiled when I finally returned my plate to the waitress spotlessly clean.

As I followed him back to his car I could not help but to wonder why he was being so nice and what he wanted from me.

He did not leave me wondering long as he spoke more seriously than before,

"Since I'm pretty sure hopeless crack-heads don't order Earl Grey tea, I can give you the $20 you wanted and drop you off in Bowen Homes, or I can take you to Fulton County Alcohol and Drug Treatment Center."

He paused only long enough to see if I was listening.

"It's up to you." He finished abruptly.

I sat back in the passenger seat unable to retain the air that expelled from my chest. He did not want sex. He did not have a hair brained scheme that would likely land me in a basement nursing a bottle of Jack Daniels. Of all guys I could run across, of all places he could have wanted to take me…it could not be a coincidence that I was sitting in a car with a man who wanted nothing more than to take me back to the detox center I walked away from to find Ray.

Unwilling to allow hesitation to rob me of the first hopeful energy I had felt in months I looked into the kindness of his eyes and accepted the mercy he was offering.

"Please, could you take me to my stepdad's house to get my stuff then take me to Fulton County?" I continued hurriedly to try and convince him of the extra stop. "We are not far from where I used to live."

He looked at me closely for a long moment as if to see if I was trying to scam him then gently nodded in agreement.

With that, he returned his gaze to the road ahead and I smiled at how cleverly God hid His angels.

35

Do-Over

Afraid to approach the double glass doors, I stood in the parking circle of Fulton County Drug and Alcohol Treatment Center and watched the man drive away. He never did tell me his name. The thought of going to the admission window made me anxious since I had already been in treatment and walked away. There was a slim chance they would let me back in, but a slim chance was better than none at all. I moved away from the light spilling out of the lobby afraid to be run off before I could get my nerve up. I tucked the garbage bag full of belongings I had retrieved from Sgt. House's storage room under my sore frame to cushion the hardness of the concrete curb and settled in to think. As I smoked one of the cigarettes the man was nice enough to buy me I decided that so far today my luck had been good. Maybe it would last long enough for me to convince the center to give me another chance.

I tossed the hot-boxed cigarette butt into the grated drain opening and shuffled up to the reception window and told the woman I wanted help for drug abuse. After filling out the perfunctory paperwork on the chipped clipboard I waited for her eyes to scan to the middle of the page. *Have you been a patient at Fulton County Alcohol & DrugTreatment Center before? If yes, how long ago?* My shoulders dropped as she began her reasons why I would not be able to get in.

As I walked away from the window I thought about the IHOP man. It was no mistake that I was back at 265 Boulevard. The projects and alleyways of Atlanta had become more familiar to me that the neighborhoods and schools I used to know. More than once I saw a woman who looked a lot like me pushing her wheeled cart and arguing with her invisible friend about which way 'they' should go. The pang I felt when I saw her was just as much for me as it was for her – and as much as I felt badly looking into the empty centers of her eyes, I did not want to be her. There had to be something more and just maybe I could find it here. I crossed the lobby and took a seat just beyond the view of the reception window and settled in for a long night.

As daylight broke on day two, I stretched and headed to the window but the same night shift lady was on duty so I made a B-Line to the curve to smoke for a while. In my haste to duck the woman's view I almost knocked over the cheery looking redhead man hustling to get to his desk on time.

"Good morning." He greeted me melodiously.

"I'm not sure yet." I muttered excusing myself from his path.

The day droned on until I found myself in a choice plastic seat against the cool sheetrock wall resting almost comfortably through the night.

I roused from the fetal position by body had twisted into during the night in time to see the red haired man dashing across the lobby and through the Staff Only door. He probably thought I was a jerk.

After visiting the window I busied myself throughout the day chatting with other hopeful patrons; sometimes watching them march victoriously through the admittance door and sometimes dejectedly exiting through the double glass front door. Undeterred, I waited.

As the afternoon unfolded I stood dejected on the curb trying to savor the waning puffs of my last cigarette and looked up to find myself face-to-face with the red haired man.

"Have you eaten?" He asked in apparent concern.

Delighted at even the mention of food I vigorously shook my head "No".

"Here," he extended his hand toward me. "Take this meal ticket to the cafeteria around the corner past reception so you can grab some dinner."

Unconcerned about my plaque ridden teeth I smiled broadly and thanked him profusely. Hope began to tingle in my toes again as I watched the back of his colorful Jerry Garcia T-shirt as he walked away with a slight bounce in his step.

Day four was long and hot. The air conditioning in the lobby was blowing a lot less cool than it had in previous days. My night had been long and restless and without a drink and a cigarette I became too fidgety to sleep for very long. My restlessness had driven me to my curbside seat scouring the ground to see if there were any cigarette butts worth rescuing. There were none. Without something to take the edge off, my mind wandered places I had forbidden it to go. The army doctor haunted me with the words in his file.

"Miss Stokes, you have AIDS. This condition permanently disqualifies you from serving in any of the armed forces." He did not pause long before sealing my fate, "You are going to die before you reach 21 years old, Miss Stokes, so whatever you want to do in life, I suggest you do it now."

The numbness I felt as I sat in the gray chair at the military entrance processing station swept over me again making me want to dash across the street and down the block. I wanted to be anywhere except standing on the curve at Fulton County facing the truth in my head with nothing to make it go away.

Fear grabbed at me and squeezed until I could no longer breathe evenly. I had to do something. What if I died today? I am already a year older than the man said I would see. Was it happening now and I just couldn't feel it? Afraid to tell anyone but unable to bear the thought of dying alone on the streets, I made my daily shuffle to the reception window and the woman greeted me with a tolerant scoff.

"I'd like to get into drug treatment please." I muttered my daily mantra.

I watched her shuffle her papers and begin the same response I had heard for 3 days in a row. I politely waited for to her to finish but this time I did not shuffle away from the window. The fear of dying kept me pinned to the spot.

I found my voice under the pounding of my pulse, "Listen," I pleaded. "I know that I have been here before. And I know that I didn't finish the program - but Ma'am I really do want help." I fought tears as I continued trying to even my cracked tone.

"I know a lot of people need help, and yeah, I blew it. But Miss, I have HIV and I and I don't want to die on the streets using crack. I really want to get clean and get my life together."

I expelled the last of the wind that fear had not squeezed out of me and stood there half looking into her unreadable expression and half looking past her at the people who had stopped shuffling their daily paperwork to see what was happening at the reception window.

She spoke in a low and serious tone, "You have AIDS?"

Ashamed to confirm it but terrified to shuffle away from the window again, I steeled myself and answered. "Yes, I have HIV."

Her expression seemed to stiffen and soften all at once. Not knowing what to think I began to turn away in shame.

"Wait," she called after me. "Don't go anywhere. Just have a seat and someone will come out to talk to you."

No longer concerned with what her expression meant I dashed across the small lobby and took a seat in the plastic chair on the front row closest to the Staff Only door and waited. Someone will come out to talk to you she had said. With nothing else to hold onto, I repeated the words in my mind and the rhythm of them kept me planted in the chair.

After what seemed like hours, the cheery red-haired man opened the Staff Only door and motioned for me to come back. My heart raced with a mix of fear and excitement but I fought the faint spell that threatened and gathered my plastic bag. I had finally gained access to the coveted doorway.

As he introduced himself, Gary's words were pleasant and his questions were without accusation. How long have you had HIV? How long have you been using? What kind of drugs do you use? There is no address in the file we have from your first stay here, do you have one? On and on, he pried making his way through the thick stack of admission papers. I wasn't sure if Gary Dreyfuss knew anymore about HIV than I did or what he thought of me, but his expression was open and his tone was kind.

I sat attentively answering every question to the best of my ability. No, I don't know much about HIV. Yes, I got it the first time I had sex. No, I was raped. Yes, but we broke up and I told him he should go see if he had it too. No, he doesn't have it.

Today was not the day for attitude and it was not a time to keep secrets. I needed to let everything inside me out so that I could see it – stop it from haunting me. After long years of hopelessness and longer nights of horror, the time had finally come for me to grab whatever chance God had decided to give me again and hold on to it for dear life.

36

Detox

I shifted in the twin hospital style bed grateful for the longest and most restful sleep I'd had in months.

"I see the dead has arisen." A short dark brown woman called to me from the doorway.

With sleep still in my eyes I struggled to focus on her while I drug myself from my comfy nest. She could not have been more than 5 feet tall but had a stance that said she was not one to play with. Her medium brown skin was riddled with black freckles that seemed to give you an out if you could not stand to look into her direct gaze. But in spite of her deep, authoritative voice and strong body language I could also see an unmistakable kindness in her face.

"I'm Barbara, one of the counselors here – and you've been sleeping for almost 2 days, child." she caught me up matter-of-factly.

"Two days!" I repeated dumb-founded. "I'm sorry Ms. Barbara, I didn't know." I apologized.

"Well, I put a few toiletries on your night stand." she said pointing to the gray two-drawer metal cabinet by my bunk.

"Go get washed up. I'm taking the ladies downstairs for breakfast in 10 minutes." She directed.

With that she scurried down the hall to attend to the loud voices that had drawn her attention.

Having been in Fulton County before I knew that staying in bed all day was strictly against the rules and gathered I must have been in pretty poor shape for the day counselors and the night shift nurses to let me sleep for so long. Feeling like the luck that met me at the intersection of Campbellton Road and I-285 was still lingering, I quickly gathered the hospital tray full of personal items and dashed across the hall to be in the breakfast line on time.

The smell of grits and bacon permeated my mind as I quick-stepped behind the heavy set girl in front of me to get a glimpse of the goodies under the cafeteria lights. My eyes widened as the white-clad, hair-netted woman behind the breakfast line plopped a healthy serving on my tray. Without stopping for a milk carton I dashed to the nearest table to engulf the feast. I unceremoniously plunged the plastic spoon into the steamy grits but before I could bring it to my mouth I yelped in pain. The electricity shooting through my jaw and toward the center of my brain made my eyes tear up and the spoon fall limply from my fingers.

My jaw had gotten worse. The dinner from two days ago was as much of a challenge as the eggs and toast at IHOP, but at least I was able to open my jaws wide enough to take small bites at a time and mush the food against the roof of my mouth with my tongue until I could swallow it. Now, the throbbing ache that accompanied my attempt to open wide enough for a spoon was excruciating. Disappointed but unscathed, I picked up the plastic knife and slathered the end of it with a flat paste of grits and gently slid the food past my lips until my tongue could take over. Breakfast was a painfully slow process and the bacon was impossible, but my stomach was glad for the efforts I made. As I cleared my tray and joined the group to march back upstairs I hoped that mashed potatoes or the like was on the lunch menu.

The days droned on as we assembled for group after group. Some of the women cried as they answered questions from the group leader and others sat staring into nothing. I made my best effort to speak up and follow the topics of conversation but only bits and pieces stuck to my still fuzzy mind. On my fifth day I put my name on the list to enter the 28-day intensive residential treatment program offered on the other side of the building and was thankful for the long groups when I was awarded a bed to continue my treatment.

No sooner than I settled into my new room I posted outside the door to wait for the doctor. He did not make rounds on the detox side but now that I was in level two maybe I could finally talk to someone about my jaw. He scuttled from room to room checking to see if any of the residents had medical complaints and when he came to me I barreled over his words eager to tell him about my nagging pain. He wrote something on his clipboard and scurried off to ask the same question to the next client. I guessed that he had to consult with someone before he could tell me what to do. It did not dawn on me until the third day that he was not listening to my complaint so when he turned to move on to the next client, the throbbing pain that would not go away made me speak up.

"Hey doc, what can I do about my broken jaw?" I asked earnestly."It really hurts." I added hopefully.

He stared at me for a long moment before pulling a yellow pad from his pocket and scribbling hurriedly.

"Look," he barked accusingly. "If you don't want to be in treatment no one is keeping you here." He glared at me disapprovingly before continuing."

Take this to the nurse's station and they'll give you a bus token and a pass to go to Grady emergency." He shoved the paper toward me.

I took it and lowered my head. As I turned to follow his instructions he called after me,

"That's an 8 hour pass. If you're late or don't pass the urine test when you come back, your bed will go to someone who wants it."

I wanted to defend myself but decided that both my jaw and my pride hurt too much. He was probably a very nice man ordinarily, but people like me lied and stole things and never appreciated people who tried to help them. I decided to focus on my jaw and leave the other battles for another day.

For the entire time I was on the bus to Grady my fingers and toes tingled. The butterflies in my stomach threatened to squeeze through the opening in my lips and yelp. I watched the man two rows in front of me nod and finger his pocket. It was not hard to figure that he was on his way to or from the dope house. I counted each letter "A' I could find on the bus bulletin boards to ignore the overpowering need to ask where he was headed.

Most of the people in the emergency waiting room grew impatient waiting for their number to be called but after three days in the hard plastic chairs at Fulton County the deep curve and thin cushion outside triage felt just fine to me.

"A-304, Number A-304" The intercom blared.

I scurried to replace the magazine I was browsing and dashed toward the doorway where the nurse waited.

"Have a seat and roll up your sleeve," She directed. "I need to get your vitals."

I plopped into the recliner seat and followed her guidance.

She flipped through her charts to fill out the blanks in my new Grady file. "I see you have been here before but I need to get some more medical history on you Miss Stokes." She announced.

My heart raced with fear that was so noticeable she glanced at the blood pressure machine and asked if I had ever been diagnoses with hypertension.

"No, I'm just nervous." I admitted.

"Well, let me start this over so we can get a true reading." She readjusted the cuff and continued."No need to be nervous Miss Stokes, we're here to take care of you." She consoled while having me point out my discomfort on the pain chart.

I relaxed enough for her to get the reading she needed but I could still feel my heart pounding. The more questions she asked, the louder it thumped in my chest – until finally, she reached the dreaded question,

"Have you been tested for HIV/AIDS?" she asked almost rhetorically.

It seemed she was writing before I could answer.

"Y-yes," I stammered. "I'm positive."

Her pen paused mid-dash and she stared up at me as if she wasn't sure she hear me correctly.

"You got AIDS? She grunted. All the previous politeness in her tone had dissipated.

I paused and looked at her wishing I could take my statement back. But it was too late. "Yes, I took an HIV test a few years ago while trying to get into the army and it came back positive." I stated in a quiet voice that did not seem quite my own.

Her hand slipped gently away from the position it had been near my face and she took several steps away from me. It seemed her movements were involuntary – as if she knew that she shouldn't but could not help herself.

Unable to address the information she passed me along to the next station. "Well," she mumbled. "You can have a seat back in the waiting room." She tidied her forms in a veiled attempt to dismiss her reaction. "Someone from oral surgery will be out to see you soon.

Hours passed. No one had called my name or number again and I was concerned that my eight hour pass would soon expire. I strode to the window and asked if I could use the phone. After a tough negotiation the woman looked up the number to the treatment facility and informed the staff that I was indeed at Grady and was waiting for outpatient surgery.

After the longest wait imaginable I was finally ushered off through the Grady corridors and placed in a dental chair to wait for the surgeon. I snuck looks of myself in the shiny chrome of the overhead light and vaguely wondered it fixing my jaw would change my face at all.

"Miss Stokes? The short curvaceous brunette called from the doorway.

"Yes." I called back.

Wasting no time she filled the room with activity while citing passages from my medical file. The woman assisting her paused along with her when she read my HIV status out loud. The atmosphere quickly went from dispassionate to apathetic. Her movements became choppy as she hurriedly checked her surgical tools and filled the needle from a bottle labeled Xylocain. She neatly avoided my eyes as she unceremoniously shoved it into my gums near the source of my swelling.

"Let's give that a minute to kick in and I'll be back to wire you." she barked already turning her heels to leave the room.

I had a hundred questions about the procedure she was going to perform but nothing in her mannerism told me that she wanted to be bothered. I worriedly amused myself by running my tongue over the place she pricked my gums.

It was not long before she returned with the same choppy movements and began taking instruments from her tray and prying into my mouth.

"Aaargh!" I bellowed as the sharp pressure exploded in my head.

She rocked back on her heel and stared at me as if I had just dented her brand new car.

"You're telling me that you can feel that?" she asked in an accusatory tone.

"Yes, and it hurts really bad." I muttered through the spittle.

She let out an exasperated sigh and grabbed the Xylocain bottle and reloaded her needle. I flinched as it broke the surface of my gums and unceremoniously met the bone.

"You feel this needle too I suppose?" she asked incredulously.

Unable to control my now heavy tongue I nodded 'Yes'.

She scoffed and waved her hand dismissively before reaching for the tool she was working with before. As she began to scrape and clip at the inside of my mouth she ushered a lesson with each gruff motion of her hand.

"You know that you can spread HIV to other people so I hope you are not having sex."

Crunch. Scrape.

"Oh, no wonder you complained about the local anesthetic." She accused glancing up from my open file, "I see that you're in a drug treatment center."

Grind. Crunch. Squeak.

"I really hope the work I'm doing on your jaw isn't a waste of my time." She delivered her sermon while her assistant nodded in agreement. "We just don't have resources to waste...."

I tuned out her attacks and focused on the high pitched scream of the drill and the tiny shards of bone spattering against the inside of my jaw. This is only for a moment, I consoled myself. The pain will not last and she is not the whole world. I was unable to stop the tears that rolled down my cheeks into her work area but I would not break down. I kept my eyes open and rode the waves of pain past the glare of the light, across the white room and focused my attention on tomorrow.

37

Revelations

The bus ride back from Grady was uneventful and I was grateful as I watched the warm light of the sun prepare to break through the pre-dawn sky. I was not sure how long I sat in the dentist chair under assault but it felt like hours. I was happy to finally have my jaw fixed but it seemed that what I could not pay in insurance the ER doctor was sure to pull from me in humiliation.

I shuddered slightly as I recalled her voice of doom and tried to shake it off as I showed my time-stamped discharge papers to the lady in the admission window. The nurses on the second floor met me at the elevator to check for contraband and quickly confiscated my unopened bottle of liquid codeine. They said the Antabuse they were giving me along with the vitamins would react to the codeine and they would give me Tylenol for any pain I had.

As I stood there dumb-founded and unable to speak through my wired jaws the only thing I could think to do was to open my mouth and show them the metal plates at the top and bottom of my jaws held securely in place with surgical steel wires looped through like industrial spaghetti.

One of the nurses nodded in understanding and proceeded to crush a Tylenol and mix it with warm water. I gratefully sucked it through the cracks in my teeth and obediently hobbled off toward my room.

Tired and sore I eased myself onto the side of my cot and reached for my charity lotion to put around the cracked corners of my mouth. My hands connected with nothing. Sure I had left it on the corner of my nightstand I reached for the hospital light over the bed and sat numbed by what it revealed. Gone! All the toiletries I left waiting for me were gone. I scrambled to my feet and pulled the top drawer open to see if maybe someone had put them away for me but it too was empty. By the time I snatched open the bottom drawer and peeked into the closet I knew that I had been robbed.

The sinking feeling in my stomach deepened as I approached the desk and voiced my complaint with the help of the nurse's pencil and the blank space at the bottom of her crossword puzzle.

"Are you sure you did not take your things with you?" she asked reaching for an answer.

I stared at her wide eyed but managed to shake my head 'No'.

"Well, Miss Stokes, we won't be able to do anything about it until the day staff gets here in a couple of hours." She dismissed the crisis.

Uninterested in scribbling any more complaints I retreated back to my room and stared into the empty nightstand. Gone! Everything is finally gone. Over the years I lost things here and there and Rod made sure to help seperate me from the bulk of it, but there were tiny pieces of my life that I had managed to hold onto thanks to Sgt. House. My Prince T-Shirts and summer pants, my pretty yellow sleeveless sweater with the cute eyelet opening at the neck, even the outdated gold poof pants I used to look so good in back in the day ... all gone. My chest pounded and my temples throbbed as I tried to reconcile the loss. It felt like life was snatching my identity away and I tried fiercely to hold on to it. I closed my eyes and envisioned the newspaper clippings from the poetry column I penned in Savannah and remembered the cracked binding of my hand written poetry ledger. Why would someone take that?

I crawled into the bed and wedged my back against the wall and could not help the squeal that escaped my almost immobile lips.

"Noooo! No. No. No. NO!!!" The pain came in a long unstoppable mantra. I leaned the heaviness of my head against the wall and stopped trying to control my cries.

"Peeease, peaase gimme my 'uff back." I gurgled for the whole floor to hear if they could.

The nurse popped into the doorway as if I would be issued a spanking for the outburst but I did not care. It was not her stuff. She had stuff at home where she went when she left work. Her family was there and she had not hurt and abandoned them. The last remnants of any evidence of my life before wandering the streets had disappeared and I wanted to touch them again. I needed to know that I was not dreaming about Germany and Oklahoma and I had not imagined the lines of poetry and long walks with my Walkman blasting Prince into my ears.

Her words were lost to my sobs and she finally retreated back to her crossword puzzle to let someone else deal with the chaos. I sobbed and muttered incoherencies to my waking roommate and the vicious line of giggling women who popped their heads into our door on their way to morning wash-up routine. I did not care about their giggles and I would not leave my room for breakfast or any other meal until my things were back.

After hours of threats from staff and racking sobs my body finally buckled under the pressure. The bitter vile in my stomach rose to the back of my throat and demanded a way to abandon ship. The wires looping through the metal plates along my jaw line strained to allow passage for the vomit to escape but could not. The nurse watched in horror before dashing off to call someone. I leaned my heavy head forward to try and let some of the pressure through my teeth and managed to regain enough control to swallow what did not squirt through the cracks in my teeth. Before I could succumb to the wave of weakness I found myself looking into kind but concerned face of the red-haired Grateful Dead counselor. Gary's hands shook as he positioned the needle but he held steady until he hit his mark.

"This is phenegan – it will stop the nausea and relax you." He patiently explained even under the harried circumstance.

He eased my calming body into the bed and snatched pillows from the other bed to elevate my head. My sobs subsided as the injection worked its' way through my veins.

"Denise, you have to stay calm. We don't have any way of removing your wires." He explained in a serious tone.

"If you throw up, you could choke to death before we could do anything about it." He stared into my eyes waiting for the information to sink in.

Just before the drug dimmed the early morning light I connected with his eyes and nodded in grateful agreement before falling into the arms of a long sleep.

I peeled myself from the thin white sheets and examined the brown patch of blood that dried under my mouth during the night. Worried, I scrambled to the bathroom to soap my washcloth and clean it up before anyone saw. Judging from the doctor's reaction at the ER I wouldn't be surprised if the laundry staff burned the whole set if they knew it came from an HIV positive person's bed.

Tears spilled into the soapy mix as I scrubbed my sheet and I was overcome by the shame of my outburst. I was glad that the counselors were helping me and I did not want to cause trouble, but I did not know how to stop the emptiness and fear I was feeling. As I fretted in my task I did not notice Barbra walk into the room and stand behind me.

"We do have laundry service you know?"She poked good-naturedly.

As I tried to respond to her the metal plates tin my mouth retaliated against my attempt. I clutched my face with one hand and pointed to the disappearing stain on my sheet with the other hand hoping she would understand.

She paused and searched my face before continuing, "I know that you disclosed your HIV status when you did intake. And I also know that you can't get it from old blood on sheets." She finished in an understanding voice.

I stared at her shocked that she would say it out loud. Feeling a tinge of hope trying to chase away the despair I ignored the protest from my wired jaws and squeezed the words through my teeth.

"I have it" I slobbered, "but don' know 'bout it" I admitted almost incomprehensibly.

She nodded her head comfortable with the conversation. "We have a staff person who can give you a lot of information about HIV." she paused before continuing, "If you want it."

She waited for my response.

Unable to just nod I sloshed, "I wanna know 'erytang."

Something flashed across her eyes that told me she was pleased with my response and I smiled over the wires.

"Okay." she smiled back. "Fred Locklear is the epidemiologist. I'll let him know you want to see him."

"Is all your stuff gone?" she queried.

Surprised that she did not scold me for my tantrum I just hung my head and nodded. As she turned to leave the room she grunted, "Humph. I got it" before scurrying off.

I plopped on my bed and looked across the room at the bulging bag under my roommate's bed. I didn't remember her having so much stuff before I went to Grady. I wanted to drag it out and pour over the contents to see if some of it was mine, but something about Barbara's demeanor made me think twice about taking matters in my own hands. I held on to the serenity prayer they taught us in day group;

God grant me the serenity
To accept the things I cannot change,
The courage to change the things I can,
And the wisdom to know the difference.

I repeated it in my head over and over again trying to figure out which thing God was going to grant me before finally accepting that going through her things would only cause trouble - with her and with the staff. Maybe I was just supposed to wait and see what happened next.

Over the next days I was so busy going to Mr. Locklear's office learning about HIV that I forgot to worry about my stuff. Barbara was right. Fred Locklear had a lot of information. He made me wonder if maybe I could beat HIV when he said things like you can learn to manage it. I wasn't sure what to do next but I could see that the more pamphlets and articles Fred gave me the more I began to feel like putting together a strategy of things to try would help me more than just waiting to see what HIV would do.

I woke early on the morning that the bulk of my group was being discharged. Sleep did not come easily anyway since I was not allowed to have anything stronger than Tylenol for my jaw I had taken to walking the halls most of the night to comfort my pain. Morning meditation group was tense but uneventful. I kept watching Barbara wondering how she could just ignore the thieves who had taken everything I had left. Almost sure that she did not care I fought the anger that was building up in me as I watched them giggle and share about how they are going to stay clean when the left the program. I began to doubt that "*acceptance*" was such a good idea. Maybe it was just a trick to keep me from fighting for my rights. To keep from snapping at the lot of them I ignored their banter and refused to share when it was my turn.

I hung my head as mediation group disbanded and the women were sent to their rooms to get their bags and line up at the elevator. As I shuffled toward the door to hide out in my room Barbara stopped me in my tracks.

"You might want to stick around." She stated matter-of-factly.

Wondering what she had up her sleeves I glued my back to the desk by the elevator and waited for the women to come back, bags in tow.

"Ladies, I wish you all well and hope that you decide you want to stay clean more than you want to use" she preached while walking back and forth in front of the elevator line-up like a drill sergeant sending her young topps to war.

"But I need to remind you that the first step in the program we work is honesty." She continued making eye contact with each of the ladies.

I watched them shift nervously under her x-ray eye as they waited for the other shoe to drop.

"Before we complete your discharge I'm going to need each of you ladies to empty your bags for inspection." She delivered her blow swiftly over a choir of moans and mumbling.

I stood taller against the desk and eye-balled the women as they each reluctantly emptied their bulging parcels for the entire floor to see.

Barbara approached me and spoke volumes in the brief look she gave me before proceeding with her instructions,

"Denise, do you see anything that belongs to you in these bags?"

Half ashamed of my earlier anger and half excited at the prospect of recovering some of my things I slowly left my post at the desk and picked out what belonged to me. Every single woman had something of mine as if they had raided my room and divvied up their bounty. I guess nobody thought I was coming back from the emergency room. Not one of them protested as I piled my T-shirts and pants in a heap. As I approached the last girl my hands shook. The one thing that meant the most to me had not surfaced yet. As I poured through her bundles of Fulton County towels and sheets my fingers landed on the hard spine of a book and I drew it to me unable to stop the sobs of relief that followed. I looked up at Barbara from my crouched position and she accepted my thanks with a slight brush against my shoulder before continuing her closing sermon. The last of her words were lost to the flood of emotion that spilled from me.

She had stood up for me. This woman I had never seen in my life before being accepted into detox went out of her way to help me! And so did Gary and Fred Locklear. It seemed that only a short time ago I was surrounded by people who smiled widely until I passed before tripping me or plunging a dagger into my spine. I was befriended by the guy who professed his love until my panties came off and then disappeared. I was encircled by the well-meaning street buddy who could not think of a better way to show concern than to reward me with a sack of dope. The man from the IHOP and the people at Fulton County were the kind of people I had either not seen or not noticed in a very long time. And the one thing they all had in common was the 12-step program they kept telling me I needed to work!

I gathered my things and told the ladies on line to 'keep coming back' before marching off to my room where the silence of the white walled sanctuary spoke to me. People were doing something that meant more than having all the money in the world. They were touching people and giving them a chance to get their life back. I doubted that many of them sported Gucci purses after work or fingered fine Waterman pens as they filled out her paperwork but they looked happy. If the group I had been lucky enough to fall in with had made anyone else feel as safe and cared for as I felt right now, I wanted to stay with them.

I smiled as I fingered the dry spot where my blood had been and clutched my poetry book closer to me. Flashes of old abandoned buildings filled my head. I remembered the prayers I used to recite into the darkness hoping that something would change - prayers that God might forgive me and save me. I remembered wishing that I would wake up to find out I had only been having a bad dream. Then I had stopped talking to God because I thought He wasn't listening to a sinner like me.

But as I relaxed my shoulders in the safe place I had found I reconsidered. Maybe He did hear me and maybe heaven was not a cosmic event that unfolds after you take your last breath. Maybe heaven was giving a lost girl a safe ride or a meal ticket. I thought about all the horrible things I did to my body trying to get drugs and understood that salvation might come from standing up for people who don't know how to do it for themselves.

My smile grew wider than my jaws wanted to allow and I knew that no man, no fear and no bad memory could make me walk away this time. I knew I wanted to stay clean – and quietly set my sights on the outpatient program I had been hearing that some people go to after Fulton County. Tomorrow, I would talk to Barbara about St. Jude's.

The House of Pain

I ran my tongue across my front teeth and savored the absence of pain that used to accompany the habit. Since I had gotten the wires removed from my jaws I was eating everything in sight! St. Jude's Recovery Center had been kind to me. When I met with Ed, the house manager, I knew immediately the staff did not tolerate excuses. I had a long interview filled with questions about where I saw myself and what I wanted from recovery – but more urgently, how I would take care of myself in my convalescent state.

I remembered what Barbara told me, be honest during my interview. I told Ed that yes, the pain bothered me but I could take care of myself, I could eat soft foods from the house cafeteria and I could manage my pain with only Tylenol or Goody's. When he asked me about HIV I told him that I learned a lot from Fred Locklear but I needed more information. To my delight my honest answers were enough to get me into St. Jude's.

As I sat in the lower level classroom waiting for the group leader my grateful state was shrouded with the doubt that maybe my honesty had lead Ed to be just a little hard on me. A part of my treatment plan was to follow all the rules and attend all the groups everyone else did but to also go to an outside HIV support group and take AIDS101 class. The outside group was easy since Fred's sister-in-law, Faye Brown, lead a support group for HIV. Our Common Welfare was an amazing place where Faye and Skip introduced me to other people with HIV and gave me more information than I knew what to do with. Still, I struggled with my requirement to attend the AIDS101 class I was begrudgingly waiting for. What could I learn that I didn't already know?

My restless state was interrupted by a talkative brown-skinned woman with a slight swagger. I had never seen a feminine woman swagger before, but she did. It was like watching two people occupying the same space. I sat up in my circled group chair and watched her interact with my housemates as she unpacked her overburdened arms. She scattered stacks of pamphlets and condoms across the table as she ushered the clinging crowd to their seats then slammed an object in the middle of the table causing the room to hush.

We stared at the big brown rubber penis in silent shock before a succession of reactions began to emit from the crowd. Giggles and gasps settled under the sound of the now serious boom of her voice.

"This is a penis. Does anyone know why and how to put a condom on it?" she shot at the stunned group.

Blocks away from the bored indifference I felt only moments before I stared in wide-eyed silence as she began to work the room. Though there was no trace of arrogance or exhibitionism in her mannerism, yet the 40 or so of us sat glued to her every word. Even when I was on drugs I knew that I needed to use a condom every time I had sex, but she weaved a medical and behavioral science lesson into a best-selling drama not one of us could ignore. Against my vow to just brush her off and sit through the class for credit, I found myself chiming in with the rest of the room, eager to ask and answer questions.

At first, I could not hide my frustration and shot my questions at her in an attempt to prove to myself that this was just a useless repeat of information.

"Well," I interrupted her attempt to explain what someone with HIV goes through. "My girlfriend has HIV and it's not like that for her." I sat back smugly sure that I had broken her flow.

"Well sweetie," she responded patiently, "not everyone with HIV goes through the same thing but I want to make sure you guys know the basics."

I sat back for a while still trying to pretend not to be fascinated until she started talking about medicine.

"Well," I interjected, "AZT does help to fight HIV, but the side-effects sometimes make people sicker than the HIV."

I waited for her response. She shifted on her feet and looked into the center of my gaze as if to say I'm not moved. Then she responded.

"You know, you have a good point about the medication but there are two things to keep in mind."

She broke my gaze and included the rest of the group in our private sparring session.

"There is no cure for HIV so for many people some medicine is better than not having any options at all. And the exciting news is that they are working on better medications all the time." She concluded skillfully.

I could not help but to nod along with the rest of the class as she continued.

"When it comes to those who are already infected, we have to keep people alive long enough to see better medicines." She scanned the room with what could only be described as love in her eyes before she closed her group.

"When it comes to those of you who are not infected, we have to learn about HIV, take responsibility for our behaviors so we don't get infected, and we have to treat people who have HIV with the love and respect that we all deserve."

I jumped to my feet and beat the rest of my housemates in the thunderous applause she had earned from the group. I could only shake my head and kick myself for the funky attitude I had when she first came. St. Jude's and the 12-step program was teaching me a lot but it was more clear to me every day that I still had a lot to learn.

I waited for her to give and receive hugs from the overwhelmed group that smothered her into the corner by her table of goodies. She shot me a knowing glance and I understood.

As the last of my newfound friends cleared the group room I stood near the door waiting for her response.

"So," she said in a mock whisper, "did your *friend* learn anything new about her HIV?"

I raised my chin to be sure that I met her gaze evenly before responding.

"Yes, Dottie, I learned a lot about my HIV from your class." I contiunued bravely knowing that she would not judge me,

"I even learned that using a condom isn't enough, I have to tell people I have HIV before sex so they have a choice and not just a condom."

She smiled and I knew that I was in desperate need of what she had to offer me. Her walk, her confidence, her compassion – I wanted to know how Dottie Thomas became who she was and everything in her smile told me that she was willing to show me.

She broke her smile as we walked through the front door of St. Jude's to place her packages in her trunk.

"Denise," she spoke with the same passion she did in front of the class, "there are a lot of people living with HIV. A lot of them are women who look just like you."

I hung on her every word as she schooled me.

"They are alone and in the closet and they will die in that closet if nothing brings them out of it."

She looked me up and down and smiled again.

"You a bony lil something, but you can help those women come out of the closet and live Denise." She nodded her head vigorously while laughing from her gut. "You can carry a message of hope to them that will make them believe they have something to fight for."

Her battle cry reached beyond the surface of my skin and deep beneath the layers of shame and pain I had walked around in since the military doctor told me I was going to die. I was dazzled by the flare in her eyes and sucked into the energy of her powerful stance. I wanted to do more than stay clean. I wanted to live before I died with HIV or anything else, and I knew that Dottie would show me how.

I stood in the parking lot of St. Jude's and looked squarely into the shadow that HIV had cast over my life and vowed to walk out of that shadow and bring as many people with me as I could. Just like everyone else from detox I had struggled against the burning desire to get high until it became a daily decision I embraced gratefully. I had talked to people and began to let go of the things I had lost with the understanding that things could be replaced – and though difficult, I was learning that I knew little about really living sober. But as Dotte's battle cry became my own, the real work began.

I met 23 with a vengance. With 9 months clean, I went about my daily routine with a renewed sense of hope and responsibility. I finally understood that all the knowledge Fred shared with me and that I gathered in Faye and Skip Brown's support group was not just for me to live a longer time with HIV, but to pass it on to the next person in a way that they could not since they were not living with HIV themselves.

Over the next year I buried myself in information until I consumed every pamphlet and clinical study I could get my hands on. I volunteered at every walk, vigil, group, and outreach mission that would have me. Recovery was new and grand, and my youth was but a budding flower – but HIV was nipping at my heels and if it was going to catch me, it would have to run!

Enoch had passed, Vanessa had passed, Lloyd had passed, Tracy had passed... even my sweet friend Candice lost her batle to "a long illness". In my first months and years of recovery more friends with HIV had died than I could count. I had suffered emotional trauma after bitter loss – but even as I went to several funerals a week, nothing could stop me from sharing the hope that Dottie and my sponsor KJ and countless others had ingrained in my spirit.

With the fog of drugs lifted I had to face the shame of my decisions and learn to hold my head erect until I forgave myself. With the help of my new extended family I had to reach out to the boyfriends of the past and tell them I had HIV. To my relief, all of them tested negative... and forgave me for not informing them, condom or not.

12-step meetings were like intensive care for the insane emotions that surged through me at a thousand watts per second. But slowly, vigourously, I learned to channel all the reasons I had given up on myself into reasons to go on. I listened to the stories of other addicts and knew that my pain and poor choices were not unique. I shared the deepest troubles

I could be honest about and without fail found there was always a simple solution to my despair – and the solution never involved using drugs and alcohol or doing harm to myself or others.

Months gave way to years until one day I realized I was some else's "Dottie". I had let other people believe in me long enough that I believed in myself again. And once I grew up and faced life – I knew that I was unstoppable and that nothing but death could keep me from loving everything life threw at me. And it was a good thing too, because the fiercest battle was yet to come...

39

The Glass Staircase

The steady sound of the oxygen pump filled the room with questions as I tried to shift my sore body in the motorized hospital bed. In the days since I was admitted, I had gotten used to the chorus of machines that surrounded me. The bleep of the heart-rate monitor, the alarms emitting from the IV machine hungry for more antibiotics to pump through my veins, even the random code announcement over the intercom did not rattle me anymore. The scariest sound came from the steady psssh-whoosh, psssh-whoosh of the oxygen machine. My lungs could no longer find the air my body needed to survive and I stared in reverence at the accordion that had become my umbilical cord.

"How are we doing today Miss Stokes?" The smiling nurse queried on her nightly rounds.

"I've been better but I'm not complaining." I smiled back.

"The doctor is going to take a look at your labs in the morning before he comes in to see you." She explained.

The staff at Northside hospital was more attentive than anyplace I had been in the 14 years I had been living with HIV. I looked at her appreciatively.

"That's cool. Tomorrow is soon enough." I smiled broadly stretching my lips against the oxygen tube.

"I've got all the time in the world." I joked and chuckled as much as my airflow would allow.

"I'm so glad to see you're in good spirits, Miss Stokes." She nodded her head in satisfaction.

"How is your pain?" She probed as she straightened out the cords I had jumbled while trying to shift my waning weight.

"Well, it's been here so long I gave it a name." I said now weak from talking too much.

Noting my drop in energy and obvious discomfort she nodded and produced my scheduled Demerol shot. Knowing that I would not be able to fight the instant effect of the drug I waved her away.

"Let me try to fight it a little longer." I pleaded motioning for my rolling table. "I want to do some reading before you put my lights out."

She smiled and capped the needle before rolling the tray near my free arm so I could reach it.

"I'll be back in an hour or so with your shot. If you want me sooner, just buzz." She called as she darted through the door to see her next patient.

I ignored the dull throb in my back and the sharp stabbing pulses surging through my chest and pulled the tray of papers closer to my reading light. The pictures and articles fell from the bulky folder and scattered across my lap.

My eyes were drawn to a picture of me sporting a purple Outreach T-shirt plastered across the 1992 Living section of the Atlanta Journal/Constitution. I smiled as I thought about all the 12-step calls and street outreach missions I went on with Dottie and the Outreach family. Sandra McDonald was a little bitty, high-yellow woman old enough to be my grandmother but you could not tell from the powerful battle she waged against HIV with her nonprofit agency. I knew that I had been lucky to run across Dottie at St. Jude's and do all the work I did with Outreach.

Queen Latifah's blue specs glinted from the cover of the 1993 Esteem magazine they had written an article about me in. Leaving my peer counseling position at Outreach, Inc. after only a year had been a difficult decision, but even then I had known that Atlanta was not the only place I was convicted to spreading the word about HIV. There were cites across the world that were plagued by stigma and where younger and younger people were ignoring the warnings and becoming infected faster than agencies could reach them. I needed to do more and gladly answered the call from people across the country seeking someone willing to talk about living with HIV.

Some said it made me a hero, like the CNN interview. Others still called me a victim and questioned the need for such 'controversial' education, like the 1995 Washington Post article. Even my own mother was undecided on how she felt about me being so open about my HIV status. One minute she was proud and bragging to friends about my career, the next minute she was calling me up to tell me what a low-down, selfish liar I was.

As I fingered page after page of letters from teenagers and CEOs and the magazine and newspaper articles I knew that I was doing exactly what I was supposed to do, keep people talking about AIDS. I had hoped that my mother would be proud of me. But Dottie and KJ taught me that I could not spend the rest of my life waiting for her to love me. I had to set my boundaries and love her as best I could. I tried not to let it consume me but still found myself daydreaming about long chats and deep hugs from my mother.

I glanced around at the machines still churning and sighed as much as I could before allowing the stack of memorabilia to slip from my numbed fingertips. The pain was too much and the air seemed thinner and thinner. Too weak to do anything else, I stared at the bright bouquets of flowers and cards scattered along the sink and windowsill. My room was a botanical garden filled with love from my dear friends and colleagues. The doctor said it was far too much since I was a lung patient, but the deliveries would not stop flooding in and the nurse's station was full too. I let the weak smile spread around my oxygen hose. I would do my best not to make them suffer another of the sad, sad funerals many of us had attended over the years.

The scrub-clad nurse re-entered my room not a moment too soon as my head fell limply against the pile of pillows she had fluffed the last time she came. She gathered my papers and tucked them back into the folder.

"I'll put these back on the tray so you can finish reading them later." She smiled.

I gazed at the Whatzit smiling at me from the 1996 Olympic Games poster I had taped to the wall under the T.V. I had to get better so I could go to the track and field event my best friend offered me a ticket for.

The burn from the Demerol surged for only a brief moment before the warm relief came and masked the unbearable stabbing in my chest. My eyes fluttered before gently closing to the nod of the drug.

It seemed that morning came only seconds after the nurse tossed her used needle in the Sharps container on my wall. My head was still groggy but the pain was already breaking through my drug-induced sleep. I tried to focus on the gentle voice that called out to me.

"Hey lady, you finally woke up." Ron's cheery voice greeted my rising.

I smiled and slowly opened my eyes to see him stretched out in the recliner the nurses had put in my room for him. I felt badly for him but was more than grateful that he was so eager to care for me since I got sick.

Over the five years I had been clean I realized that good boyfriends were a rare find; HIV positive or not. Ron slipped into my life after a chance encounter at a Prince concert and settled in as if he had always been there. Not being HIV himself, he took as much time learning who I was as a person as he did learning about my illness and neither of us had a clue that he would need the information as soon as he did. The pneumocistis carinii pneumonia came out of nowhere – and was indeed "the big kahuna".

It was a natural progression for me to start seeing the infectious disease doctor I had been taking the clients of Outreach to and Dr. Maurice Adair made no bones about giving me the best care in Atlanta. We had discussed medicine but my T-cell count was so high that I decided to wait. No one could have guessed that my CD4 would plummet so quickly to a scant 17 and that my viral load to sky-rocket to in excess of 750 thousands copies per militer before anyone knew what hit me.

Ron had not balked. He was more of a friend to me than I could have hoped for as he took me to emergency rooms and stayed up late nights trying to break the fevers that were coming more and more frequently. Finally, the last fever I had could not be broken at home and even the ER struggled to stabilize me. Ron had settled me into my room and did not think twice as he headed home to pack a bag and stay by my side.

"Hey handsome," I smiled at him warmly "are you up for a little Super Mario Brothers?" I challenged, pointing to the Nintendo he had convinced the nurses I had to have.

"That's the spirit." he smiled already hooking the wires to the hospital T.V.

Though we were both worried, neither of us would let the concern spill into our fun as we slid down pipes and devoured power mushrooms. Like we had done since we met we played and laughed like children just happy to be together.

Ron noted my slow reaction as I struggled for the strength to hold on to my remote and tried not to let me see him switch hands so he could play poorly too. I gave him my best wicked grin and savored the moment.

"Miss Stokes I see you found a way to pass the time." The doctor called cheerily from the doorway.

"Ha-ha" I giggled weakly. "Yeah doc, I'm afraid I've learned all I can about heart disease from the hospital channel."

He smiled and scanned over my thick chart.

"Well, the spinal tap we did doesn't show any sign of meningitis so that's a plus." He announced reading the results from the barrage of tests he ordered.

"How is your breathing?" he asked still reading.

"Well," I started before realizing it had become more difficult to talk. I let the remote slip from my hands and ignored Ron's concerned face as I tried to focus on the doctor's face. "Not too good." I finished more winded than I had been before.

The doctor looked away from his chart and searched the machines for a clue to the change he was beginning to see. The light coming from behind him seemed to get brighter and it became difficult to make out his face anymore.

I felt Ron's hand on my thigh and used the last of my energy to connect to it, squeezing as tightly as I could manage to reassure him.

"I- I- can't breathe" I wheezed almost inaudibly.

My eyes refused but I could not get a fix on anything so I concentrated on trying to make out the choir of voices.

Code blue! Code blue! Let's get her to OR stat.

Denise! Can you hear me? Denise!

… acute respiratory failure…

… cardiac…

The voices merged until they were undecipherable and I turned my attention to the soothing light that had filled the room. As I gazed into the brightness all thoughts fell away except one,

Thank you, God.

I'm not afraid and I don't feel regret.

Thank you God for letting me feel love.

40

From the Crack House to the White House

The cool October wind whisked through my hair as I loaded my over-packed bag into the cavernous trunk of my classic Mercedes. Roscoe jumped in excitement waiting for me to open the car door.

"Down boy" I scolded the energetic cocker spaniel.

"Not this time buddy, mommy's going on a business trip and you have to stay with David and Shelia." I cajoled.

As if he recognized their names he immediately jetted away from the car to the end of the driveway to crane his neck across the street.

I was lucky to live in such a quiet neighborhood with neighbors like mine. Every middle-classed home on the block was neatly manicured and well cared for. Since Ron and I broke up, David and Sheila had been more than helpful in making sure that my little blonde canine child was spoiled and catered to while I traveled for business.

I watched Roscoe's beautiful blonde curls flutter in the wind and smiled against the slight sadness that always came when I thought too long. I would not trade my puppy for the world but the pang of my empty womb felt sharper and sharper as the years passed.

I had hoped that Ron and I would get married and eventually have children but sometimes good things came to an end. He was not the typical ugly break-up I had experienced while trying to navigate the tricky journey of relationships so all I could do was be happy for the seven years we spent loving each other. But it became inevitable that we would part ways since he was vehemently against having children and I had always known that I wanted to be a mother someday. I was just waiting for the narvel of modern medicine to catch up to my hope.

As I lured Roscoe into the garage and placed the key under the front mat for my neighbors I ran my hand along the flat of my stomach. Unwilling to allow the glum feeling to linger too long I gave myself the speech. In five months I would be 30. I had plenty of time to have a child. Motherhood was still a possibility and if I had not learned anything else along the way, I learned that the most wonderfully improbable things could happen in the most impossible moment.

I cruised along highway 285 noting the 166 and Campbellton exit as I passed. I had come a long way since I had walked so dangerously close to traffic nearly eight years ago. Millions of people had sat listening to me tell my story and advocate for HIV awareness. Tens of thousands of recovering addicts had made me feel at home and loved me back to life as I stayed centered in my 12-step program. My sisters and cousins had found a way to forgive my past indiscretions and opened their hearts and homes to me. Most amazing of all, tomorrow kept coming despite my long stay in intensive care in 1996 and all the other medical emergencies that followed. Even my recent HEP-C diagnosis did not have the power to cast a shadow in my life. After all – why worry about it now? It had to have been there since before I got clean so like HIV, I would just watch it and seek treatment when the time came. I shook my head, smiling - I was overwhelmed with awe as I maneuvered the Park-N-Ride and hurried toward the terminal building.

I dashed through the airport like the pro I had become. The years of flying to cities all over the world helped me breeze through the security line despite my over-stuffed suitcase and I dashed to the gate with ease.

Several men in business suits strained their necks to get a better look at my legs as I expertly maneuvered my luggage just out of reach of my tall heels. I smiled but did not stop until I reached the gate bound for Washington, DC. I was sure that romance would come again, but it would not be today; my meeting was too important.

As my fingers finally cornered my favorite MAC terracotta lip shade in the bottom of my Coach bag I froze watching my mothers eyes stare back at me from the mirror of my compact. In a flash I saw her cinnamon hair sprinkled with nutmeg swirls and felt the power of her stride parting walkways. We had come a long way. Somewhere between the hellcat bouts we had over the years to the increasingly tender talks we now shared, I had come to understand the pain and hardship she had also endured in her lifetime.

When I was a child I could only see from the eyes of a child; but as I grew into my own womanhood and made my own mistakes I knew that my mother was every bit of the goddess I always had been captivated by. I cringed as I imagined what it must have been like to me thrown away by her own mother and raised by a tyrant who seemed to take pleasure in beating her until her creamy amaretto skin was black and blue and her fingernail was torn from its' bed. Yes, despite her emotional scars my mother was a powerful woman - and I took delight in knowing that I was just like her.

The boarding call roused me from my musing and I slipped into the first class cabin and settled quickly into the comfortable seat.

"May I bring you something to drink Miss Stokes?" the flight attendant queried while delivering a glass of red wine to my harried looking seat mate.

"Yes, please." I smiled comfortably "A ginger ale."

My stomach was doing flips and I hoped the soothing liquid might help settle my nerves.

I leaned back as the plane took off and closed my eyes to take my mind off the slight waves of nausea that ensued despite the cool ale.

As the plane found its' steady altitude my mind wandered over the clouds and back to the phone call that lead me one of my now frequent trips to the capital city. At first I did not believe it was the White House calling. After all, what would they want with me? Sure I was speaking all over the country and yes, the media kindly spread the story of my journey to those it might touch. But I was still just an advocate trying to do my part. I was not a politician, I was not a powerful business woman; I was not even a high school graduate.

But only days had passed before the official invitation bearing the seal of the President of the United States arrived. Indeed, I was on the short list for President Clinton's HIV/AIDS Advisory council. After only a brief moment of doubt quelled by my always reasonable and encouraging friend, KJ, I accepted the challenge. At the time, it still seemed unreal. It was only when I arrived in D.C. for the first meeting that the gravity of the appointment dawned on me.

I smiled and eased back further in my seat as I remembered meeting Secretary of State, Donna Shalala. In her no-nonsense manner, she lined up the group appointees and made the appointment official. I repeated the sacred oath with pride and with conviction;

"I do solemnly swear that I will support and defend the Constitution of the United States against all enemies, foreign and domestic; that I will bear true faith and allegiance to the same; that I take this obligation freely, without any mental reservation or purpose of evasion; and that I will well and faithfully discharge the duties of the office on which I am about to enter: So help me God"

I woke from the light sleep and grabbed the glass of water next to my nightstand. Today was the day. My flight had landed and my trip to the Madison Hotel was thankfully short. I did not accept the invitation to dinner that was waiting for me when I checked in. My dear friend Harry Simpson understood I needed time to calm my spirit to share the podium with President Clinton.

Unable to handle the thought of breakfast I quickly showered and slipped into the well-fitted black Edie Bauer suit I had chosen for the occasion. Unwilling to allow myself time to get nervous again I focused on the headrest of the sedan as it sped me to 1600 Pennsylvania Avenue. I focused on the intricate detailing in the mosaic floors as I was guided through the secure corridors of the White House and into the outer sanctum of the press room. Minutes felt like hours as I tried to keep the conversations with my colleagues brief.

"Denise!" President Clinton boomed no sooner than the secret service opened the door and stepped aside.

"It's good to see you." He smiled as he closed the distance between us and took my hand.

"Mr. President," I smiled "how are you?"

"Just wonderful" he chimed.

A flurry of activity surrounded him as each person in the secured room vied for his attention. I folded my hands in front of me and listened to the polite comments and last minute directives from staff.

The President broke the eye-lock he was engaged in and studied my face for a brief second before giving me an encouraging smile. Every meeting I'd had with him was the same. He was sharp and warm and seemed to care as much about HIV as I did. He had quickly reassured me that he enjoyed my candor and I graciously accepted his approval since not one of my presentations or interactions was doctored. My constituency was the homeless and underinsured; the recovering addicts and the poor and middle class who struggled to live normal lives under the weight of HIV. President Clinton had always accepted my relayed comments from them with the same attention he listened to the conerns of dignitaries. I respected him and felt comfortable being myself despite my nerves.

"Great shoes Mr. President." I said muttering the first thing that came to mind.

His laughter was welcome and relaxing.

"Still nervous?" he laughed.

"Yes sir, nervous." I admitted unnecessarily.

"You'll do fine." He assured me.

The staff lined us up as the voice over the PA system began to announce our names;

The Honorable Donna Christian Green
Congressman Elijah Cummings
Congresswoman Eleanor Holmes Norton
Congressman Donald Payne.
Congresswoman Maxine Waters
Representative Lou Stokes
Senator Carol Moseley Braun

Senator Arlen Specter and
Congresswoman Nancy Pelosi
Secretary of Health and Human Services Donna Shalala
Surgeon General, David Satcher;
Director of HIV/AIDS Policy Office, Sandy Thurman

One by one the God-like voice boomed until he called me to the stage.

Denise Stokes Presidential Advisory Committe on HIV/AIDS

I took my appointed place next to Congresswoman Maxine Waters before we all rose for the next announcement,

Ladies and Gentleman, The 42nd President of the United States of America, William Jerfferson Clinton.

A roar, a long flash of lights and President Clinton took his seat to my left before rising again to stare into the small gathering of invited attendees. Harry Simpson and Reverend Edwin Saunders caught my eye from the front row. My shoulders relaxed and I focused on the encouraging and proud expressions coming from them. I was more than fortunate to be surrounded by angels.

Each speaker was more powerful and more influential than the next. Senators and Congressmen each took their turn at the important press conference until finally President Clinton rose from his seat next to me and took the podium. My mind tried to fall into doubt as I thought of following the President of the United States so I focused again on his expertly crafted shoes.. Congresswoman Waters was next to focus her passion on the issues of HIV surrounding the community and I expelled the breath I did not know I was holding as she concluded and introduced me.

I accepted kind words of encouragement from the President as she proudly beamed of my accomplishments to the room and to the tens of millions of viewers tuned in to the press conference. The panel of distinguished guests rose to their feet and applauded as I took the podium and readied myself to fight the best way I knew how. My words were strong and clear and I knew that the voices of all the people who had ever touched my life resounded from me as I spoke.

"When we talk about AIDS, we talk a lot about numbers; numbers that can be overwhelming or intimidating. But we need to look more closely at the numbers... until we begin to see the real lives they represent.

Today, I'd like to share a few personal numbers with you. The first numbers are 13 and 16. I was infected with HIV at 13 and diagnosed at 16. While my peers were planning their futures, I was being harshly told that I would not

live to see 21. That was the year I realized some children die before they have a chance live.

The next number is three. That's how many years it took for me to get the information I needed to combat my disease. I didn't learn that HIV was a sexually transmitted disease until I was almost 20. No one in my community was willing to talk to someone else's child about sex - or about AIDS. I suffered greatly with a severe case of unanswered questions. Many youth today are being tragically diagnosed in the prime of their lives because we are too timid to talk candidly about AIDS. We are too afraid to keep our children alive long enough to make healthier choices.

Thirteen. That's how many pills I take each day to help sustain my health. Pills that are not easy to take and that leave me feeling nauseated and tired. But they are all I have right now - and they keep me alive, I am happy to have them. But they are pills that are not easy to come by. Many of my peers have no access to the latest medicines. Therefore, they have no access to the hope experienced by many - with each new improvement. They sit by and watch people live longer, healthier lives while they still suffer with preventable infections.

Five. That's how many hours I sat on a hospital curb in my own urine while trying to get treatment for an allergy to an AIDS medicine; five hours of suffering when I was only a hundred feet from the source that could alleviate the fierce itching and burning that was ravaging my swollen body. But no one had the time to help me. It wasn't in anyone's job description to escort a patient to the pharmacy. Especially an un-desirable looking patient like I was that day. I experienced the same indifference that many people in my community experience when seeking care. We are not able to walk into hospitals waving insurance cards or cash. We are not able to access the good, quality healthcare that all human beings deserve. While we muster the strength and courage to take an active role in our care, we are being stripped of our dignity by the system that's supposed to help us.

One. Look into the eyes of one person being diagnosed with HIV for the 1st time. Tell a homeless young man with HIV that he has to wait one more year to get housing because the resources are not yet available. Tell one young woman that you can't fill her prescription for the medicine that will give her life - because she has no money. Tell one child that his mother won't be coming home anymore because she died today of AIDS related complications.

Do any one of these things and you will understand what this 156 million dollars means to black and other minority communities. This initiative is important because the moneys allocated and the commitments made here today

will positively impact communities in dire need of support services. And just maybe, not one more of these travesties will occur on my home-front.

The last number I want to share with you today is Zero. I demand that we be liable until there are no new infections; that we do what's necessary to save lives and not what's popular. Until there are no more people desperately seeking care only to find the doors closed. Until there are no more people suffering with AIDS, we have to stay committed; just as committed as the President, the Vice President and the Congressional Black Caucus. Just as committed as Sandra Thurman, Secretary Shalala, Dr. Satcher, the Advisory Council on AIDS and many others who worked tirelessly on this important issue.

Zero is our goal. Because no more can we sit idly by and watch AIDS consume minority communities. We must maintain the momentum that we have gained today because HIV is maintaining its momentum.

No more addicts needlessly infected with one disease simply because they have another one. Addicts should have the services AND the tools they need for effective prevention.

No more lives thrown carelessly aside
No more memorial services
No more screaming mothers
No more broken spirits... or broken hearts.
No more disparity in minority communities.
No – more - AIDS!

Part III

Out of the night that covers me,
Black as the pit from pole to pole,
I thank whatever gods may be
For my unconquerable soul.
In the fell clutch of circumstance
I have not winced nor cried aloud.
Under the bludgeonings of chance
My head is bloody, but unbowed.
Beyond this place of wrath and tears
Looms but the Horror of the shade,
And yet the menace of the years
Finds and shall find me unafraid.
It matters not how strait the gate,
How charged with punishments the scroll,
I am the master of my fate:
I am the captain of my soul.

~ **William Earnest Henkley**

41

Epilogue

"I did not write this book because I am proud of where I have been. I wrote this book because I'm grateful that I was delivered from it ... and proud of whom I have become."

Denise Stokes

It seemed as if I had spent all my young days in the shadow of death; witnessing the murder of innocence, grieving the passing of opportunity, buckling under the threat of violence. Even as the years passed the ominous shadow of AIDS still loomed over my life like a bully.

I realized that just becasue I didn't know how many days or years I had left did not make me unique, nor did it prevent me from living the best life I knew right now! I made a decision that I didn't want to live in the shadows anymore.

After all the situations that made me feel like I wanted to give up, the light of hope still found a home in my heart. I knew that I had to protect it, nurture it, and share it if I wanted the true freedom that comes from not being so afraid of death that I forget to live.

So when the student became ready, indeed, the teachers appeared. Of course, they were always there. The sound lessons of childhood, the tender tone of my grandmother's wisdom, the random kindess of a stranger. The love of God was all around me all the time – even in the darkest places. My life was never lost, my perspective was just distorted. I had delivered myself into the grip of addiction through fear and indecision. I had sat frozen by passivity while circumstance closed all the doors and windows and made my life feel small and stagnant.

Yes I was raped of my virginity with no choice in the matter. Yes, HIV would be the lifelong complication of my encounter in a dark closet with a cold steel switchblade. But I was a victim for only as long as I failed to do something to counter my circumstance.

I needed to forgive myself for what I did not do and forgive others for what they had done. Resentment and regret leave a deep taste of bitter that make it almost impossible to appreciate the sweetness of life.

I learned that it wasn't so important who loved me or didn't love me, but the measure of my life was in who and how I loved. I reflect on past reactions of people and understand that we all needed just one fundamental thing from each other – hope. Hope that tomorrow will be easier. Hope that the pains of yesterday will subside. Hope that own dreams will not always elude us.

In the tradition of hope I cannot help but live my life with passion. No matter how many times I fall short of my dreams, I know they are not lost. No matter how many lies I hear, I know the truth when it is revealed. And no matter how many times my past or my disease threaten to overshadow my life, I still cannot be what I was nor what anyone else thinks I should be. I can only stand in the supreme revelation of exactly who I am. What I know of myself is that I am a powerful woman worthy of love and full of trust. Why? Because I believe with all my heart that God lives in every one of us.

Many times I have been asked,

"Ms. Stokes how did you make it through everything you've been through – and how do you keep going?"
I always smile and tell the truth, "God." God never left me. Even amid the worst choices and hardest circumstances of my life, He was there. To answer the question you haven't asked yet,

"No!"

Even if I had a magic wand, I would not change a thing. I would not erase the rape or HIV. I would not avoid what I thought was the refuge of my uncle's apartment. I would not decide not to ride with Pluto and Randy the day I met Rod. I would not avoid the mystical white smoke in the pretty glass bowl. I wouldn't even change the strained relationship I had with my mother. Given the option to go back and make different choices, there is not one mistake I would dare change.

Everything that I am has been forged by the experiences of my past. No, I don't like pain but I am not enlightened enough to discern what should have happened in my life. I am simply responsible for what I take away from the hurdles and barriers I have faced.

Not embracing the experiences we've had in life is a lot like working hard only to walk away and leave your paycheck on the table! Whatever we have been through is done. What is left to do is to take the lesson away and live in the knowledge we now have. The beauty of earning wisdom is that it does not depreciate, and it cannot be depleted. We get to spend it again and again!

We all have scars. We have all been haunted by *"what if"* and *"if only."* But regret is an empty chasm that prevents us from standing in our purpose. It was not an easy thing to get clean from drugs and face the broken promises and outright lies of addiction; but I wasn't able to move forward until I forgave myself and took responsibility. For me, forgiveness is not just brushing aside the undesirable - but honestly understanding the impact of my faults and not repeating them.

It was a daunting task to face the shameful choices I made as a woman and the situations I was forced into - but shame is not a pretty color and I don't wear it. Dignity suits me far better than holding my 18-year-old self in front of the mirror every day and thinking that I have not grown.

I know that love can not be generated nor can it be sustained from below the belt - it must be cultivated from our higher selves. I found the saying to be true that *"we teach others how to treat us by the way we treat ourselves."* So if I'm a lady, I act like a lady. I don't ask for respect, I demand it in the way I carry myself. I understand my worth. The day you decide you want to be an honrable woman or an honorable man is the day you become just that. Regardless of your past, you are worthy so hold your head up and walk your walk!

Everything in life is not difficult, but the most valuable jewels we gather often come with a price. Hard work, an open mind, and the humiltity to learn from anyone are the greatest characteristics we can have.

My good friend Kerry oftens says,

"You've got a good life – don't mess it up."
The whole sky could be caving in and he still smiles and calmy, peacefully acknowledges that life is good. By God's grace, the company I keep, therapy, and hard work I have gained the gift of serenity in my life – and you just cant buy that.

My life is amazing and my experiences are the roadmap I use to continue the journey of becomming a better human being and reaching out to people scattered along the hard roads in their own journey.

I'd love to end by saying, "*...and she lived happily ever after*" but that's the fairy tale. Life is infinitely more abundant than an enchanting story. For all of us, happiness is a choice, and each day the sun rises I make mine...

Made in the USA
Lexington, KY
18 October 2012